THE

LIVING

WORD

SECOND EDITION

JAMES D. G. DUNN

FORTRESS PRESS
MINNEAPOLIS

THE LIVING WORD
Second Edition

Cover image: © John Woodcock / iStockphoto. Used by permission.
Cover design: The DesignWorks Group, David Uttley.
Book design: Jessica A. Puckett

Library of Congress Cataloging-in-Publication Data

Dunn, James D. G., 1939–
 The living word / James D. G. Dunn.—2nd ed.
  p. cm.
 Includes bibliographical references and index.
 ISBN 978-0-8006-6355-1 (alk. paper)
1. Bible. N.T.—Criticism, interpretation, etc. 2. Bible—Evidences, authority, etc. I. Title.
 BS2361.2.D86 2009
 225.601—dc22

                                    2008043290

Manufactured in the U.S.A.

CONTENTS

PREFACE TO THE NEW EDITION

I WELCOME THIS FRESH EDITION of *The Living Word*, twenty years after it was first published. The original lectures gave me the opportunity to gather together my reflections on scripture that had been maturing for the preceding twenty years, and which express considerations and sentiments that I believe to be still important. Indeed, if anything they may be more important, since the issue of scripture's authority seems to be in increasing danger of tearing Christians apart, particularly in the Anglican Communion. Consequently, those who want to hear the word of God in and through scripture need to think long and hard about *how* they hear that word, before attitudes become hardened and decisions become irrevocable which do lasting damage to the church as the body of Christ, to the gospel as good news of liberation, and to a common concern for the truth of God.

The crisis over scriptural authority within Christianity is a particular case of a more widespread malaise afflicting both religions and, because religions often affect politics, also national and international politics. I refer to the fact of fundamentalism and to the often baleful effects fundamentalist views and fundamentalist-inspired policies have been having since the turn of the millennium—in all three monotheistic religions not least. As I argue in chapter 7 of this volume, a primary feeder of fundamentalism is the lust for certainty and security. It is the certainty that God has spoken in particular words and formulations which are clear-cut and fixed for all time, which alone gives the fundamentalist the security (s)he craves for.

The theological tragedy is that such certainty is neither possible nor desirable. Impossible, because mere words are never adequate to express the whole truth of God. Undesirable, because such certainty and the craving for it actually undermines the faith and trust that is the mark of the truly religious, who walk by faith and not by sight. The point is that "certainty" belongs to a different "language game" from "faith." Certainty is a term that lives and moves and has its being in the artificial world of mathematics. When there are only a very limited number of variables, then it may indeed be possible to achieve a "certain" outcome—but that remains to be seen. "Faith," however, belongs with the language of relationship. Its partners are trust, confidence, and assurance. At no point in our typical daily lives is it realistic to speak in terms of "certainty"—whether eating beef, or crossing the road, or getting married. But trust, assurance—faith—is what enables us to live at all. A community that makes "certainty" its watchword is very different from the community where "faith" is the watchword. I remain very confident that the latter is a much more appropriate description of the community around Jesus and the communities established by Paul than the former. In contrast, the lust for certainty breaches the second commandment in that it makes faith in the invisible God dependent on the visibility, objectivity, and tangibility of the idol.

The ecumenical and political tragedy is that the craving for such certainty becomes itself a slippery slope which can quickly lead to disaster. The fundamentalist knows the truth in clear-cut terms. He or she sees issues in black-and-white terms—good and evil, right and wrong. When the truth of an issue can be reduced to a simple either-or, there is no room for disagreement or compromise. For the fundamentalist, I cannot be *right* unless you who disagree with me are *wrong*; those who compromise are blind and traitors; the truth does not allow of differing positions. Contrast the Jesus who came to call sinners, not the righteous: for "sinners," read those condemned by the fundamentalist; and for "the righteous"...?

Worse still, from a fundamentalist perspective, those who disagree with the fundamentalist position on any subject disagree with God. They are enemies of God. They are not simply wrong; they are evil. And if evil, opposed to God, then they are demonically motivated and should be opposed with the ruthlessness with which good must oppose evil. They can be treated with inhumanity because they have set themselves against God's truth for humankind. We don't have to go far down that slippery slope before we come to the burning of heretics, the hanging of witches, and (who would have thought it possible in the twenty-first century?) Guantánamo.

It is because I believe with a full heart that such fundamentalist attitudes among Christians both misunderstand and dishonor Christianity's own scriptures that I am glad to send this volume on its way once again into the marketplace of Christian debate and Christian contribution to wider debates.

I believe equally that to understand God's revelation in and through scripture as "the living Word" is truer to scripture than any Christian fundamentalism. And my hope is that a fuller and richer appreciation of how God's word has come to us in and through scripture, and still comes to us, may encourage a proper respect for those who differ from "us" (whoever the "us" are) and may facilitate the kind of cooperation and fellowship that should mark out Christians in their legitimate (and inevitable) diversity.

The argument in chapter 7, "God's Word in Human Speech: The Price of Certainty," was originally delivered at the Tantur Conference in Jerusalem, May 29–June 1, 1994. Chapter 8, "The Bible and Scholarship: On Bridging the Gap between the Academy and the Church," first appeared in *Anvil* 19 (2002): 109–18. Chapter 9, "What Makes a Good Exposition?" was the *Expository Times* Lecture in 2002, published in *Expository Times* 114 (2002–2003): 147–57. The final chapter, "Living Tradition," was published in *What Is It That the Scripture Says? Essays in Biblical Interpretation, Translation, and Reception in Honour of Henry Wansbrough OSB* (LNTS 316; London: T. & T. Clark, 2006), 275–89, and is reprinted here with the kind permission of T. & T. Clark.

PREFACE TO THE 1988 EDITION

IN FEBRUARY 1987 I was privileged to deliver the W. H. Griffith Thomas Lectures in Wycliffe Hall, Oxford. I am grateful to the Principal for the invitation and to his colleagues, particularly Gordon and Sylvia Ogilvie, for the splendid hospitality they provided.

The requested topic was something in the area of biblical interpretation and since the question of scriptural authority and interpretation is one that I consider of central importance within Christian theology, I was glad of the opportunity to take further part in an ongoing debate to which I had already attempted some previous contribution.

Unfortunately, the pressures under which the British University system is struggling today demand a vast amount of time in administration and committee, with less and less time available for creative work. Within the constraints of a period of heavy responsibility it became impossible to write a completely new set of lectures and I had perforce to draw on some material already to hand. Since at that time I had not contemplated publishing the lectures it seemed the most sensible course to follow.

For the first lecture I was able to adapt the opening lecture of my third-year undergraduate "Theology of the New Testament" course at Durham. This is to be published in its "Mark 1" form in a volume coauthored with Professor Mackey of Edinburgh, under the title *New Testament Theology in Dialogue* (SPCK). It was of considerable personal interest to discover that the model offered for New Testament *theology* proved so apposite for New Testament *interpretation.* But on reflection, not so much of a surprise, since I see New Testament theology as primarily a hermeneutical task.

For the second lecture I was able to supplement a lecture given to the international conference on "Jesus God and Man" at Dallas in November 1986. I am grateful to Roy Varghese, both for the invitation to that imaginative and very worthwhile conference, and for permission to reuse the lecture that was delivered there under the title "The Historicity of the Synoptic Gospels."

The third and fourth lectures were completely fresh, though I am more than happy to acknowledge the debt I owe to my Nottingham researcher, David Meade, for the insights we shared during his period of research and which he has now published in the volume mentioned in chapter 4. By drawing on it I was able to give chapter 4 a greater solidity than would otherwise have been possible in the time available. If this little volume serves to draw wider attention to Dr. Meade's most valuable work I hope he will find the *quid pro quo* acceptable.

As the series progressed I was pleased to find that the lectures seemed to hang well together and to develop a reasonably coherent and rounded position. With some encouragement from those who had heard them I began to think of possible publication. With even stronger encouragement from John Bowden of SCM Press I decided to go ahead.

At first I thought about attempting extensive revision and documentation. But that would have changed the style too much. And I have always found it very difficult to recast a text over which I had previously labored to get it "right" into a new format where I say the same things in different words. The choice between a style that makes for easy listening (and reading) and a format that cross-references and attempts to close off all loopholes is not always easy. But in this case it was a choice of offering the lectures to a wider audience as delivered, or not at all. And since I have never attempted in my work to provide "the last word" on a subject, but merely to contribute to an ongoing debate, the choice was not too difficult. I did attempt some recasting of chapter 1, to reduce the amount of overlap with the chapter in *New Testament Theology in Dialogue*, but soon found that I was moving too far from the lecture originally delivered, and so gave up the attempt. It also occurred to me that the degree of overlap served to illustrate one of the main points of the series—the adaptability of pre-formed material to different uses.

It also seemed sensible to use the opportunity of publication to give wider access to the two other essays I have contributed to the current debates on scriptural authority: "The Authority of Scripture According to Scripture," *Churchman* 96 (1982): 104–22, 201–25 (a lecture first delivered by invitation to the 1981 Conference of the Anglican Evangelical Association as an exposition of a "radical" evangelical view of scripture), together with my letter to Professor Nicole, published at the end of his response to the above in the same journal—*Churchman* 98 (1984): 208–12; and "Levels of Canonical

Authority," *Horizons in Biblical Theology* 4 (1982): 13–60. They are in effect further variations on the same theme and, having a different format, were able to interact more fully with other views in detail and in footnote. I am grateful to the editors of both these journals for permission to reproduce this material.

The final product will, I hope, help to bring home more fully the character of the scriptural tradition and of scriptural authority as it comes to clear expression, or so it seems to me, in the New Testament itself: a living tradition and a living authority. Neither disregarded nor accepted uncritically, but received with discernment as to what was its continuing force and authority in the changing circumstances of faith. A balance of continuity and discontinuity. A creative tension between old revelation and new, between authoritative tradition and prophetic Spirit. To locate oneself, so far as that is possible, within that process, is to gain invaluable insights on how scriptural authority can still function today. To hear the living word of God as it was heard in the beginnings of Christianity, so far as that is possible by present-day empathetic exegesis, is an invaluable aid toward hearing the living word of God today. If this little volume helps even in the smallest measure toward that end I will be more than satisfied.

PART 1

1. THE TASK OF NEW TESTAMENT INTERPRETATION

1. Introduction

I BEGIN BY ASKING TWO STARTER QUESTIONS.

(a) What Is the New Testament?

The immediate subject matter of New Testament interpretation is obviously the New Testament. But what is the New Testament? The nature of the discipline is bound to be determined in large measure at least by the character of the subject matter. Yet all too often the question is not asked. The answer is simply taken for granted. The question, after all, is a beginner's question, and by the time we are ready to tackle the larger subject of how we should *interpret* the New Testament we have left such elementary matters far behind us. But on this occasion at least we must pause and be prepared to begin by asking the naïvely fundamental question. For if the task is, in large part, determined by its subject matter, we must have a clear grasp of the dimensions of that subject matter. Otherwise we may end up charting only the Atlantic and not the Pacific as well, only the land and not the sea.

I normally begin my final year course on New Testament theology by asking this question. After the initial surprise the class's scatter of answers can usually be grouped around two aspects or perspectives.

1. The New Testament is a collection of *historical documents*—in fact, most of the Christian writings from the first century of our era.

As such they are invaluable source documents for any study of the beginnings of Christianity. Almost all our knowledge regarding Jesus and the initial spread of Christianity derives directly from them. Without them we would lose all possibility of direct access to these foundational events.

2. The New Testament is also *scripture*. The New Testament writings have been regarded by the Christian churches as their primary authority down through the centuries, and still are today. Since the earliest centuries the New Testament documents have functioned as "canon," that is, as rule or yardstick or norm for faith and life. They belong to the class of sacred writings. For generations of Christians they have been heard to speak as the word of God written.

As we shall soon see, there are controversial features about both these ways of regarding the New Testament. But that should not cause us to blank out one or other aspect from the start. To do so would reduce our problems, but would not help in their solution. For unless we begin by acknowledging this twofold historic character of the New Testament documents we will run the risk of ignoring dimensions of our subject matter and so of undermining our task from the outset.

With this preliminary answer to our first question we can go on to our second:

(b) What Is New Testament Interpretation?

Of course we cannot expect a complete or final answer right away. A good deal more clarification and discussion will be necessary before we can hope for that. But it is worth attempting a first approximation to an answer at this stage since that will provide the parameters for the rest of our discussion, or the broad outline that we will hope to fill out as we proceed.

Unfortunately even at this stage we find ourselves caught in a fundamental conflict. The disagreement arises from the two answers given to our first question. For, as we would expect, different views of New Testament interpretation arise out of the different ways of regarding the New Testament.

1. For some, interpretation of New Testament texts is a purely *descriptive* exercise. It is the task of the historian, not of the theologian. The concern should be to lay out the history of early Christian religion and theology. The objective should not be to

derive observations of continuing theological significance from these writings, but simply to describe the theologies of the New Testament writers, what was believed, thought, taught, hoped, required, and striven for in the earliest period of Christianity. Wilhelm Wrede and Krister Stendahl have provided classic statements of this understanding of the task of New Testament scholarship.[1]

2. For others, interpretation of the New Testament will inevitably have a *prescriptive* role within the larger discipline of Christian or dogmatic theology. This arises not simply from a dogma of canonical authority, but from the *fact* of canonical authority. By this I mean the fact that the New Testament has always determined the character and emphases of all subsequent Christian faith and theology in greater or less degree. Even those theologians who have denied the dogma of canonical authority have found it necessary to appeal to the content of the New Testament (Jesus, Paul, John, etc.) to justify their own theological reconstructions. The fact is that the New Testament writings have served as a crucial determinant for the whole of Christian faith and life. From this perspective, then, the subject matter of New Testament interpretation is not simply first-century ideas of antiquarian interest but the convictions and experiences which came to expression in the New Testament writings and which can still speak directly to contemporary Christian concerns. New Testament interpretation means not merely describing the theology of the New Testament but doing theology through the New Testament. The classic response to Wrede at this point is the essay of Adolf Schlatter.[2]

It would be all too easy to develop these two perspectives as polar alternatives, to save ourselves further trouble by simply labeling them respectively "liberal" and "conservative." That done, we could then each retreat safely into our own theological and ecclesiastical traditions and either ignore the other or snipe away at the other's exposed flanks. The more demanding task is to recognize that there is truth in both ways of viewing the task of treating the New Testament. Since the New Testament *is* both historical source *and* scripture, we must take proper account of both aspects. Of course, there is a potential tension between these two aspects—seen at its most extreme in the contrast between the academic scholar with narrow historical interests on the one hand, and the "simple believer" on the other reading the Bible as God's voice speaking directly to one in the here and now. But the task of New

Testament interpretation is precisely to handle that tension and to ensure that it is a creative rather than a destructive tension.

2. New Testament Interpretation as a Dialogue

The most hopeful way forward is to begin a dialogue between these two different perspectives on the task of New Testament interpretation. In larger terms that will involve a dialogue between past and present, between first century and twentieth century, between the standpoints of the New Testament writers and their readers on the one hand, and that of the modern exegete on the other.

The descriptive aspect of the task of New Testament interpretation requires us to recognize that the New Testament belongs to the first century, with all that that involves (a subject to which we must return). But we cannot get far in the dialogue until we as exegetes also recognize that *we* ourselves belong to the twenty-first century, with all that *that* involves. Apart from anything else, the understanding we bring to the task of exegesis has been shaped by our upbringing and education, by our inherited culture and traditions—including our own theological tradition in its particular distinctiveness.

To cite a few examples. When British students first come across the word *kingdom* in the biblical writings, their understanding is bound to be influenced by the fact that they belong to the United Kingdom, that their country is a monarchy with an imperial past. Their history as Britons will give shape and content to that word. Or again, their initial understanding of the word *law* may be influenced by the issue of "law and order" or by their Reformation heritage. No one is surprised when Roman Catholic and Protestant exegetes come to different conclusions, for everyone knows that they have come to the text from different starting points.

This is precisely why Rudolf Bultmann asked his famous question: Is presuppositionless exegesis possible?[3] His answer is clear and obvious: No! Exegesis without presuppositions is an impossibility. We *all*, whoever we are, bring to the text our own "pre-understanding"—our pre-understanding not just of what its words mean but also of what we expect it to say. To change the metaphor to one made more familiar by the work of Anthony Thiselton:[4] what we see in a text is limited by the horizon of our own understanding; when we read the text we see only what lies within the horizon which bounds our understanding; we can "cash" the language of the text only in the currency of our own linguistic heritage and world.

Consequently, a crucial part of the dialogue of New Testament interpretation is to recognize *that* we have presuppositions, *that* we have horizons—or more precisely, to recognize that our perception will be limited by our presuppositions, our vision limited by our horizons. And to recognize this not simply as a first step which can then be left behind, but to recognize that it will always be true. Our perception of what is there in the text will always be shaped by the language or experience "bank" from which we draw to "cash" the words and phrases read. Our understanding will always be limited by our horizons however much these horizons may have expanded in the meantime. If initially we cannot recognize *what* the limits of our horizons are, at least we can recognize *that* they are limited.

And thus we will begin to realize that a sharp antithesis between the alternatives posed above (descriptive versus prescriptive) is somewhat unrealistic. Even the descriptive exercise cannot escape a significant input from the exegete's own viewpoint. That is to say, whether we like it or not, some element of dialogue is essential, if only because it is unavoidable. Better then to engage in the dialogue in positive mood rather than to waste time wishing it could be otherwise.

But is "dialogue" the right word? For many the alternative to "scientific objectivity" is the despair of the "hermeneutical circle." If we see only what we are able to see from our twenty-first-century perspective, or through our Protestant or Catholic spectacles, then are we not simply staring in a sequence of mirrors? If the starting point determines what we find, if the presuppositions determine the conclusions, are we not simply going round in circles? We find what *we* are looking for, answers to *our* questions, and, surprise, surprise, the answers as a rule tend to support our presuppositions. The "hermeneutical circle" looks to be too much like one of those children's trains at a fun fair, going round and round and round always on the same track, and never getting anywhere. Can we escape?

Yes! The simple answer is that we can *correct* or *improve* our pre-understanding. We can broaden our horizons. For example, although a British student begins his New Testament study with a particular idea of what a "kingdom" is, there is sufficient evidence of the way in which the Aramaic equivalent was used at the time of Jesus for him to develop a new understanding of the word, one more informed by the first-century material and less by his twenty-first-century heritage. Or again, someone may come to his study of the New Testament with the presupposition of what the "gospel" says, that evangelistic preaching should always speak of repentance for sins and of God's provision of atonement for sins on the cross. Such a person can check whether this was always so within the New Testament writings. And when he recognizes that Paul hardly speaks of repentance and John never, and that the evangelistic sermons in Acts never present the cross as an act of atonement, he may well find it necessary to redefine his understanding of how the gospel may be preached.

In other words, there is no need for us to keep going round in a circle. We can alter our perspective, refocus our questions. The circle, if you like, can become more like a spiral and in pursuing the line of questioning we may hope to find ourselves spiraling in towards the center.

"Dialogue," however, is the more appropriate metaphor. Our initial questioning should lead to some clearer understanding of the subject matter and to some correction of our initial viewpoint. This in turn should enable us to pose the question afresh, or to pose the original question more sharply.

At the same time we should remember that it *is* a dialogue. For we may well find that the New Testament writings do not merely answer back to our questions. The New Testament may put *us* in question. And may do so in such a radical manner that conversion is the only answer possible for us. So Francis of Assisi found with regard to the words of Jesus: "Sell all that you have and distribute to the poor, and you will have treasure in heaven" (Luke 18:22). Words that he had no doubt heard before now came to him as the word of God and called for total assent. The Reformation's insistence on "scripture alone" is an expression of the same experience repeated many times over, when the words of scripture were heard to speak in a way that challenged generally accepted presuppositions and practices. Or we might reflect on why it is that liberation theology has arisen in Latin America. For liberation theology is itself an expression of this same dialogue—where questions have been posed to traditional authorities (including scripture) by the conditions in these countries, to be met by even sharper questions posed in turn by an important strand of biblical teaching.

To put it another way, New Testament interpretation is a dialogue, simply because any twentieth-century attempt to inquire into first-century writings is bound to be a dialogue. A dialogue that starts by recognizing the inescapable distance between the first century and the twentieth, which begins with the recognition that a first-century text is bound to be in some degree or other strange and foreign to us. For if it is not, the likelihood is that we have assimilated the one to the other too quickly; we have allowed the voice of the twentieth century to drown out the distinctive tones of the first century; or the words of the first century to drown out the questions of the twentieth. If the former is the temptation of the too critical, the latter is the failing of the too uncritical. But if we want to hear the distinctive voice of the New Testament writings, whether in terms of what marks them out from other first-century writings, or in terms of hearing the otherliness of the word of God addressing us now, some sort of dialogue is unavoidable: a dialogue in which we find our own questions being clarified and redefined and in which we allow ourselves to be put in question.

3. The Complexity of the Dialogue

So far we have set out only the basic character of New Testament interpretation as dialogue. Now we must begin to look at it more carefully and at its complexity. What appears in the initial statement as something fairly straightforward, on closer examination quickly proves to be more complicated. Here we can make use of two words that have proved useful, if not indispensable, in previous attempts to understand the process of New Testament interpretation: the words *historical* and *critical*. The dialogue of New Testament interpretation must be both historical and critical.

(a) Historical

Under this heading I want simply to describe more fully what is involved in the recognition of the first-centuriness of the New Testament writings. Much can be said on this subject, but I will confine myself to three main points.

1. The New Testament writings are all in greater or less degree *occasional writings:* they contain particular emphases because they were addressed to particular situations. It seems to be a fair working assumption that the authors were not composing "in the air" but with a view to the needs of at least some congregation(s). To what extent then were the language and emphases of each writer determined by the needs and situations addressed?

The answer is clear enough in the case of most of Paul's letters. In particular, it is beyond dispute that 1 Corinthians was written because there were a variety of problems troubling the infant congregation in Corinth. As has often been noted, our knowledge of the role and importance of the Lord's Supper in the first Gentile congregations is dependent almost entirely on the "accidental" fact that there was serious abuse of the common meal at Corinth. What is less appreciated is that since the particular points and emphases Paul makes were addressed to that abuse, we today will not be able to appreciate their full force without a reasonably clear idea of in what the abuse consisted.

To take another example, Paul's letter to the Christians in Rome has traditionally been regarded as much less tied to a particular situation, in which case our understanding of it would be less dependent on our knowledge of that situation. But in recent years it has come to be recognized more and more that here too is a letter which arises out of a particular phase in Paul's mission and whose theology reflects that stage in his thinking. Even with Romans, therefore, it will be necessary to inquire into the particular context in Paul's work and thought if we are to appreciate all the various nuances and overtones in the letter.

What about the other New Testament writings? Is the Gospel of John quite so timeless as it has often seemed? Or do we need here too to become aware of particular tendencies and tensions in the Christian assemblies to which the Fourth Evangelist belonged, or to which he was writing, before we can properly tune in to the message he intended his readers to hear? What about Acts? A history of Christian beginnings, yes, indeed. But a history with a purpose or a bias, like all histories. So that if we miss the purpose or misconceive the bias we read the text with blinkers, unaware of all that is going on in the text. What indeed of Jesus' words themselves? Were they not addressed to particular individuals, often making a point specific to that individual? Without some appreciation of that particular context the words will be open to misunderstanding. Even here, if we are to pursue the dialogue responsibly, we must ask to what extent particular words of Jesus were addressed to particular situations and can be properly understood only in specific contexts.

There can be no escape then from the task of careful historical exegesis. In particular, we must beware of abusing the benefit of hindsight or the privilege of being able to set these writings within a much broader horizon than was visible to the writers themselves. Our evidence may be fragmentary for the first-century Graeco-Roman world as a whole. But at least we can set it all out before us. We can take note of what was happening in Rome and in Jerusalem at the same time, in a way that was quite impossible then. We can trace large-scale patterns and slow-moving cultural transformations of which those active in only one part would hardly have been aware. We can see now how certain tendencies developed into Gnostic sects on the one hand or into catholic Christianity on the other. The danger of the hindsight perspective or of too broad horizons is that we not only see the end *from* the beginning, but we also see the end *in* the beginning. We too readily assume that such developments were inevitable and that the writers involved at the earlier stages of the development must have been somehow aware of it and intended that it should be so. A properly historical exegesis will ever recall how limited a particular author's horizon must have been and seek to respect that limitation when enquiring what the author intended to say and what his first readers heard him say.

The challenge of the word *historical* in the task of interpretation, therefore, is for the exegete to locate him or herself as firmly as possible within the historical context of the document or passage under study—both the broader context of the culture and the time, which I perhaps need not go into more fully here, and the particular context that called forth the writing or to which it was addressed.

2. Historical conditionedness is another and larger aspect of the same point. The issue here is the extent to which biblical writings are expressions of their age. I do not say *simply* expressions of their age. But it seems a fair working assumption that the New Testament documents were written to be understood by people with different frames of reference from ours—different history, politics and social conditions, different thought patterns, customs and symbols, different education, language and idiom—everything, in other words, that shapes conceptuality and language reference, everything that is involved in the difference of the first century from the twentieth century. The question therefore is: To what extent were the writings of the New Testament conditioned by the times within which and for which they were written?

The point has usually been taken well enough with regard to much *Old* Testament writing. For example, the widespread recognition of the opening chapters of Genesis as a kind of myth—that is, an explanation for the perceived reality of man and his world using simple symbolic narrative such as would be understandable even to quite primitive societies. Or again, the extent to which the law codes of the Pentateuch reflect a nomadic or agrarian stage of civilization. Or how a particular law like the *lex talionis* ("eye for an eye, tooth for a tooth") has to be understood within the context of the conventions of the day. Equivalently in the New Testament we can recognize that Jesus' teaching bears the stamp of an itinerant ministry among the villages and small towns of Galilee; whereas Paul's reflects an essentially urban mission in the larger cities of the eastern Mediterranean. And like the account of creation's beginnings, so with the account of the climax of human history, since Revelation has to be understood in the symbolism of apocalyptic rather than literally.

The point is perhaps most obvious with regard to various ethical issues. For example, Paul's counsel of complete submission to the authority of the state in Romans 13 can easily be misconceived and misapplied, unless we remember the vast gulf between the political realities of the Roman state in the first century and that of the ancient and developed democracies of the twenty-frist. We who can exercise political power through the ballot box and through pressure groups need to make an effort of historical imagination to appreciate the political powerlessness of the great mass of the populace in Paul's day. It simply did not lie within the bounds of possibility for Paul to exercise political power. He did not advocate a more pro-active political stance simply because such a possibility would not have occurred to him; such a possibility was not contained within the horizon of thinkable thoughts for Paul.

Similarly with the issue of slavery. We need not wonder at the earliest Christian assumption of slavery as an unavoidable and therefore acceptable part of society. For that is what it was—simply the lowest level of the socioeconomic ladder. The conviction that slavery is morally repulsive was a much later growth within Christian consciousness, and if we are rightly to appreciate what the New Testament says on the subject we must avoid judging it by the standards of another and later time. Otherwise the dialogue of New Testament interpretation becomes merely a twenty-first-century monologue.

The relevance of the same point has been recognized to at least some extent on the still vexed question of the role of women in the church—particularly with regard to Paul's counsel in 1 Corinthians that in praying or prophesying women should wear a covering on their heads. Few Christian women today feel bound by that counsel since it is generally appreciated that this particular instruction was determined by the social conventions relating to women in first-century Corinth and therefore is of limited applicability.

3. At the same time we dare not forget the other dimension of these writings—that they are scripture as well as historical sources. It is the historical character of these writings that forces us to recognize their occasional quality and context conditionedness. But that is only one side of the picture. By calling them scripture I do not refer merely to the fact that generations of Christians have read them as the word of God written. I refer much more to the fact that, however occasional and contingent these documents were in their composition, they were also recognized as having greater and more lasting significance than is implied by these two words.

The fact is that it was these and just these documents which were preserved. Other letters of Paul and other first-century Christian writings were not preserved. Why so? The obvious answer is that they were preserved precisely because their significance for faith was recognized as going beyond the immediate situation which occasioned them. Other examples of earliest Christian writing were allowed to disappear from view because they were not used, because they did not outlast the occasion or need for which they were written. But these were preserved as having more than temporary importance. And their later acceptance as canon was in most cases simply an acknowledgment of the authority they had been increasingly accorded from the first. To that extent we can certainly speak of a canonical authority attaching to these documents from the first. Or in alternative terms, since these writings were heard to speak with more than ordinary authority, and with an authority that outlasted the occasionalness and conditionedness of their origins, since the word of God was heard in them from the beginning and beyond the circumstances of their initial reception, to that extent they were accorded the status of scripture from the first.

And this too, be it noted, is a *historical* observation, as much rooted in history and validated by historical study as the observation of the same writings' occasional and contingent character.

Thus we can begin to see just how complex is the dialogue of New Testament interpretation. For here we have writings that are limited in applicability by their historicalness, by the fact that they belong firmly to the first century and to a variety of particular contexts and circumstances. But at the same time we have to recognize that these writings, the very same writings, have been recognized to speak with the voice of scriptural authority more or less from the first. The unconditioned word of God expressed in words of man limited in reference and scope.

This is why, of course, New Testament interpretation *must* be a dialogue. The correlation between the word of God and the words of the New Testament is not a simple one-to-one correlation. We cannot simply read a text from the New Testament and assume that it is the word of God for ourselves today. We must recognize that the limited scope of the text may limit its applicability to the different circumstances of our own time; that its scriptural authority functions by showing us how the word of God was heard in particular circumstances of the first century, not by having prescriptive force for us today. Only by engaging in dialogue with the text, a dialogue that takes full account of the historical character of the text, will we be prevented from abusing the text and from jumping to wrong conclusions.

This brings us to the other key word in describing the dialogue of New Testament interpretation.

(b) Critical

The word *critical* often has a negative tone, as though it meant "looking for some fault in order to condemn." But, of course, it can have a much more positive note as well—"looking for some weakness in order to improve." Writers often speak of their spouses as their "best critic." A teacher should be the typical critic in this sense. The word itself then simply means a readiness to attempt an evaluation of that being examined. Linked with the previous word it is often used to describe the task of the historian—the "historical critical method." As such it need only mean a readiness to question and evaluate all the data that comes before the historian. It has, of course, been used in a still narrower sense to include the criteria by which such an evaluation may proceed—in particular, the presupposition that all events should be explained in terms of a closed sequence of cause and effect. But here it is used in the more neutral sense of readiness to probe, question, and evaluate.

1. In the first place that means being critical of the *text*. That is to say, the New Testament critic must be willing to treat the New Testament texts as products of the first century, and as such to analyze them in the same way as one would other historical texts. Such an examination is not antithetical or hostile to their further role as scripture. For its purpose is to clarify the character of the documents that were to be recognized as scripture, to cut

through any mystique or dogmatic insistence regarding how things must have been, to appreciate so far as possible the impact that they actually had, without ignoring any features that may now raise an eyebrow. To be properly critical is not to ignore or deny any claims to inspiration on the part of the authors. On the contrary, it is to gain a clearer understanding of how inspiration worked and what it produced. Since it is also a historical fact that the New Testament writings were heard to speak with more than occasional and contingent authority from the first, it is also a properly critical concern to want to hear again, so far as possible, the word of God that was heard within and through the circumscribed and circumstantial categories of the New Testament text. Indeed, we might well say that within the church the New Testament critic is simply helping to carry out the churches' continuing need to "test the spirits," to evaluate and assess *whatever* claims to speak here and now with authoritative voice as the word of God.

There are many aspects in a critical study of the New Testament. All that we put under the heads of "textual criticism," "tradition criticism," "source criticism," and "redaction criticism," for a start. But here I will take up only one example of what is involved. I have in mind particularly the *diversity* of the New Testament writings. I take up this example not so much because I have written on the subject, but rather because what I have written has been so misunderstood—almost wholly on the conservative side. And misunderstood precisely because the sort of points I have been making above have not been grasped, or at least not in their full extent. Permit me the indulgence of some self-defense.

In *Unity and Diversity in the New Testament*[5] one of the points I tried to make is that the gospel is never expressed in the New Testament in precisely the same terms. That when we compare the gospel as presented by Jesus, by the sermons of Acts, by Paul, and by John, it is not strictly speaking the same gospel. There is what we might call a "core gospel"—the proclamation of Jesus as risen from the dead, the call for faith in this Jesus, and the promise of God to that faith. But no New Testament writer reduces his proclamation of the gospel to quite so bare a skeleton. In each New Testament writer that common core is expanded and elaborated. And it is in these fuller proclamations that the difference and diversity comes. Why so? For the very reason that we have already elaborated above—because each New Testament writer has in view different circumstances and needs, and it is these differences that are mirrored in their particular statements of the gospel. Different circumstances called forth different emphases. Diverse and divergent needs were met by elaborating the "core gospel" in diverse and divergent proportions. The classic case is that of the strikingly different emphases on the interplay of faith and works which we find in Paul and James.

More than one conservative critic has immediately reached for the word *contradiction*.[6] "Dunn accuses the New Testament of innumerable contradictions," would be a fairly common opinion. But such a comment shows that the reviewer has missed the point and evidences a disturbing lack of historical consciousness. In that book I never used words like *contradiction* or *error*, because that was not what I was talking about. What I had in view was the historical conditionedness of the various proclamations of the gospel in the New Testament—the different and divergent emphases that arise between particular expanded statements of the gospel because they are addressed to different circumstances and divergent needs. What I had in mind was the fact that there is no such thing in the New Testament as an absolute and unchanging form of the gospel which is independent of circumstance and occasion and which therefore can be abstracted from the New Testament for use in every and any circumstance thereafter. We only "hear" the gospel in the New Testament when we hear it in its conditionedness and relativity, in its *different* expressions. If we hear any particular expression of the gospel as though it was wholly independent of the historical circumstances for which it was spoken and written, then we do not hear it as the New Testament author intended it to be heard. We run the danger of imposing an alien voice upon the voice of the New Testament and so of distorting the hermeneutical dialogue.

In short, to recognize the diversity within the New Testament is simply to take the historical relativity of the New Testament documents seriously. It is to be properly critical, since it takes proper account of the historical nature of the words in which the word of God was heard. And by so doing, by recognizing the conditioned and occasional character of the word of God, it becomes more possible to hear that word of God afresh.

2. In the second place New Testament critics must be critical of *themselves*. This means, basically, being willing to recognize the *possibility* that the text will speak with a different voice and message from what they had presupposed— being willing to take this seriously as a methodological possibility. So if the New Testament critic is inclined to come to the text from a "strictly historical" viewpoint, or using the historical critical method in the narrower sense, one must be open to the possibility that the texts do have an extra dimension, whether described in terms of inspiration, revelation, or word of God. To be properly critical New Testament critics must be critical of their own viewpoint, of their own historical critical method. If, on the other hand, their inclination is to come to scripture with an already established pattern of faith, they must be open to the possibility that that pattern is inadequately grounded in the text, that exegesis may point to conclusions which call important aspects of that faith in question.

In other words, an essential characteristic of the New Testament critic (as of any critic) is *open-mindedness*—a willingness to ask questions and to follow through the answers and their corollaries. Open-mindedness is not the same as empty-mindedness, though some teachers have made the mistake of confusing them. Empty-mindedness asks for the impossibility of offering the mind as a blank sheet, on which new truths may be imprinted with pristine freshness. Open-mindedness recognizes that presuppositionless enquiry is impossible, takes into account that the New Testament critic will approach his or her task with some sort of faith. Open-mindedness is what makes a true dialogue possible—a dialogue between the student of the New Testament, wherever he or she is, and the text itself, whatever it is. An *open* dialogue, which allows *all* questions to be asked, and which is ready to consider all potential answers. An open *dialogue,* which allows answers to react back on the starting point, to criticize the faith that prompted the initial question, to correct or abandon presuppositions that the dialogue shows to be faulty.

For example, what if 2 Peter was *not* written by the apostle Peter? What would that say about 2 Peter? About its canonical status? About the canon? What if Matthew and Mark actually do disagree about Jesus and the law? Is one more "right" than the other? Or can both be "right"? What if there is real estrangement and even some antagonism between Paul and the law? What does that tell us about Paul? About the Old Testament in relation to the New? What if, on the other hand, we find that even after all our critical work Jesus does not seem to fit any normal category? If after all rationalization of various miracle stories there still seems to be something more? If the resurrection faith of the first Christians makes no sense without postulating that something had happened to Jesus, "the resurrection of Jesus"? What if after the most penetrating analysis of a text which sets it firmly in its first-century context it still leaps from the page and addresses us as God's word?

To be properly critical, to be genuinely open-minded can make an interesting historical inquiry into a dialogue of discovery, where the discovery is as much about oneself as about the text being questioned.

4. Partners in the Dialogue

I have already stressed the complexity of the dialogue, but there are two further dimensions to it which ought not to be ignored, even though they make it still more complex.

(a) The first is the further historical fact that the dialogue has already been in progress for nearly two thousand years. This means, as I hardly need remind you again, that these writings have functioned as scripture, and been heard to

speak with personal and canonical authority all down through the centuries of our era. So we have other contributers to the dialogue. The dialogue is not simply a matter of our shouting from the twentieth century across a vast empty canyon to the first century. We have many dialogue partners on the way who can contribute to our own dialogue, and not uncommonly provide cautionary tales of misunderstandings and dialogues distorted.

These diverse partners also introduce a further diversity in interpretation and insight. For the same New Testament writings have been heard to speak with different emphasis and effect, as the diversity of our different denominational traditions makes clear beyond dispute. The diversity of God's word as originally spoken has been compounded by the diversity of the interpretations that have been attached to or read from the New Testament texts. And, for the same reason, the interpretations have been diverse in large part because the questions addressed to the texts and the needs to which they ministered were equally occasional and conditioned—just as we operate in our turn within the relativities of our different twentieth-century contexts. The dialogue is complex because the various partners in it are all speaking in the language of their own times and circumstances so that communication is never perfect.

In drawing attention to this further dimension of the dialogue I do not mean to imply that the whole dialogue is in danger of collapsing into a cacophony of competing voices, all with as much right to be heard as the other. There is a surprisingly large measure of agreement between all the different traditions on a number of key issues: one need only think, for example, of the ecumenical creeds of the undivided church, or the relative success of the WCC's Lima text, *Baptism, Eucharist, and Ministry*. But more important for our present purposes, I would wish to emphasize that within the dialogue as a whole the original meaning as intended by the author and heard by his first readers should have normative status. That is not to rule out other interpretations, other expressions of the word of God as heard through these texts. But it is to say that all interpretations should be able to justify themselves in the face of the author's original intention.

I am, of course, fully aware of the problems of speaking of an author's "original intention"; I have already outlined some of them above. But in any dispute as to a text's meaning, the author of the text must surely be given first claim to it—it is *his* text. And that means also first claim to its meaning. His meaning is *the* meaning. And if other meanings are to be read from the text, they must always be measured against his meaning. The further they are from the meaning he intended, the more open to question are they. At the end of the day, it is the author's intended meaning that must serve as the normative meaning, the check against imposing meaning on the text, the check against using the text like a ventriloquist's dummy. Only exegesis can prevent eisegesis.

(b) If the historical tradition of the churches is a further dimension in the dialogue of New Testament interpretation, it is equally important to realize that New Testament interpretation is not a matter of you and I engaging in the dialogue in isolation from each other. The task of New Testament interpretation is a *corporate* one. The New Testament interpreter operates within a double context, reflecting the two-sided character of his primary subject matter—the community of scholarship and the community of faith. He is responsible to both—to share his insights and to accept their criticism.

Truth is seldom simple enough to be grasped fully by a single mind. And when that truth is the truth of a particular first-century context and meaning, of whose complexity we cannot now be fully aware, it is of critical importance that different individuals engaging in dialogue with that text from all their different twenty-first-century contexts engage also in dialogue with one another. Insights gleaned by different viewpoints and different expertise will provide a stereoscopic view of increased depth that would be impossible for the individual working on one's own. Of course, the individual specialist naturally tends to honor his own discipline by attributing as much significance to it as he can in explaining the data under examination—this applies as much to the theologian as to the psychologist or sociologist. But such professional pride will almost certainly lead more often than not to a distorted picture of the whole. The individual specialist needs to bear in mind one's own limited horizons, and for the sake of truth needs to be open to the fuller view provided by the diversity of specialisms and to the correction to one's own more limited perspective that they make possible.

The same is true within the community of faith. The New Testament interpreter has a responsibility to the community of faith to speak the truth as he or she sees it, to unfold the reality of the New Testament, its strangeness as historical documentation as well as its claim on faith as scripture. And since the meaning intended by the original author should have normative significance in all matters of interpretation, the New Testament interpreter has the particular responsibility constantly to recall the community of faith to that meaning and to provide a lead in the task of reexpressing the faith of the New Testament in words and ways more appropriate to today. But that is only one gift and function within the community of faith. And if the New Testament interpreter exalts his or her role too highly the result will again be distortion and imbalance. For theological truth, like all truth, is many-faceted. And it needs the different roles and gifts of the body of Christ to bring that truth out in its fullness.

Moreover, no claim to make an authoritative pronouncement has ever been accepted at face value or been regarded as self-authenticating within the Judeo-Christian tradition. The words of prophets were tested to eliminate false prophecy. The words of Jesus have been subjected to interpretation from the beginning. The word of God has to be heard as such before it is obeyed or reckoned worthy of preservation. How much more then the offering of exegete and teacher, of interpreter and theologian. To function within the community of faith the interpreter of the New Testament requires and depends on the evaluation and assent of the community. The dialogue of New Testament interpretation takes place within the community, with all the possibility of correction and sharpened insight that this involves.

(c) This brings us to one final observation. What has been described so far has been principally the task of the trained interpreter. In relation to the community of faith that task has just been circumscribed and qualified by pointing out that it is only one gift or function within the community of faith, which needs to be evaluated and complemented by other gifts and roles if it is to make its proper contribution to the upbuilding of faith.

But it has to be qualified in at least one other way. For to confine the task of New Testament interpretation to the professional scholar would be as unjustified and inaccurate as it is to confine theology to the academic world. Of course the professional has a special expertise and calling that is not widely shared within the community of faith. That is why the New Testament scholar and theologian must be willing to put his or her historical and critical expertise at the service of the community as a whole, to be one element in the community's theological dialogue, as I have just said. But *everyone* who tries to bring the New Testament writings to bear on their own thought and life and social context is doing New Testament theology, whether they describe it as such or not. And that applies to most if not all members of the Christian churches at some time or other.

To discern an author's meaning, to hear the New Testament properly as scripture need not by any means depend on a vast apparatus of scholarly expertise. On the contrary, the scholar can often become so caught up in the complexity of his analysis that he loses sight of the meaning clearly intended by the author. The faith that enters the dialogue of New Testament interpretation uncluttered with details of doubtful disputes can often hear what the text has to say with a freshness and a simplicity which the professional scholar has missed or forgotten. This, too, is part of the dialogue at a community level.

The point here, however, is that *whoever* engages in New Testament interpretation must recognize that New Testament interpretation is a dialogue, involving the same problems as were outlined above, needing the same kind of historical and critical involvement in one degree or other. There is no virtue in simplicity for simplicity's sake, if the truth involved is in fact more complex. "Ordinary believers" should by no means regard themselves as excluded from the dialogue of New Testament interpretation. But they should recognize that they are subject to the same dangers as the professional theologian—of the dialogue becoming unbalanced, of the bridge of New Testament interpretation losing its footing in either first or twentieth centuries—or both.

Here again it needs to be said, the dialogue of New Testament interpretation is a dialogue within the community of faith. New Testament scholars can only offer their own insights and interpretations for evaluation by the whole community. To do less is to arrogate claims of truth to oneself. But this applies as much to the "lay" theologian as to the professional. The community needs to respect expertise where that is present, and to be sensitive to the aspects of the dialogue that the professional can provide. But it has also to encourage all its members to engage in the daily dialogue of New Testament interpretation, to be open to critical comments from all participants, and to play its own part in evaluating and assessing all claims on its attention. Only so can the task of New Testament interpretation fulfill its proper role.

2. THE GOSPELS AS ORAL TRADITION

1. Introduction

IN THE FIRST CHAPTER I spoke of New Testament interpretation as a dialogue. The point I want to develop in different ways over the next three chapters is that this dialogue was already happening *within* the biblical material itself, and not least within the New Testament. First, what we might describe as the dialogue between the *historical concern of the Evangelists in preserving the tradition of Jesus* and *their concern also to use* and so also to *interpret* that tradition for their own times.

Although New Testament scholarship is already well into the second generation beyond Rudolf Bultmann, the study of the Gospels continues to be largely influenced by the tremendous impact of his work—and particularly on the matter under discussion, the historicity of the Gospels. Bultmann's impact is still felt at two points in particular—two points of principle that largely governed his own analyses.

(a) The first can be summed up in the distinction between the Jesus of history and the Christ of faith. That is to say, the conviction that the first Christians were not really concerned with the earthly Jesus; the life and expression of faith focused rather on the exalted Christ. Jesus was not remembered as a teacher of the past (even of the recent past), but as the living Lord of the here and now. Only so can we make sense of the fact that Paul and the other letter writers in the New Testament show no interest whatsoever in the life of Jesus as such, and bother to quote only a minimal handful of sayings spoken by Jesus during his earthly ministry. As has often

been observed, if we had to depend on the letters of Paul for our knowledge of Jesus' life and ministry we could write it all down on the back of a postcard—descended from David, meek and gentle, two sayings about divorce and support for evangelists, the institution of the Lord's Supper, his suffering and atoning death—and that's about it.

(b) The second point of principle has become one of the basic axioms of form criticism—that the tradition preserved in the Gospels reflects first and foremost the life-setting of the early church rather than that of Jesus. The literary forms in which the Jesus tradition is now set are the forms used by the early churches in their worship, evangelism, catechetical training, and apologetic. So they reflect primarily these concerns, and not those of a merely historical or archival interest in Jesus.

When these two principles are put together the almost inevitable conclusion is that the Gospels cannot be taken as immediate or direct evidence for the life and teaching of Jesus. Despite appearances, the Gospels do *not* reflect a desire to remember Jesus as he was and what he said while on earth. The material they contain is testimony first and foremost to the early Christian faith in Christ as crucified, risen, and ascended Lord. The traditions they contain have been shaped by that faith and in accordance with the needs of the believing communities. This does not mean that Gospel tradition cannot be traced back to "the historical Jesus." But it does mean that the traditions have almost certainly been shaped and elaborated and added to—Bultmann would say, considerably added to—in the light of the Easter faith and in response to the changing needs of the Christian congregations.

The practical effect of this conclusion can be most simply stated in "burden of proof" terms. According to this logic the burden of proof lies with those who want to maintain that some particular tradition or saying goes back to Jesus. Given the two principles just outlined, it can no longer be simply assumed that a passage in any Gospel is historical until proved otherwise. Rather, it must be recognized primarily as an expression of the faith of the early church. For it to be accepted as evidence of something Jesus said or did a case has to be argued. The burden of proof lies with those who want to argue for historicity.

This outcome has some unfortunate consequences. For one thing, it tends to make a New Testament scholar uneasy when he or she cites some text as evidence of what Jesus said or did, lest one be thought to handle the text too simplistically or superficially. So in order to justify one's use of a text he or she has to engage in an elaborate analysis and discussion. To the layperson the scholar appears to be devious and embarrassed about something straightforward. This in turn increases the Christian layperson's suspicion of scholarship: it appears to be systematically skeptical and unbelieving. Thus the breach between the lectern and the pew becomes deeper and wider, with the poor occupant of the pulpit often caught uncomfortably in the middle. Such polarization between faith and scholarship benefits no one.

But it need not be so! Insofar as both faith and scholarship are concerned with truth they should be allies, not enemies. And in fact there need be no such polarization over this issue. Not by rejecting the Bultmann legacy wholesale—that would simply create a new polarization—but by retaining the best insights in the Bultmann legacy while eliminating the overstatements. We can do this most simply by developing two main points—picking up only a few aspects in the space available.

2. The probability that the first Christians were keen to retain and to pass on memories of Jesus' ministry

(a) There is a basic plausibility in the assertion that the earliest desciples *must* have been interested in stories about Jesus and in what he said. Whatever we think of Jesus, it is hardly open to question that he made a profound impact on his immediate followers. We need not become involved in complex christological questions in order to recognize Jesus as the founder of a new religious movement. In terms of human nature as we know it today, it would have been very unusual indeed if the followers of such a leader had not been concerned to preserve memories of the exploits and utterances that first drew them to him and sustained their loyalty to him.

The claim should not be exaggerated, of course. It is not universally true. We see it borne out to some extent at least in the case of other significant religious or philosophical figures like Jeremiah or Socrates or Diogenes. But it is not true of the mysterious Teacher of Righteousness in the Dead Sea Scrolls about whom we know virtually nothing. On the other hand, there were two factors operative in the case of Jesus that were not present in regard to the Teacher of Righteousness and which would go a long way toward quickening the element of "human interest" in Jesus.

The first is the degree to which Jesus himself featured as part of the earliest Christian proclamation. Jesus was not remembered merely as one who had provided a system of teaching or a philosophy or a spirituality that could be preserved and practiced without reference to the original teacher. It is true that the focus of evangelistic preaching centered very strongly on the end events of his life on earth (death and resurrection). Nevertheless, it would be surprising indeed if the disciples had not looked to Jesus' own earlier ministry and pattern of teaching and lifestyle to provide some kind of guidelines for their own life of faith.

The second is the fact that Christianity from the beginning was an evangelistic faith. It did not withdraw into the desert as a closed sect where all the members would know the facts of its founding and there would be no need to record them. From the first it sought to gain converts, and very soon converts from further afield than Palestine, including Gentiles. Human curiosity being what it is, most of these converts would almost certainly have wanted to hear more about the Jesus in whom they had believed.

In short, on *a priori* grounds it is more likely than not that the first Christians were concerned to preserve memories of Jesus and to inform their converts of them. Of course, an *a priori* argument like this does not take us very far unless it is backed up by actual evidence. But in this case there is such evidence.

(b) It is clear that in the earliest Christian communities an important role was filled by *teachers and tradition*. Luke characterizes the earliest Jerusalem church from Pentecost onwards as devoting themselves to "the teaching of the apostles" (Acts 2:42). And the importance of teachers is strongly attested elsewhere. In the earliest church at Antioch the two most prominent ministries were prophets and teachers (Acts 13:1). In 1 Cor. 12:28 Paul takes it for granted that teachers are next in importance in the life of the church to apostles and prophets. And in one of the earliest documents in the New Testament it is already assumed that the teacher must spend so much time on his task that he will have to depend for support on those he teaches (Gal. 6:6).

The task of a teacher, almost by definition, would have been to preserve and instruct in the matters regarded as important by the community. It is in very large measure a conserving function. In the case of the Christian congregations the teaching in question would not simply have been about the Torah. They would be responsible, no doubt, to search the scriptures for prophecies regarding Jesus. But instruction about Jesus, about what he said and did, must have played a prominent part in their teaching. In sociological terms the teacher in a sect plays an absolutely crucial role in consolidating and preserving the sect's self-identity, by recalling the sect to its distinctive character and to the reasons for its separate identity. Unless we wish to argue that Jesus' life prior to his death was undistinctive (but then why was he crucified?), we must accept the probability that the earliest Christian teachers were charged with the task of preserving and retelling the distinctive features of Jesus' ministry which first drew disciples to him.

This is confirmed by the prominence given to *tradition* in the earliest churches. The earliest Christian writer, Paul, speaks on a number of occasions about the traditions he passed on to his churches (1 Cor. 11:2; 15:3; Col. 2:6; 1 Thess. 4:1; 2 Thess. 2:15; 3:6). He clearly saw this as an important part of the task of an apostle—to ensure that the congregations he founded were properly informed of the traditions which characterized the Christian churches. These must have included the founding traditions that all Christian communities shared as part of their common heritage and which marked them off from other sects and synagogues. And since Paul was adamant that his understanding of the gospel was received first and foremost from God and not man (Gal. 1:11-12), the traditions he refers to cannot simply have been the proclamation of Jesus' death and resurrection itself, but must at least have included stories about the teaching of Jesus.

This is further borne out by Paul's own testimony that three years after his conversion he went up to Jersualem "to visit Peter" (Gal. 1:18). The verb used means more precisely, "to get to know, find out about." Since Peter was best known as the most prominent of Jesus' disciples and as one of the "inner circle" (Peter, James, and John) who evidently had been closest to Jesus, getting to know him must have included learning about his time with Jesus. And since "he stayed with Peter for fifteen days" he would certainly have been able to learn a great deal—including stories of what Jesus did and said when Peter was present. It is scarcely conceivable that such traditions were not included by Paul among the traditions he passed on to the churches he founded.

It would be odd indeed to imagine Christian congregations meeting throughout the eastern Mediterranean, who in their regular gatherings were concerned only with study of the (Jewish) scriptures, with the message of Jesus' death and resurrection, and with waiting on the risen Lord—and who were quite unconcerned to recall and reflect on the ministry and teaching of Jesus while on earth. On the contrary, it was precisely these memories and traditions that they were most likely to want to share and celebrate together—the founding traditions that gave them their distinctive identity.

(c) All this can be deduced without looking at the Gospels themselves. When we do turn to them these plausible but still provisional conclusions are confirmed. For the Synoptic Gospels in particular contain just the sort of traditions about Jesus that we would expect the early Christian teachers to take responsibility for preserving and passing on. I refer, first of all, to the nature of the Gospels as *biographies of Jesus*.

Bultmann himself was strongly of the view that the Gospels should *not* be regarded as biographies. To understand why, we must remember that he was in fact reacting strongly against his own theological education. It was one of the fashions in the heyday of liberal Protestantism in the latter decades of the nineteenth century to write lives of Jesus, with the Gospels treated as sources for a modern biographical study. That is to say, these lives of Jesus felt free to reconstruct a fairly detailed chronological outline of his life and ministry, to speculate about Jesus' inner life, and to discuss the development of his self-consciousness. Bultmann saw this as a complete misunderstanding of the character of the Gospels. They were *not* biographies!

What he meant or should have said was that they are not *modern* biographies. Unfortunately, this qualification was not recognized and the blanket dictum (the Gospels are not biographies) became a basic axiom in most form-critical studies for the next two generations. It seemed to confirm rather neatly the twofold assumption outlined at the beginning: the earliest Christians were interested only in the exalted Christ and their own contemporary needs. They had no biographical interest in Jesus as he had been prior to his death and resurrection.

In fact, however, the Synoptic Gospels conform quite closely to the form and function of the *ancient* biography. The nearest parallel in the Graeco-Roman world to the genre of Gospel is the *bios* or *vita* ("life"). Whereas modern biography has a central concern with personality development and chronological framework within which it occurs, ancient biography had a much more static concept of personality and only rarely expressed interest in such development. On the contrary, human personality was thought of as fixed and unchanging. Moreover, a deeply rooted assumption of the ancients was that a person's character was clearly revealed in his actions and words. Consequently, it was the principal task of the biographer to portray his subject by relating things he did and said and thus to depict his character.

But this is very much what we find in the Gospels. No particular, or at least consistent, concern with chronology. And certainly no attempt to describe development in Jesus' character or self-understanding. But a thoroughgoing attempt to portray Jesus by means of what he said and what he did. In terms of the categories of the time, therefore, the Gospels, or the Synoptic Gospels in particular, *can* be described as biographies. And precisely as such they indicate a considerable concern on the part of the Evangelists to recall and record Jesus as his first disciples remembered him.

(d) Finally, we may reflect a little further on the character of the Synoptic Gospels as *collections of oral memories about Jesus.* This is one of the most positive features of the form-critical approach. It has made us much more conscious of the period of oral tradition that lies *behind* the written Gospels, the tradition as it was being used *before* it was written down. Such an awareness immediately relieves us from over-dependence on arguments about the precise dates of the Gospels. Whatever dates we determine for the Gospels, it is hardly to be disputed that the earliest Christian churches were *oral* communities before the Gospels were written. And, as already noted, as with all oral societies then and since, they would inevitably have sought to retain and express their founding traditions, for it was these traditions that justified and explained (to themselves as to others) the reason for their

separate and distinctive existence. And not only to retain these traditions, but to retell them too, to seek and create opportunities to rehearse and celebrate their sacred tradition. So the Jews have celebrated the Passover for millennia. So the Qumran community preserved its Damascus Document. And so the first Christians no doubt recalled and relived the events of the last days of Jesus' life in the memories that now form the passion narratives in particular.

Equally important, the recognition of the oral character of so much at least of the tradition used in the Gospels frees us from an over-dependence on arguments based solely on literary dependence. Despite the recognition of an oral period of the Jesus tradition, too many Gospel analysts have continued their task as though the relationships between the Gospels could be understood solely in terms of literary sources—of a scissors-and-paste type of editing. As though the traditions used by Mark, for example, ceased to exist as oral traditions all over the eastern Mediterranean, simply because Mark writing in Rome, say, had written them down! But of course Matthew and Luke, assuming they had copies of Mark to hand, also had access to oral tradition, including oral versions of much of what Mark had recorded. When churches in Syria, for example, received their copies of Mark's Gospel, that was hardly the first time they had heard much or most of what Mark contains.

Being made thus alert to the oral background of the Gospel traditions, it becomes fairly easy to spot characteristics that were probably first oral before they were literary. For example, the "pronouncement story," where the episode related builds up to a memorable saying of Jesus as its climax. Or the account of some encounter, as between Jesus and the centurion in Matthew 8, where the central focus is clearly the snatch of dialogue between the centurion and Jesus, and the other details are clearly subsidiary to that. Storytellers the world over will recognize the basic rule of thumb of good storytelling—to get the punchline right, whatever else. Another example would be the use of link-words or linking themes: for example, the words *fire* and *salt,* which link together the final verses of Mark 9; and the neat way Matthew uses the theme of "following" to tie together the sayings about discipleship with the account of the disciples being caught in a storm on Galilee—an effective way of illustrating what "following Jesus" will mean for the would-be disciple.

Mark's Gospel itself has many "oral" features, and may be fairly described as oral tradition written down. Indeed, bearing in mind that Mark would write his Gospel to be read out loud, the Gospel itself can properly be regarded as an extended oral presentation of the traditions of Jesus, little different in character from the many celebrations of the new movement's "founding traditions." I think in particular of Mark 1:21-29, structured on the pattern of "twenty-four hours in the ministry of Jesus." Or 2:1—3:6, a collection of controversy stories, charting the areas of disagreement between Jesus and groups of Pharisees, and building up dramatically to the climax of the complete breach between them. Or chapter 4 on the theme of Jesus' parables, illustrating and expounding their rationale. Or 4:35—5:43, a collection of miracle stories on and around the Sea of Galilee, and linked together by the motif of crossing back and forth "to the other side." And not to forget Mark's own characteristic "immediately"—immediately Jesus did this, or immediately he went there—which keeps the tale told by Mark moving along at a brisk pace and never allows the listener's attention to wander.

The point is this. The Gospel traditions themselves show that their present form is the outcome of a well-established practice of oral use. In other words, they bear witness to a strong and widely prevalent concern among the first Christians to *remember* Jesus, to celebrate their memories, to retain them in appropriate forms, to structure their traditions for easy recall, but above all to remember.

In short, the idea that the first Christians were *not* interested in the pre-Easter Jesus is little short of ludicrous. On the contrary, they would certainly have been concerned that the memories of "all that Jesus said and did" should be passed on to new converts and retold in new churches. The "biographical" interest of the Evangelists in portraying the character of Jesus by recounting his words and deeds did not begin first with them. In the concern of the new congregations to formulate and celebrate their founding traditions, it was no doubt there from the first. In burden-of-proof terms, it is this recognition that should be the starting point of investigation of the Synoptic traditions of Jesus' ministry.

3. We can also see how the first Christians passed on the traditions about Jesus and gain a clearer perspective on what their concern to remember Jesus meant in terms of historicity

In the first chapter of *The Evidence for Jesus*[1] I have discussed and documented this topic in some detail and so may be permitted here to treat it more briefly. The point is this. The recognition of the oral character of the Synoptic tradition also involves recognition of a degree of freedom on the part of the storyteller to shape his material with a view to the needs of his audience. Often and again the story teller or teacher will have been concerned more with themes and high points of the tradition being used than with details he would regard as subsidiary to these themes and high points. He will have grouped his material in order to illustrate a theme rather than to preserve a chronological sequence. He will have told his story in a longer or shorter version depending on time available. He will have slanted his account in detail or tone so that it might better serve the needs of the group to which he ministered.

None of this cuts across what has already been said. The probability that the first Christians were concerned to retain and pass on the memory of what Jesus said and did remains undiminished. What we are now looking at is how they did so. We can illustrate the character of these orally recounted memories by simply comparing our own Synoptic Gospels, since, as we have seen, their contents consist in large part of oral traditions written down.

(a) For one thing they grouped the traditions in different ways. As is well known, the material that makes up the Sermon on the Mount in Matthew 5–7 is scattered throughout four or so of Luke's chapters. And, for the most part, it is clearly the same material. The most likely explanation of this phenomenon is not that Luke broke up and scattered Matthew's Sermon, but that Matthew has *constructed* the Sermon by grouping together elements of Jesus' teaching which were actually delivered at different points during his ministry. This is simply good teaching technique—to group coherent and complementary material together to make it easier to remember. In fact, Matthew seems to have made some attempt to group almost all of Jesus' teaching into five blocks, probably as a sort of echo of the five books of Moses. If this is indeed the case, the point which bears upon us is that the grouping of this material was determined by teaching technique rather than by historical considerations.

In particular, it is unlikely that Matthew intended his readers to think of the Sermon on the Mount as actually delivered by Jesus on a single occasion. He has simply constructed a framework in which to set these important memories of what Jesus said—a quite understandable and acceptable teaching device that would have misled no one. In short, such an example confirms the earliest Christians' concern to preserve and pass on the memory of what Jesus had said by grouping it in easily remembered forms. To insist that the framework be accorded the same historical status as the content of the Sermon is probably to misconceive the character of the remembering process and to misunderstand the intention of Matthew.

A similar conclusion would have to be drawn, for example, from the collection of mini-parables in Mark 4:21-25. The fact is that the four one-verse parables or wisdom sayings occur at quite different places in Matthew, scattered through Matthew's Gospel. And Luke has evidently followed *both* Mark and the Matthean source in using the sayings twice, once in Mark's grouping, the other scattered through the Gospel like Matthew. The most obvious conclusion to draw is that these sayings of Jesus were remembered both individually and as grouped together for convenience, by means of linking devices.

(b) Second, we may note examples where the Evangelists preserve the same account but in different lengths or with different emphases. The account of Jesus' disciples plucking ears of grain on the sabbath is a case in point (Mark 2:23-28 pars.). Matthew and Mark both have material in their versions that is found in neither of the other Gospels. It is clearly the same incident in each case, but in each case the storyteller has either abbreviated a longer tale or expanded a briefer tale. Another example is the story of Jairus's daughter and the woman with the hemorrhage (Mark 5:21-43 pars.). Luke's version is twice as long as Matthew's and Mark's nearly three times as long. Again, either one has abbreviated a fuller account, or another has lengthened a briefer account. This is the art of storytelling—not to reproduce an account always in the same words and with parrot-like precision, but as the needs of occasion and audience may demand.

An example of an episode from Jesus' life retold with different emphases is the account of the healing of the centurion's servant (Matt. 8:5-13//Luke 7:1-10). As already noted, the focus is on the exchange between Jesus and the centurion, but the build-up to that central section is rather different in each case. In Matthew's briefer version the centurion meets Jesus and addresses him personally; it would appear from the rest of the account that this is partly because Matthew wants to stress the immediacy of the centurion's faith. Luke, however, in his longer introduction, emphasizes the fact that the centurion did *not* come to Jesus personally but sent others; and it is clear from the details Luke includes that he wants to stress the centurion's humility. It is certainly the same event that is thus related in these two different ways, but the accompanying details were evidently less important than the central exchange and need not be recounted with the same precision. As in all good storytelling, the story is lost if the main point is distorted or forgotten, but the subsidiary details can be modified without spoiling the story or misleading the listeners.

Another example would be the account of Peter's denial of Jesus (Mark 14:66-72 pars.). What was important was the fact that Peter denied Jesus no fewer than three times and that when he heard the cock crow he remembered Jesus' prediction and wept. The details which make up that vivid story are less important—who it was who accused Peter, whether the cock crowed once or twice. The accusers are indicated with casual, vague descriptions which shows that it was no part of the storyteller's purpose to identify the who and the when with precision—"a maid," "someone else," "the bystanders." To insist that these details can be pressed to yield firm historical facts is to misconceive the purpose of the Evangelists and to distort their emphases. It is like insisting that symbolic language be understood literally or a hymn be read as prose.

(c) Third, it is also clear that the words of Jesus could be remembered in different versions. This, of course, would be inevitable to some extent at least since translation was often involved. Words of Jesus spoken in Aramaic would be translated into Greek, and since no translation can produce a complete set of precise equivalents, in word or idiom, it is inevitable that different Greek renderings of Jesus' words would be in circulation. What was important was the sense of what Jesus had said, not a precision of verbal form. And in order to express that sense the translation might need to be longer than the original, with some explanatory expansion to make an unfamiliar idiom clear. Anyone familiar with the range of modern translations of the Bible will take the point without difficulty.

We see something of this even with two of the most precious and most used of Jesus' words. As is well known, the Lord's Prayer comes to us in two versions—Matthew 6:9-15 and Luke 11:2-4. As the prayer taught by Jesus, to serve as the special prayer and badge of Jesus' disciples, we might have thought great care would have been taken to keep the words the same for all. But Matthew's version has the longer address—"Our Father, who art in heaven"—whereas Luke simply has "Father." And Matthew has two more petitions than Luke, although they seem chiefly to fill out the preceding petitions. Luke's version is generally thought to be closer to the original in length, while Matthew is closer in idiom. What has probably happened is that Luke's translation has not been at pains to reproduce the Aramaic idiom, while Matthew's version has been elaborated in the course of earliest Christian usage—to make it more rounded and easier to say in congregational worship. We see the same thing continuing thereafter with the addition of the now familiar ending at a still later stage—"For thine is the Kingdom, and the power, and the glory. Amen." This is just the sort of polishing and refining we would expect in liturgical usage. After all, Jesus had given them the prayer to *use,* and use it they did. It was intended to serve as their prayer, not just as a memory of something Jesus had said. And in being thus used its details changed a little, without changing the sense, in order to serve more effectively as their prayer. The process is no different today. In a day when there are three or four English versions of the Matthew 6 prayer we can understand and appreciate well enough the concerns and priorities of the first bearers of the tradition.

The other example is the words of Jesus at the Last Supper (Mark 14:22-25 pars; 1 Cor. 11:24-25). As is well known here also the tradition comes to us in two main forms—a Matthew/Mark version and a Paul/Luke version. One of the principal differences comes in the word over the cup. According to

Matthew and Mark Jesus says, "This is my blood of the covenant." According to Paul and Luke Jesus says, "This cup is the new covenant in my blood." The sense is more or less the same, but the emphasis is slightly different. Here, too, even in what was probably one of the most precious words of Jesus, there was no attempt to preserve strict conformity. The sense was more important than the form. So, too, it is probably significant that only Paul's version adds the command, "Do this, as often as you drink it, in remembrance of me." Probably a further example of liturgical polishing—the spelling out explicitly of what was understood to be implied in the shorter formula.

In these cases what we see is tradition not merely being remembered, but tradition used. And tradition valued not simply because it was first given by Jesus, but because it continued to provide a medium of encounter between the divine and the human. Just so, we might say, with the psalms of the Old Testament. They were treasured down through the generations not simply because they were composed by David or Asaph or whoever, but because they continued to serve as an inspired means of worship and of grace.

(d) This insight probably helps provide an answer to the problem mentioned at the beginning: the fact that the earliest New Testament author (Paul) seems to have been so little concerned to refer his readers to what Jesus said and did. The fact is that there are a good many exhortations in Paul where he is most probably *echoing* words originally given by Jesus and remembered for that reason. Romans 12–14 and 1 Thessalonians 5 contain a number of examples. The point is that Paul used the Jesus tradition in this way presumably because he saw it as *living* tradition, valued not merely because it had spoken to them in the past, but because it still spoke to them with the force of inspired authority. Paul spoke it afresh, not because it had been heard as the word of God twenty years earlier, but because he still heard and experienced it as the living word of God there and then.

On this point we can see a parallel with the way the Old Testament scriptures were heard and functioned as authority. Of course, there are very many instances where an Old Testament scripture is cited as such, regularly with the formula "as it was written" or an equivalent. However, there are very many more instances where there is no explicit citation as such, but where the scripture has clearly influenced and molded the words and images used. In such cases, we may say, the scripture has exercised its authority in shaping the thought and language of the New Testament author—no doubt in many cases without conscious intention. The scripture has functioned authoritatively, and that authority stems from the original inspiration, but it has been experienced as a living authority and not as a casual echo of the dead past.

So with the memory of what Jesus said and did. We have already noted how highly probable it is that the material contained in the Synoptic Gospels was fairly widely known in the earliest Christian congregations. The fact that Paul makes so little explicit reference to it almost certainly means that he could take knowledge of it for granted. Now we may add that he could also make allusion to the Jesus tradition, just as he often made allusion to Old Testament scripture, and for the same reason. The words of Jesus were not merely remembered but experienced afresh as words of the Lord. This sense of a *living* tradition is crucial for our understanding of the earliest handing on and use of the corporate memories of Jesus. For the first Christians the words of Jesus were not like some dead corpse, with limbs stiffened and fixed by *rigor mortis,* to be conveyed from place to place like some revered relics, but a living voice which was heard again and again speaking with ever new force and effect in a variety of fresh situations.

(e) Finally, this helps us to begin to understand what is almost certainly the most difficult case of all for Christians who hold the Bible in high regard. I refer to the Fourth Gospel. Here the matter is peculiarly sensitive, since so much seems to depend on it. For if John's Gospel is straightforward history, then we have in it the most amazing and powerful self-testimony of Jesus. If John's Gospel is unvarnished history then all that Christians need ever claim for Jesus is clearly attested there, and by Jesus himself. If John is correct, then the old apologetic-evangelistic question is unavoidable: the one who makes such claims for himself is either mad, bad, or God.

But the very starkness and unequivocalness of these claims is what begins to raise the nagging question in the mind. If Jesus made such claims, why do the other Gospels make no use of them? What Evangelist having among the traditions which had been passed to him such wonderful sayings as the "I ams"—"I am the resurrection and the life"; "I am the way, the truth, and the life"; "Before Abraham was, I am"; and so on—what Evangelist having to hand such sayings could ignore them completely? The question, once raised, cannot be squashed into silence, since the integrity of that whole apologetic-evangelistic approach is at stake.

Once raised, that question leads to others. For we begin to realize more clearly that the style of Jesus' teaching in John's Gospel is very distinctive, and very different from that in the other Gospels. There we have a Jesus who speaks in short, pungent sayings, like the one-verse parables mentioned above. Or whose longer, connected statements consist in longer parables, or what look like collections of shorter sayings, like the Sermon on the Mount. But in John's Gospel we have these lengthy discourses, which often seem to take a theme and develop it in a sort of circular motion, as in the Bread of Life discourse in chapter 6, returning more than once to the earlier subthemes and elaborating them afresh. Rather in the way a theme like love is elaborated in the First Epistle of John.

At the same time we recognize elements within these discourses that strongly recall particular sayings of Jesus found in the Synoptics. The new birth discourse in chapter 3 echoes Jesus' saying about entry into the kingdom being possible only for one who becomes as a little child (Matt. 18:3 pars.). The Father-Son discourse of chapter 5 seems to build on the way Jesus was remembered as addressing God as Father in intimate terms (as in Mark 14:36). And the discourse about Jesus as the good shepherd in chapter 10 seems to be a natural and (in Christian perspective) inevitable deduction from Jesus' parable about the lost sheep and the caring shepherd preserved in Luke 15. So the teaching of the Johannine Jesus is not so far removed from that of the Synoptic Jesus, at least in core sayings and themes.

These twin features in John seem at first puzzling—the striking *dis*-similarity between the Johannine discourses in boldness and style of statement and the teaching of Jesus in the Synoptics, *and* the *similarity* provided by central elements of these same discourses. The puzzle is resolved when we realize that these Johannine discourses are probably just a more developed example of the sort of thing we have already seen in the Synoptics themselves. The Johannine discourses are probably best understood as extended meditations or reflections on the significance of various typical events in Jesus' ministry and sayings of Jesus remembered within the communities from which John's Gospel came. They are but a further example of the oral tradition process and of how it was a living process where the richness and significance of the earlier tradition was spelled out, in story form, perhaps even actual sermons, by one who had been present at such events and perhaps even heard these sayings and who had meditated long and hard on them.

This seems to me to be a very fair understanding of what John in effect claims for his own writing, when he describes the task of the Paraclete—an inspired "*re*-proclamation" of the truth of Jesus (John 16:13-15), a recalling of the signs Jesus performed (John 20:31), a spelling out of the significance of what he had said (e.g., John 2:21), and a leading into the fuller truth of things his disciples had not been able to hear or understand when Jesus was with them (John 16:12-13).

Some Christians find such conclusions rather threatening, because they seem to undermine the trustworthiness of John's Gospel. But that is to miss the point. That is to assume that John's intention was to provide straightforward, unvarnished history. Nothing that he says compels us to that conclusion. That he is speaking about a historical person who actually lived and ministered in Galilee and Judea and who died on a cross in Jerusalem is, of course, fundamental to his message. But his concern seems to be to give us the truth about Jesus, the reality now visible to the eye of faith but not to those whose eyes were too blind to see. To make this truth of Jesus dependent on whether

Jesus actually said the words ascribed to him in John's Gospel or not is almost certainly to misunderstand that truth, perhaps even to undermine that truth. It is almost certainly to misunderstand John's intention and to make it harder for his message of Jesus to be heard. Whereas, to recognize the character of John's Gospel as a reflective remembering enables us to appreciate the dynamic impact made by Jesus on his disciples and the living quality of their memory of him.

In all these areas illustrated above there are many other and often more complex cases. But hopefully sufficient has been said to give a clear enough flavor of the character of the earliest Christian remembering of Jesus in his life and ministry.

4. Conclusion

To sum up. It is clear from all this that the earliest Christians *were* concerned to remember Jesus and to pass on these memories to new converts and churches. But again and again it is equally clear that they were more concerned with the substance and meaning of what Jesus had said and done than with a meticulous level of verbal precision or with a pedantic level of historical detail. It is important to recognize the force of both points. To underestimate the former is to cut Christianity off from its historical foundation and fountainhead. But to misplace the emphasis in the latter stands in equal danger of distorting the concerns of the first Christians. The Synoptic tradition as history—yes, indeed! But the Gospels also as the living tradition of the earliest churches—that, too.

We therefore can make the strong and confident affirmation that the Synoptic Gospels in particular *are* a source of historical information about Jesus; the Evangelists were concerned with the historicity of what they remembered; in burden-of-proof terms we can start from the assumption that the Synoptic tradition is a good witness to the historical Jesus unless proved otherwise. But we must be careful not to overstate our case. To claim that the Evangelists had the same level of historical concern in every phrase and sentence they used runs counter to the evidence and almost certainly misunderstands their intention. Equally serious, such a claim *undermines* the case for the historicity of the Gospels, since it makes that case depend on a series of implausible harmonizations. Properly to recognize the Evangelists' concern for historicity in their own terms means recognizing also their other concerns and above all the character of that earliest remembering as a living word.

3. WAS JESUS A LIBERAL? WAS PAUL A HERETIC?

1. Introduction

IN CHAPTERS 2 THROUGH 4 we are looking at the dialogue of theological interpretation *within* scripture. In chapter 2 our concern was to look at the dialogue between the Jesus tradition and the use made of it by the Evangelists. In this chapter we look at the dialogue between Old Testament and New.

One of the most amazing features of Christianity is its incorporation of the Old Testament within its collection of sacred writings—the fact that it treats the Old Testament as part of its scripture, its normative canon. For the Old Testament is primarily *Jewish* scripture. It is only *Christian* scripture in a derived and contested sense. It was not written by Christians. It is pre-Christian. Of course, Christians claim a strong line of continuity between Old Testament and New—the whole claim that Christ and Christianity are the fulfillment of the promises and prophecies which lie at the heart of the Old Testament. But even if we maximize that claim, we cannot shut our eyes to the *also* strong *dis*continuity between Old and New Testaments. The fact, for example, that most Jews did not recognize Christ and Christianity to be the fulfillment of these promises and prophecies—and still do not. The Christian argument that Christ is the expected fulfillment has evidently not been sufficiently clear-cut or compelling to convince the bulk of his own people. That should at least give us pause in our too little examined assumption that the Old Testament is Christian scripture clear and simple.

Or again, the fact that Christianity has, like it or not, abandoned so much of the Old Testament. To take only the most obvious example: we no longer regard the laws of sacrifice as binding on us. There is a whole swath of the law that was fundamental to the faith of the Old Testament which we dismiss as no longer relevant to us. Of course, Judaism itself no longer sacrifices, and has not done so since the destruction of the Temple in 70 c.e. But that is a case of Judaism having to rationalize an unexpected and unwelcome development. And strong strands of Judaism would regard the sacrificial laws as only in temporary suspension, *force majeure,* ready to be reenacted with all the old fervor when the Temple is restored, whereas Christianity regards it as a matter of principle that the sacrifices are no longer to be offered. To revive the law of sacrifice would be to cut at the heart of Christianity's distinctive claim that Christ by the sacrifice of himself has made an end to all shedding of blood in sacrifice.

The point is that we have here a set of laws which belong very much to the essence of the Old Testament and the religion it inculcates. The Torah, we should recall, is the heart of the Old Testament. This is not simply the claim of later Judaism, but is integral to the self-understanding of all parts of the Old Testament. The prophets who call for a deeper observance of the law, not for its abolition. The Wisdom writers who see the law as the embodiment of divine wisdom. And so on. None of these prepares us for this step that the first Christians take of actually abandoning, counting as null and void, crucial elements of the law.

So clearly we have something of a problem in regard to the Old Testament as Christian scripture. We cannot regard it as Christian scripture *tout simple.* There is a fundamental tension between Christianity and its Jewish roots and origins, which lies very much at the heart of Christianity. And nowhere does it come to clearer expression than at this point. What does it mean to call Christian canonical scripture laws and observances that Christianity no longer observes or wants to observe?

Of course we can construct some kind of rational defense by spiritualizing the Old Testament laws and observances in question. Allegorizing has a long and well-regarded history within Christian circles. But it is also open to much abuse and raises awkward questions about the ground and authority for the allegorical meaning offered. And self-evidently it is *not* taking the Old Testament text in question at its most obvious and intended meaning. The more we stress that the normative meaning of a text is the meaning intended by its author, as I certainly want to do in talking of the New Testament writings, the more embarrassing becomes the device of spiritualizing those laws we no longer want to obey. It certainly introduces a nervous-making precedent for any hermeneutic since it actually locates the meaning of the text *outside* the text, reads the allegorical meaning in varying degrees by arbitrariness into the text. So the issue and problem remains: What does it mean for Christianity that it includes the Old Testament within its canon? What does this say about the character and force of scriptural authority?

2. Jesus and the Old Testament

What then of Jesus? The question is particularly sensitive if we want to see in Jesus' use of the Old Testament a pattern and norm for all Christian usage. This is certainly the case in many attempts to argue for a strong sense of scriptural authority—in terms of "infallibility" or "inerrancy."

The line here might well start with a text like John 10:34-36:

> Jesus answered them, "Is it not written in your law, 'I said, you are gods'? If he called them gods to whom the word of God came (and the scripture cannot be broken), do you say of him whom the Father consecrated and sent into the world, 'You are blaspheming,' because I said, 'I am the Son of God'?"

Here, it would be said, Jesus (or the Fourth Evangelist, if the parenthesis is his addition) clearly takes a strong view of scriptural authority: "the scripture cannot be broken." That is, its force cannot be set aside or nullified. Jesus (or John) here proclaims that the binding character of a scriptural pronouncement cannot be loosed by human wish or weakened by human interpretation.

Similarly with Matthew 5:17-18:

> Think not that I have come to abolish the law and the prophets; I have come not to abolish them but to fulfill them. For truly, I say to you, till heaven and earth pass away, not an iota, not a dot, will pass from the law until all is accomplished.

The conclusion is the same. Jesus sets himself under the authority of the Old Testament. He affirms its continuing force and validity. The argument would, of course, be much elaborated. But this is the heart of it.

Yet how can we argue so? As we have already noted, Christianity *did* abandon important parts of the Old Testament. It did not regard the laws of sacrifice as a continuing force and validity. It has broken the force of these scriptural injunctions in the sense in which they were intended, and still understood at the time of Jesus. If we insist on saying that Jesus set himself *under* the authority of the Old Testament in this undifferentiated way then we have to accept the unpalatable corollary that the Christianity which subsequently abandoned so much of the Old Testament was actually going against Jesus. The more we argue for the continuity between the Old Testament and Jesus, the more awkward the *dis*continuity between Jesus and subsequent Christianity. The more we press John 10:35 and Matthew 5:17-18 in terms of infallibility and inerrancy, the more embarrassing the Christian refusal to observe the laws of sacrifice becomes. Of course, we can argue a theology of fulfillment; but that is simply another form of *dis*continuity which does not actually resolve the problem. Or we can argue for a canonical coherence, which means that a clear principle enunciated in the New Testament can be used to justify such a reinterpretation of these Old Testament passages. But it still does not weaken the basic fact that, whatever John 10 and Matthew 5 mean, Christianity has abandoned the plain sense and prescriptive force of Old Testament scripture.

Clearly, then, we cannot simply base our view of Jesus' attitude to the authority of the Old Testament on a "strong" reading of passages like John 10 and Matthew 5. We must look more closely at how the Gospels show Jesus *actually* to have used the Old Testament *in practice*. Unless we want to drive a wedge between Jesus and subsequent Christianity we cannot simply assume that such a "strong" reading of John 10 and Matthew 5 is the only legitimate reading of these texts. And the only way to check whether there are other legitimate readings, or indeed other readings which come closer to their intended sense, is to check the other evidence of how Jesus *used* the Old Testament, not merely how he spoke about it.

(a) First, we should note the way Jesus dealt with the issues raised by the oral tradition, and oral Torah. According to Mark Jesus fell afoul of the Pharisees on a number of points. Over the sabbath law he was heavily criticized for allowing his disciples to pluck and eat grain on the sabbath (Mark 2:23-28) and for healing a man with a withered hand on the sabbath (Mark 3:1-6). In Mark 7 he is heavily criticized for failing to encourage his disciples to observe the traditions of purity in the case in point—eating food without first washing hands to cleanse away any impurities that might have attached to the hand while mixing with others in the open or in the marketplace (Mark 7:1-5). In the same chapter Jesus himself attacks the tradition of corban—the ruling which insisted that a vow must be fulfilled, even if it was made in thoughtlessness or in spite regarding one's obligations to others (7:10-13). In each case it is the Pharisaic interpretation of particular points of the written Torah that he disputes.

The relevance of this sequence of evidence could be disputed. Precisely for that reason: because the issue here is *not* the Torah, but a particular sequence of *interpretations* of the Torah. Indeed, according to Mark 7:13, Jesus' complaint against the Pharisees is that they have made void a particular *written* command ("Honor your father and mother") by this interpretation of the law of vows.

This is certainly a fair point. But it only softens the issue to some extent. For one thing, it underscores the fact that there was a debate about how the law should be interpreted, and that Jesus took part in that debate. And for another, the Pharisees would not have accepted such a clear distinction between the written law and the oral law. The oral law was simply their exposition of the law. Their whole concern was to show how the law written so many centuries before, in and for rather different circumstances than their own, still applied to their own day. These were simple examples of case-law, rulings that had been made by previous legal experts and as such had gained the weight of the law themselves. So the Pharisees would certainly have regarded Jesus as dangerously minimalist or reductionist with regard to the law—too casual, by half. Dangerously liberal, in fact.

And if the Pharisees, so much more the Essenes, whose particular interpretation of the law was even tighter and more binding. In the eyes of two of the principal sects, the most active theological schools within first-century Judaism, Jesus was highly suspect.

(b) But what about Jesus' attitude to the law as such—the written Torah? We have seen Jesus in dispute with two of the main theological groupings in first-century Judaism. Another passage shows him in dispute with the third main body of thinking opinion at that time—the Sadducees. According to Mark 12:24-27 Jesus disputed with the Sadducees regarding the resurrection from the dead. The Pharisees believed in resurrection; they thought it a legitimate interpretation from the scriptures. The Sadducees did not: it was nowhere clearly attested in the Torah. In this dispute between Sadducees and Pharisees it was the Sadducees who were being more fundamentalist: only what was clearly written in the law should be part of faith. But Jesus here sides with the Pharisees. On this issue Jesus, like the Pharisees, would have been regarded by the Bible loyalists as a dangerous innovator—someone who *read into* the text he quoted ("I am the God of Abraham, and the God of Isaac, and the God of Jacob," Mark 12:26) what was not self-evidently there.

A sharper example is the *lex talionis* in Matthew 5:38-41. The law said clearly, "An eye for an eye and a tooth for a tooth." But Jesus sets this law aside as relativized by a higher principle—that of love of neighbor. Judaism at the time of Jesus was certainly not averse to the idea of summing up the law in terms of first or basic principle. And love of neighbor was an obvious choice for such a first principle. But not in such a way as to set it in opposition or antithesis to other parts of the law. To love the neighbor was to act toward him within the terms of the law, or to bring him nigh to the law. But in this and the following antithesis Jesus exalts the one principle of love of neighbor in such a way as to limit the applicability of another law and render it ineffective in its prescriptive force. To select a particular law from within the range of laws and to exalt it over the rest without scriptural warrant would be regarded by many at the time of Jesus as arbitrary. And to set it in opposition to another clearly stated law would be regarded as dangerously liberal.

For a final example we might return to Mark 7 and the word of Jesus about true cleanliness—Mark 7:18-19:

> Do you not see that whatever goes into a man from outside cannot defile him, since it enters, not his heart but his stomach, and so passes on?

Here there is some disagreement between Mark and Matthew as to whether Jesus' saying was really so radical. Where Mark says, "*Nothing* from outside *can* defile . . . ," Matthew has in effect, "Defilement comes not so much from without as from within." Without going into the issue of what Jesus actually said, the point is that Mark can present the saying of Jesus in such a sharply antithetical form. Indeed, Mark can go on to add *his* interpretation: "Thus he declared all foods clean." According to Mark, what Jesus said amounted to a denial that there was such a thing as unclean food—an abrogation of another whole segment of the Torah, the very important laws on clean and unclean foods (particularly Leviticus 13; Deuteronomy 14). Whether it was Jesus or Mark who did it, the author of Mark 7 certainly intends his readers to see Jesus as approving the abandonment of the law of unclean foods. The issue was no slight matter of particular dietary laws. Unclean foods had been at the heart of the Maccabean crisis: observance of these food laws was a mark of a loyal Jew, a faithful member of the covenant—1 Maccabees 1:62-63:

> Many in Israel stood firm and were resolved in their hearts not to eat unclean food. They chose to die rather than to be defiled by food or to profane the holy covenant; and they did die.

Anyone who called on or encouraged Jews to abandon such laws as these was being unfaithful, a dangerous subversive and apostate. But this is evidently how Mark believes Jesus should be understood.

So the issue of whether Jesus thought the law was eternal and eternally valid cannot be settled by reference to John 10 and Matthew 5. He certainly seems to have thought that some at least of the law was not so. And he is remembered as encouraging others to sit loose to some laws and to abandon others.

(c) The point becomes more complex still when we remember that a strong characteristic of Jesus' ministry was his *openness*. He was remembered in both polemic and admiration as "a friend of tax collectors and sinners" (Matt. 11:19 par.). His table-fellowship was notoriously open to such disreputables (Mark

2:16). Here we have to recall what was so shocking about such conduct. A tax collector would be widely regarded as a traitor, a collaborator with and agent of the occupying armies of Rome, a quisling. A loyal and faithful Jew could hardly help despising such a person, and would certainly not want to welcome him into his company. And "sinner" was a favorite word used in the various factions within Judaism at that time to describe those who were outside their group, outside their boundaries, unacceptable to the right thinking and right doing, the "righteous." A sinner was one who did not observe the law as the particular group thought it should be observed. For the Pharisees the non-Pharisee was a sinner, including the Sadducee. For the Essenes the non-Essene was a sinner—including the Pharisee!

What we see in Jesus' ministry, therefore, is one who was ready to cut across the conventions that governed the different and dominant subgroups within his society. He was one who flouted the prevailing religious sentiment and conventions. The point should not be exaggerated, of course. He was not an anarchist. He should not be presented as a kind of first-century hippie. Nevertheless, a flouter of conventions is a dangerous figure in a situation where the rules of acceptable social conduct are so clearly drawn.

Or to put it in different terms, Jesus was a boundary breaker. The religious society of his day had drawn clear boundaries around it. The Essenes and Pharisees are simply the clearest examples of such careful drawing of the boundary lines to mark out who is *in* and who is *out*. As modern social anthropological studies have reminded us, ritual acts and concern for ritual purity are one important way of drawing such boundaries—between acceptable and unacceptable, righteous and sinner, the in and the out, us and them. Even John the Baptist's insistence on baptism was of this order—a necessary boundary to be crossed for those who wanted to be found faithful in the end.

But with Jesus there is none of that. He frequently crosses the boundaries drawn by others. He refuses to draw any such boundaries for himself: unlike John the Baptist he did not even require baptism of his would-be disciples; and his table-fellowship was in no sense a ritual act for the insiders from which the outsiders were excluded. On the contrary, Jesus' ministry was marked by an *in*clusiveness rather than an *ex*clusiveness. To those who pressed the claims of family upon him, he says, "My mother and brother and sister are *whoever* does the will of God" (Mark 3:35). To disciples who want him to tell off an exorcist who exorcises in Jesus' name but who does not follow Jesus, he says, "Do *not* forbid him. . . . He that is not against us is for us" (Mark 9:38-40). The despised half-breed heretic Samaritan is his model for the loving neighbor, rather than the priest or Levite (Luke 10:29-37). In face of the austere purity of the Qumran sect who will not allow any physical blemishment to render the eschatological assembly of God less than perfect,

Jesus says, "The messianic banquet is precisely for the maimed, the blind, the lame" (Luke 14:12-24).

Once again we should not exaggerate the point. Jesus certainly demanded commitment on the part of those he called to follow him. His demands were high and in terms of priorities uncompromising. But in his relations with wider circles with whom he came in contact his attitude was remarkably relaxed—or should we say "liberal"?

(d) What then of John 10:35 and Matthew 5:17-18? The problem with John is less severe since the phrase translated "cannot be broken" is not specific and may mean simply "cannot be nullified, rendered futile, emptied of its force and significance." Jesus, in other words, would be appealing to a belief that he shared in common with his fellow Jews—that no scripture was empty of significance. Since that is common ground the question then becomes what its significance is—a question of right interpretation. In the event the use made of the text has a strong *ad hominem* emphasis: since scripture speaks of men as "gods," why should it be offensive to call Jesus "the Son of God"? In short, the contribution of this text to our current discussion becomes much less clear-cut.

With Matthew 5 the position taken up seems more cut and dried: not a jot or a tittle is to pass from the law until all has been accomplished; Jesus came not to destroy but to fulfill. Clearly the key to right understanding lies with the words *fulfill* and *accomplish*. But whatever they might mean, it seems that Matthew, no less Mark, wants to present Jesus as interpreting the law, and indeed relativizing the law by the principle of unselfish love. As in Mark, so in Matthew, Leviticus 19:18 ("Love your neighbor as yourself") provides a governing principle by which such laws as the sabbath are to be understood and obeyed. And even more than Mark, Matthew brings this principle to prominence: in Mark Leviticus 19:18 is cited in only one passage (Mark 12:31, 33); Matthew cites it in no less than three passages (Matt. 5:43; 19:19; 22:39). The command to love the neighbor as oneself is evidently a "canon within the canon" by which other laws are to be interpreted. Likewise, Matthew is the only Evangelist to make explicit use of Hosea 6:6: "I desire mercy and not sacrifice" (Matt. 9:13; 12:7). And the effect is the same—to relativize in terms of applicability some commands of the law by reference to a higher principle. So even in Matthew Jesus himself provides a clear authority for the abandoning of some actual laws of the Old Testament. At this point Matthew and Mark or Matthew and Paul are not so far apart as is sometimes argued.

What, then, of the question in the title? Was Jesus a liberal? The answer that I think is appropriate will already be obvious.

What, after all, is a "liberal"? It is a relative term. It has to be defined in relation to some antonym by antithesis—liberal in relation to some matters of dispute, liberal in contrast to conservative. In the religious terms appropriate on this occasion, a conservative is one who conserves, who wishes to retain the tradition of his society or church with as little change as possible, one who stresses continuity as a matter of primary concern, one who wants to be as faithful to the great truths of earlier days so far as possible. A liberal, in contrast, will feel free from such a blanket obligation; he or she will want to be free to make distinctions between what is more important and what is less; he or she will not feel bound equally or bound in the same way by all scriptures. The conservative will tend to emphasize the wholeness and integrated character of the revelation: to abandon one part can lead too easily to abandoning all. The liberal will want to say that only by making some distinction between essentials and nonessentials within the whole can the essentials be defined and the whole retained. He or she will want to sit loose to some beliefs and formulations that the conservative regards as important, perhaps even as fundamental.

If this is a fair characterization, it is hard to deny Jesus the title "liberal." Within the religious context, in relation to the dominant traditions and beliefs of his day, Jesus was certainly not conservative. The kind of readiness he showed to reduce the criteria of acceptability to a simple principle—love of neighbor, doing the will of God—is more the mark of a liberal attitude than of a conservative attitude. His kind of openness to the recognition that those whose commitment differs from our own can be equally acceptable to God is too threatening to the conservative who wants his or her boundaries to be much more clearly defined. If some form of exclusiveness is a prime mark of the conservative temperament, the sort of inclusiveness preferred by Jesus is the mark more of what we have to call a "liberal" temperament.

Again, the point must not be overstated. Jesus clearly was nurtured in his own faith and self-understanding by the scriptures we call the Old Testament. He used these scriptures in teaching and debate. He commends them to the rich young man as a guide for living (Mark 10). To call Jesus a "liberal" is not to consign him to the bottom of the slippery slope of constantly slipping standards of faith and life. On the contrary, he undermines the whole scenario of the "slippery slope" threat and warning—that once the integrated wholeness of the conservative system is breached at any point, the collapse of all the rest of faith is inevitable. For he *is* one who questioned *some* scriptures. He *is* one who put his foot at the beginning of the slippery slope beloved of fundamentalist polemic. And yet who is to say that he slid to the bottom?— whatever the bottom might be in this case. No! The example of Jesus is a clear indication that the "slippery slope" polemic is basically flawed in approach and out of sympathy with the mind of Jesus— piece of scare-mongering that betokens the insecurity of the more conservative temperament more than the vulnerability of the truth or the liberty of the Christian person.

3. Paul and the Old Testament

What then of Paul? If Jesus was a liberal in relation to the authority of the Old Testament, what about Paul?

Even more clearly than Jesus, Paul was dependent on the Old Testament. It is only necessary to glance at the pages of Paul's letters in the New Testament to see that when he gets into a theological argument one of his first and primary concerns is to validate his points from scripture. Despite the fact that Marcion thought himself a good Paulinist, Paul would have been absolutely horrified at Marcion's attitude to the Old Testament. For Paul it was a matter of fundamental importance to be able to demonstrate, at least to his own satisfaction, that his Christian faith and gospel were fully consistent with the Old Testament and, indeed, were the most appropriate understanding of it. The formula "as it is written" is no mere concession to a belief in scriptural authority that he has actually abandoned in favor of faith in Christ. It is a genuine expression of his conviction that the gospel was "preached beforehand through the prophets in the sacred writings" (Rom. 1:1), and in Christ the promises of the Old Testament have been fulfilled (Romans 4), that in the gospel of faith the law has been properly understood and confirmed (Rom. 3:31). Many of the arguments made for a "strong" view of scripture from Paul are good: in Paul's eyes, what scripture said, God said. For Paul scripture was the word of God written.

Yet at the same time, Paul it is, more than anyone else of the New Testament writers, whose work has resulted in the separation of Judaism and Christianity. Judaism would certainly regard him as a heretic. Hyam Maccoby's *The Mythmaker: Paul and the Invention of* Christianity,[1] in its outright attack on the dismissal of Paul, is simply an extreme version of a polemic that is an almost inevitable consequence of what Paul did. We see such a polemic already in the Pseudo-Clementine literature of the second and third centuries, where Paul is depicted in the guise of Simon Magus—a deluded visionary who is no match for Peter. And the depth of hostility is already reflected in Galatians, 2 Corinthians 10–13, and Philippians 3, not to mention Acts 21. The Paul who in these passages dismisses so passionately and scornfully those judaizing missionaries and apostles who must have come from Palestine, if not from James and Jerusalem as such, was certainly denounced in turn in similar and perhaps even more virulent terms—preacher of another Jesus, purveyor of another gospel, peddler of another Spirit—a false apostle, a deceitful workman, servant and dupe of Satan.

Paul certainly did not wish for the breach that has come about between Judaism and Christianity. His hope was that through the conversion of the Gentiles his fellow countrymen would be provoked to jealousy and so come to accept Jesus as Messiah (Romans 11). He labored long and hard, as one of his top priorities, to maintain a strong bridge between the Gentile mission and Jerusalem, putting his life at hazard in his determination to take the collection of the Gentile churches back to Jerusalem, come what may. But his hope was not realized, and still has not been. The people of God is still split into two streams—the ancient stream of Israel and the newer stream of Christianity. And Paul's part in the coming about of that split was decisive.

So the question cannot be avoided. Was Paul faithful to his Jewish heritage? Or did he sell it for a mess of Christian pottage? Did Christ so bowl him over on the Damascus road that all his use of the Old Testament has to be judged at the end of the day nothing more than an arbitrary attempt to rationalize that experience? Is Christianity as he presents it the true successor of the religion of the Old Testament, or at the end of the day, an aberration? Who has the greater claim to the Old Testament—the Christianity that takes its lead from Paul, or rabbinic Judaism? To tackle these sorts of questions in the depth they require would take us well beyond the space available. But at least the impact and measure of Paul can be sampled and illustrated at three key points.

(a) As we have seen, the food laws were a matter of great importance for the Jews of Paul's day. The appeal to the blood of the martyrs, the Maccabean martyrs in this case, would have been as powerful then as the equivalent appeal within the Protestant or Catholic traditions. In the days of the Maccabees people were put to death because of their observance of the food laws. This was no minor matter of idle dispute and inconsequential disagreement. People had died for these beliefs. Similarly, the very popular hero and heroine stories on which Jewish children were no doubt brought up made the same point. Daniel, Tobit, and Judith were all great heroes, not least because they had been faithful in their refusal to eat the food of Gentiles by which they would have been rendered unclean. All these stories must have entered deeply into the Jewish psyche of Paul's day. A good reflection of it, no doubt, is Peter's reaction on the housetop in Joppa, when he saw the vision of clean and unclean animals and was told to "Rise, kill and eat"—"I have *never* eaten *anything* common or unclean" (Acts 10:14).

But this was one of the issues where Paul believed the truth of the gospel was at stake. As we see in the Antioch incident in Galatians 2:11ff., for Peter and Barnabas and the other Jewish Christians to insist on observing the Jewish food laws was to abandon the fundamental principle that God accepted Jew and Gentile alike by faith, faith in Jesus Christ. In his later treatment of the issue within his own congregations he was a good deal more relaxed. In 1 Corinthians 8–10 and Romans 14 he wants the stronger members who have dispensed with or disregard such food laws to be considerate for the weaker brethren who still want to observe them. The strong should be ready to limit their freedom for the sake of the weak. Paul himself is still clearly of the opinion that all foods have been provided by God richly to be enjoyed by God's creatures (1 Cor. 10:25-26). To be sure, he does not insist that others must share the same opinion. But he has certainly abandoned the law of clean and unclean foods for himself: "I know and am persuaded in the Lord Jesus that nothing is unclean in itself" (Rom. 14:14, 20). Such an abandonment would certainly be regarded as unfounded and treacherous by most of his fellow Jews, and indeed by many of his fellow Jewish Christians.

(b) A second example would be the *sabbath law*. This was in many ways even more fundamental for the devout Jew. It was one of the Ten Commandments. It had been observed by Yahweh himself in creating the world. In effect, therefore, it was not merely a Jewish or covenant requirement; it was an ordinance of creation. But it was also a particularly important expression of Israel's obligation under the covenant—a perpetual covenant between Israel and God to be observed throughout their generations (Exod. 31:16-17). And in the much-loved prophet Isaiah, more used by the Christians than any other, it was precisely observance of the sabbath that would be the great mark of the ingathering of the Gentiles—a text that Paul could hardly ignore for that very reason—Isaiah 56:6: foreigners who join themselves to the Lord to keep the sabbath and not profane it, to hold fast the covenant.

And yet it is in Paul that we have the clearest indication of any New Testament writer that the sabbath was soon abandoned or at least was being regarded as of little consequence for many of the first-generation Christians—Paul himself included, no doubt. In the same passage already referred to, Romans 14, Paul speaks of those Christians who regard all days alike, no day as special—an attitude that no devout Jew could espouse. Here was a clear commandment of the Old Testament, one of the Ten Commandments no less, which was being treated as though it had never been said. How could a loyal Jew justify this? What criterion external to the scriptures could he use to discount so completely such an explicit word of scripture?

The problem is not his alone, we might add. For there is actually no clear word in the New Testament that validates the abandonment of the sabbath law or transformation of it into a Sunday celebration. Here is an interesting test case for the Reformation principle of the perspicacity of scripture, the rule that the unclear must be interpreted by clear. For in this case it is the Christian observance of Sunday coordinated with the disregard for the sabbath which is less than explicit, that is, less than clear; whereas the scriptural command to keep the seventh day holy is clear beyond dispute. And yet we follow the unclear New Testament and disregard the clear Torah.

(c) Above all there was the test case of *circumcision*. Here if anywhere the scriptural authorization was clear-cut and unequivocal beyond peradventure.

Not simply as a commandment of the Sinai covenant that might be relativized by an argument which places the Abrahamic covenant earlier. The problem for Paul's interpretation is that circumcision is so clearly affixed to the promise to Abraham. I refer of course to Genesis 17:9-14:

> And God said to Abraham, "As for you, you shall keep my covenant, you and your descendants after you throughout their generations. This is my covenant, which you shall keep, between me and you and your descendants after you: Every male among you shall be circumcised. You shall be circumcised in the flesh of your foreskins, and it shall be a sign of the covenant between me and you. . . . So shall my covenant be in your flesh an everlasting covenant. Any uncircumcised male who is not circumcised in the flesh of his foreskin shall be cut off from his people; he has broken my covenant."

Here, one might think, is a command whose lasting authority is beyond doubt—Abraham's seed to observe it "throughout their generations," "an everlasting covenant." But we know very well that Paul resisted in this issue more fiercely than in any other. How can you foolish Galatians want to be circumcised? Don't you see that if you receive circumcision you destroy your faith in Christ? You are cut off from Christ! Circumcision now means nothing for the person in Christ. "I wish those who are trying to have you circumcised would go the whole way and castrate themselves!" (Gal. 5:2-12).

How could any good Jew who heard Paul speak like this doubt that Paul had "gone off the rails"? The law was the great mark of God's electing love of God's people Israel. It marked Israel out as God's peculiar people. And the boundary was most clearly marked by these distinctive Jewish rituals and customs—circumcision, sabbath, particular food laws. Yet here was Paul calling in effect for an abandoning of all three. It had been bad enough that Jesus broke down boundaries between factions *within* the chosen people. But Paul was now breaking down the boundaries *around* the chosen people, breaching the walls of the covenant that distinguished and protected Israel as God's special people. Clearly Paul was being *un*faithful to his Jewish heritage. He was rejecting Israel's election, whatever he might say. In the view of many of Paul's Jewish contemporaries Paul was a renegade and apostate. His reinterpretation was not simply a *re*-interpretation but an abandoning of the law, of clear, indisputable, and fundamental commands of scripture. He was a heretic! No wonder Marcion thought he was simply following the logic of Paul's position.

4. Conclusions

We began by asking the questions: Was Jesus a liberal? Was Paul a heretic? To both questions the answer has clearly been, Yes! Does that seem to some a disturbing conclusion? Perhaps even a shocking conclusion? Or just bizarre? If so, that is only because we see these issues from our own perspective. From the perspective of nearly two thousand years of Christianity, the questions are, of course, ridiculous. Jesus and Paul provide the norm, the ideal, the definition of divine revelation, that from which *others* depart, not the model of different degrees of departure from the norm. But this is true, of course, only if we see the issue from our perspective. Within their *own* contexts these questions as they relate to Jesus and Paul are quite respectable and the answers valid. Over against the current religiosity and system of faith and religion, Jesus *was* liberal, and Paul *was* a heretic. And that is the only contemporary context we can set them within.

In other words, we cannot *assume* that Jesus and Paul would have been "conservative" and "orthodox" thereafter, however these words might be defined subsequently, simply because various stripes of conservative theology claim Paul for themselves and simply because the several orthodoxies of Christian history have set Jesus at the center. The fact is that Jesus and Paul were disturbing presences in their own time. And the disturbing character was an integral part of their ministry and witness—the unnerving unexpectedness of claiming that the kingdom of God is *here,* of claiming that Christ alone is the seed of Abraham. Jesus and Paul were nothing if they were not nonconformists. The probability is that to see them as a model for a new conformity is to misperceive them. For example, to take Jesus' actions with regard to the sabbath law as in effect a new law (what may and what may not be done on Sunday) is to set oneself at odds with the spirit of Jesus' ministry and to corrupt Jesus' liberty into a new form of Pharisaism. Or to set Paul's gospel into a fixed and unyielding outline that must be followed if the gospel is to be properly preached is to have Paul erect again the same sorts of rules and restrictions on the liberty of the Christian man which Christ had broken down for him. If Jesus and Paul provide a model, it is of a surprising, disturbing, boundary crossing, breaking down or disregarding of religious conventions; and to lose that is to lose something very much at the heart of their respective ministries.

The fact is that Jesus and Paul were themselves on the boundary. They both stand at the interface and overlap between two great religions—Judaism and Christianity. They are the fulcrum points on which salvation-history turns into a new course. They were "outsiders," people who did not fit neatly into the pigeonholes and categories of their time, people who challenge and break an old paradigm and around which a new paradigm coheres. Jesus was a disturber of false peace; and we may assume he would still be the same were he to come again as he did before, in whatever context of religious faith and practice he found himself. Of Paul it was said fifteen centuries before Luther, "Are you alone right and a thousand years wrong?" Like Luther, Paul was one who stood for what had grasped him as divine truth even if that meant standing in the face of certainties of centuries-old truth and revelation.

The questions we ask in this chapter are still relevant. And the answers more so than we may realize. But let me in closing simply sketch out some of the important points that arise for our theme of the living word.

(a) The effects are clearest with regard to the Old Testament. For, on the one hand, we have the Old Testament as part of holy scripture. On the other we have a Jesus and a Paul who prevent us from taking these same scriptures as still having prescriptive force for us. We must hold the two together. We cannot "do a Marcion" and reject the Old Testament. But we cannot treat the Old Testament as though what Jesus and Paul did and said was irrelevant to the question of how *we* understand and use the Old Testament. Can we still speak of the Old Testament commandments that Jesus and Paul disregarded and discarded as the word of God? There is no reason why not. So long as we tie it into what I said before about the historical conditionedness of all scripture, including these commands. In this case that means recognizing that the description of them as word of God is itself a historical description. They *were* the word of God to millions of Israelites down through many centuries. But they no longer are so for us—certainly not in their obvious and intended sense. We honor these passages as God's word in a historic sense, invaluable as ways of understanding how God dealt with his people in times past. We do not honor them by calling them God's word in the same sense today.

What is true with regard to these particular commandments shows us how we must evaluate the Old Testament as a whole. The Old Testament does not stand for us as word of God independent of the New Testament and of Jesus. As Christians the Old Testament continues to exercise normative authority for us only when we read it in the light of the revelation of Christ. And that means being ready to recognize that some teaching and some requirements laid down in the Old Testament are no longer of prescriptive authority for us. Of course, the Old Testament remains indispensable for our understanding of the New; it is the foundation of the New. But for us it takes its significance from the superstructure that Jesus, Paul, and the others built on it. In a word, the New Testament relativizes the Old.

This also means that the Christian operates with a canon within the canon, like it or not. The canon within the canon for the Christian is, of course, the New Testament, or more precisely the revelation of Christ as presented in the New Testament. We read the Old Testament through the New. We interpret the Old Testament in the light of Christ. He is the clear by which the now unclear Old Testament must be understood. For Paul and Christians then and since, the brilliance of the light of Christ has cast the Old Testament into shadow. The new revelation has relativized the old and so also relativized the authority of the old.

(b) But is this true only of the Old Testament? Is the New Testament a once-for-all revision of the old revelation that now serves as itself the finished and final paradigm? Is there any sense in which the New Testament's relativizing of the Old becomes a paradigm for the way in which new revelation might relativize the authority of the New Testament? Here we must take care lest we erode the definitive role of the New Testament for Christianity. But we can give a cautious yes at two points. Part of what the paradigm of the New Testament's relativizing of the Old teaches us is that the message of God's saving grace can be too easily obscured and rendered less effective by an over-evaluation of certain scriptures; that good and authoritative scriptures can be so understood as to narrow and misdirect God's grace. For example, circumcision was not abandoned simply because Christians believed they had received the circumcision of the heart. As well might they have left baptism behind with John the Baptist since they had experienced the Coming One's baptism in Spirit. Nor was there any reason within scripture for the food laws to be abandoned. In both cases it was the historical circumstance that these rules and practices had become too much identified with a narrow, inward-looking, Israel-centered faith, which relativized them and rendered them obsolete for the new covenant.

The obvious corollary is that it must be entirely possible that certain New Testament requirements, good words of God in their time, in the same way become restrictive and corruptive of the grace of God today. As did slavery. And, as many today would say, as does the scriptural subordination of women to men. If we define the canon within the canon not just as the New Testament as a whole but the revelation of Christ to which the New Testament bears normative and definitive witness, we must allow that canon to exercise a similar sifting and evaluating function of our faith and lives, our proclamation of the gospel and our ordering of our common lives today.

Was Jesus a liberal? Was Paul a heretic? We answer yes to these questions not least because we wish to highlight and maintain the character of God's revelation as "the living word." We wish to say that God spoke with a specificity of reference to God's people in the past. With such a specificity that often the word spoken has reference only to that past and not to the present. Only so can we continue to claim that God speaks with specificity of reference to us today, and at the same time, save ourselves from the old mistake of erecting what has been the word of God to us into a restrictive and stultifying dogma for others. Only so can we rejoice in "the living word."

4. THE PROBLEM
OF PSEUDONYMITY

1. Introduction

THE PROBLEM OF PSEUDONYMITY refers to the problem of pseudonymous literature. Pseudonymous literature is usually understood to mean writings whose authorship has been concealed for one reason or another by a fictitious name. The problem is that such a practice almost inevitably seems to us to have a motive of insincerity and falsehood. When used of biblical literature pseudonymity raises the question of an author's integrity. Does pseudonymity not imply the intention to pass off one's work as the work of someone else? Does it not therefore necessarily imply an intention to deceive? It is this implication that pseudonymity involves deception which causes the problem. How can one attribute such a motive to a biblical author? What would the acceptance of the presence of pseudonymous writings within the canon mean for our understanding of scripture and for the authority of the writing in question? Is the status of scripture compatible with such an immoral motivation?

There have been various attempts to defuse the problem.

(a) Some have tried to *deny* that there is a problem. The problem does not exist, because there are no examples of pseudepigraphy in the Bible. Every book that claims to be by a particular author was written by that author or at least dictated by him. Here the issue is transposed into a different problem—the problem of the gap between the conservative and the rest of New Testament scholarship. Since almost all New Testament scholars would dispute the Petrine authorship of 2 Peter, and most accept that the Pastorals are post-Pauline, the

insistence of the conservative scholar that these documents *are* nevertheless written by the person named tends to isolate such conservatives toward one end of the critical spectrum and to make the resultant dialogue more difficult. Here I cannot go into questions of authorship of individual books. What I want to do is to ask for an open-mindedness to the possibility that there may be pseudonymous writings in the New Testament, to examine what that would mean within the historical context of the times, and to think through a little of what it would mean for our understanding of these scriptures and for our whole understanding of the living word.

(b) A second approach to the problem of pseudonymity in biblical writings is the attempt to alleviate it. The problem is not so serious, since there is very little in the Bible that might properly fall under the head of pseudepigraphy. The problem has been perceived as serious because pseudonymity has been confused so much with anonymity. There are many anonymous writings in the Bible, more than the alleged pseudonymous writings. We simply do not know *who* was responsible for many biblical texts. This is quite true. But it does not help us very much. For one thing, there is still the problem, on the conservative side, that Jesus and Paul do ascribe authorship to various passages which might be regarded critically as from the hand of an unknown author. For example, they attribute Deuteronomic passages to Moses and various psalms to David. And for another, the recognition that much of the Bible is anonymous in terms of human authorship does not help with the problem of pseudonymity if and where it does actually occur.

(c) There have also been many attempts to resolve the problem. The most common one has involved what we might call a psychological-mystical approach. The unknown author felt himself to be one with the author named. Since pseudonymity usually means attribution to someone of a past generation, someone now dead, the suggestion is that the actual author believed himself to be inspired by the spirit of this person, caught up in ecstatic inspiration into a mystical identity with the person named. The flaw in this thesis is that it seems to have no hard evidence in its favor. It generalizes a theory of ecstatic mysticism from Graeco-Roman literature, especially the orphic, hermetic, and sibylline material, and imposes it on the dissimilar Jewish material. Jewish writers thought themselves inspired by God, but never as identified with God. And there is no evidence whatsoever, outside the data which the hypothesis is trying to explain, that a Jewish pseudepigrapher thought he was possessed by the spirit of some other and long dead person. Despite its popularity this attempt to explain the phenomenon of pseudepigraphy in biblical writing must be regarded as a failure for lack of supporting evidence.

The weakness of most discussions of pseudonymity in the Bible is that they have focused the discussion too much on Graeco-Roman parallels. They have not paid enough attention to the Jewish nature of these writings or to the Jewish context from which they came. Here in particular we need to take account of the tradition process that lies behind so many biblical documents— and not least its character as living tradition. Hence, the importance of the subject for this book. Fortunately, we are in a position to draw on an important monograph by David G. Meade, *Pseudonymity and Canon*,[1] a thesis which it was my privilege to supervise during my time at Nottingham, and which has made an important breakthrough in the study of biblical pseudepigraphy.

2. Pseudepigraphy and Apocrypha

We can start with the obvious fact that within the Jewish tradition at the time of Jesus and Paul there was a clearly established pattern of pseudepigraphy. It is seen most clearly in the apocalyptic writings—the cycles attributed to Enoch, Ezra, and Baruch. These are clearly pseudonymous, at least in the sense that despite their claim to contain and express the words of those just named, they were clearly written long after the time of these persons' sojourn on Earth. The Enoch cycle may start well back before the New Testament period, even in the third century B.C.E., but can hardly be attributed to the pre-deluvian patriarch himself. IV Ezra and II Baruch clearly reflect the situation following the fall of Jerusalem and the destruction of the Temple in 70 C.E., and so can hardly have been written by those who lived five or six centuries earlier.

But would anyone think they were? Would not most if not all readers of such works recognize what is patently an artistic device? A revelation of the mysteries of heaven attributed to the famous patriarch who had been translated to heaven without seeing death. Visions arising out of the fall of Jerusalem attributed to two famous figures, especially remembered for two things—their divinely commissioned ministries associated with the fall and restoration of Jerusalem the time before (sixth century B.C.E.), and for their activity as scribes. At the very least this would be recognized as a literary technique, with an underlying message in the case of the last two: Jerusalem had fallen and the Temple been destroyed before, in accordance with the will of God; but it was not long before both Jerusalem and Temple had been restored, by the same divine will. The attribution to Ezra and Baruch was as much as anything an attestation of faith—one of the means used by the actual authors to express the conviction that God had not finally and completely abandoned Israel on this occasion either.

Such reflections immediately raise the question as to whether pseudepig-raphy is the right word—particularly if the word contains any implication of deliberate deceit and forgery. If that is what pseudonymity necessarily implied, then these writings should almost certainly *not* be called pseudonymous. Because they would have fooled nobody! But if pseudonymity means attribution for the purpose of making a theological point—in the case of 4 Ezra and 2 Baruch, the affirmation of the continuity of God's purpose, of the continuing faithfulness of God, despite appearances—then that forces us to regard pseudonymity in a different light: as an acceptable practice, *not* intended to deceive, but a means of affirming the continuity of God's purpose between the circumstances of the named author and the circumstances of the actual author.

Someone might say: but these are not biblical books. They provide no precedent for a concept of *scriptural* pseudonymity. And that may be a fair point, although they do seem to point us to a certain technique and understanding of pseudepigraphy within the same Jewish context from which the New Testament writings emerged. And that cannot be without relevance when we look at the New Testament writings themselves.

But of course the phenomenon is *not* confined to the so-called Jewish pseudepigrapha. Something not too dissimilar is also present within the Apocrypha. And when we speak of the Apocrypha it is well to recall that this was part of the Bible used by Greek-speaking Jews. Take, for example, the Wisdom of Solomon. Written in Greek, almost certainly in Alexandria, it is the classic expression of Hellenistic Jewish wisdom. To be sure, it does not claim to have been written by Solomon in so many words. But the autobiographical section in chapters 6–9 is clearly intended as a first-person account of Solomon's own experiences. Here again there would be little chance of deception, even if that had been the intention: the whole is too much pervaded by the spirit of Hellenistic thought, even if transposed into a Jewish matrix. But deception is hardly the point. What the author is presumably attempting to convey by his pseudonymous technique is that this expression of Jewish wisdom is fully in line with the wisdom tradition with which Solomon was identified in Jewish memory. Even when transposed into Hellenistic language and form it is coherent and continuous with the wisdom of Solomon. It *is*, as those who first gave the book its present name rightly perceived, the Wisdom of Solomon.

Equally interesting and relevant is the phenomenon of septuagintal expansions. The fact that in the LXX there are expanded versions of Esther and Daniel; also the Letter of Jeremiah (= Baruch 6); and not to mention the reordering of the chapters of Jeremiah. Here we see a willingness to make substantial additions to earlier writings. There was evidently no sense that a document once written was complete and closed, that additions to it would violate its character or the integrity of the original author. And certainly talk of deception and forgery would be inappropriate. What we have, rather, is a sense that earlier traditions can be expanded and elaborated in a way wholly appropriate to that tradition, so that the elaborations and expansions can be retained within that tradition, continuous with it, part of a larger integrated whole which can be regarded as belonging to the original author's corpus without impropriety.

If we make the point in terms of canon, then we have the interesting fact that the canon of the Greek-speaking Jew and of the Greek-speaking Jewish Christian was larger than the canon of the Hebrew Bible. This does not diminish any sense of canonical authority: we could still speak, if we so wished, of the canonical authority of both the Hebrew version *and* the Greek version. What it does put in question is the idea that "canon" always meant "closed canon"—that the recognition of a particular writing as having what we may fairly call canonical authority meant thereby that it could be neither added to nor abstracted from. On the contrary, we have a concept of what we might better call *open* canon, or open-ended canonical authority: a writing, an oracle, which could be regarded as speaking with word-of-God authority, but whose content could be developed or elaborated without loss of canonical authority, presumably to adapt the earlier word to different circumstances or help retain its continuing force, or simply because the new material was coherent with the earlier.

Here, in other words, we have a variation on the idea of living word, living tradition. Open-ended canonical authority is just another way of saying the same thing.

But what about the scriptures themselves, those scriptures that actually do belong to the Christian, or at least Protestant canon of Old and New Testaments? The question still arises: Are they not of a different order from what we have been looking at? Does any of this apply to or throw light on our sacred writings and on the problem of canonical pseudepigraphy in particular? I will look first at some Old Testament examples before turning to the New Testament.

3. The Old Testament

The simplest procedure is to take three examples from the three main sections of the Old Testament: the Law, the Prophets, and the Writings.

(a) The Law. It is now widely agreed that the Pentateuch is the end product of a quite lengthy tradition process. We do not need to argue over particular points. The consensus of modern scholarship would include recognition that the earliest level of tradition goes back before the Mosaic

period, and that there is no good reason to rule out the hand of Moses in the earliest stages of the Pentateuch itself. But the importance of Deuteronomy and of a Deuteronomic school in the Josianic reformation is also a matter of widespread consensus, and likewise the role of Ezra in establishing the Pentateuch in more or less its present form in the postexilic period.

The point is that whatever might be the result of disputes over innumerable details, it would be flying in the face of too much evidence and good scholarship to deny the basic affirmation: that the Pentateuch is the product of a lengthy process of tradition.

But if this is accepted, notice what it means. Once again we have an example of a tradition that grew and developed. Indeed, we can speak quite properly of a *canonical* tradition that grew and developed. For the earliest forms of the tradition were obviously cherished and passed down because of their importance in explaining the community that preserved them to itself, because they served to express the self-identity of the community. And the influence of Moses in putting his stamp on the earliest stages of the law gave these formulations an abiding authority for the life, social, and religious structures of the community. But once again not a closed authority, but a living authority that could be and *was* expanded and elaborated as new insights emerged and that could be and evidently was adapted and modified as circumstances changed. Deuteronomy could become a complete and distinct block within the whole, with its material, be it noted, set out in terms of addresses given by Moses at the time of Israel's entry into the promised land. And the whole complex reworked and rewritten in a final, or sequence of final editings.

How did those who made such elaborations, additions, editings regard their role? Not as something inadmissible, to be sure. This was simply the way in which canonical tradition functioned. Not as a fixed deposit from the past to be relayed with meticulous scrupulosity to the next generation, almost certainly. But as a living interaction of older tradition and newer insight into that tradition and fresh revelation coherent with that tradition. Unknown, anonymous scribes and teachers have played an important part in that process—but not with contributions that they would regard as distinctively theirs, for which they should be honored by subsequent history. They would see their role simply in terms of filling out what had not been clearly enough said in the earlier tradition, or what had not been envisaged at the earlier stage, or saying again in different form and more appropriate mode what had always been part of the tradition. It was still the law of *Moses*. The continuum of tradition, coherence with what Moses had been the first to put together formally, that was the criterion. Such workers with the tradition would no doubt regard themselves as inspired, but it was not a fresh revelation that might run at cross purposes to the revelation given through Moses, not a different revelation which required to be validated by that scribe's own claim to inspiration, to be set down like a prophet's call narrative. It was validated by the community indeed, not as the work of some specific scribe, but simply as the community's recognition that this elaboration or addition still spoke with the authoritative voice of Moses.

There were, of course, other inspired utterances all during this period, which were not simply filling out the older tradition and where the continuity with the law of Moses was not so immediate or of a different nature. These were prophetic oracles, wisdom sayings, psalms, and so forth, remembered as such, and often attributed to the one who spoke them. But the same logic did not apply to the elaboration of the Moses tradition, simply because it was not regarded as theirs, but as still the law of Moses.

Of course, the time came when that particular canon was regarded as closed, when the Pentateuch took its more or less final form, and could no longer be added to. That happened, as we have already noted, almost certainly in the period immediately following the exile. Presumably the continuum was seen to be becoming too stretched out, the continuity too thin. The tradition had solidified into a single, normative form. That is not to say, however, that the sense of living tradition had ceased, or that the need to interpret the earlier tradition was any less. It simply took a different form, as the Pharisees demonstrate. The sense of a living tradition is still there, as the Pharisees attempted to fill out and clarify, to develop and adapt the now written Torah. The dynamics are only different in degree. In the earlier stages the interaction between old revelation and new was more fluid, since the old revelation was itself not in final form. In the hands of the Pharisees the only difference is that the old revelation was in a more fixed form. But the need to interpret and reexpress it was just the same. And just the same was the clear sense that this was still the law of Moses, not merely a secondary explanation of it, inferior and dispensable. The early Pharisees are not much remembered in the early stages of the rabbinic traditions, and even in the period of Jesus there were many more *un*attributed sayings than attributed, for the same reason. The authority of these Pharisaic rulings lay much more in the tradition being interpreted and in the continuity of the interpretation with the earlier words of Moses, than with the inspiration of the particular teacher who gave the ruling.

Here again then we have the same clear sense of a living word, which, once spoken, can be heard to speak again in different circumstances and with different variations and where the elaborators of that word saw themselves as that, spokesmen for the living tradition which bears the name of Moses.

(b) The Prophets. Here we have space to take only one example—the case of Isaiah. As with the Pentateuch, so here, and perhaps even more so here, we can

speak of an overwhelming consensus of biblical scholarship that the present Isaiah is not the work of a single author. While much of chapters 1–39 can be referred back to the eighth-century Isaiah of Jerusalem, there is widespread agreement that chapters 40–55 come from the hand of an unknown prophet of the exilic period, and that chapters 56–66 are probably a collection of multiauthored oracles. Even more conservative scholarship today would not necessarily find it essential to argue for a single eighth-century authorship. It is not simply a question of whether predictive prophecy is possible or not. It is rather that the message of Second Isaiah would have been largely meaningless to an eighth-century Jerusalem audience. It is so clearly directed to the situation of exile. Consequently, had it been delivered a century and a half before the exile, it would be unlike the rest of Jewish prophecy, marked out as that is by the relevance of what is said to the speaker's present. A more typical modern conservative line, therefore, would be to argue that the core of chapters 40–66 goes back to the original Isaiah, but has been considerably(?) worked over by disciples of the great prophet who felt what they were doing was done in the spirit of Isaiah.

Such a step toward "critical orthodoxy" would be quite sufficient for my present purpose. For my main point would again be illustrated: a core original that has been expanded and elaborated, over a period of one and a half, two, or more centuries, but within the tradition of the original Isaiah and so attributed to him, reworking and all, without any sense of impropriety, and certainly without any intention to deceive.

And if we follow the majority line of critical consensus, the point becomes even clearer. For it looks as though the case just mentioned for chapters 40–66 was actually true of chapters 1–39. Oracles of the original Isaiah seem to have been worked up and redacted in the light of Second Isaiah. Chapters 36–39 have been borrowed from 2 Kings 18–20 to provide a bridge to chapters 40–66. Moreover, the continuity between First and Second Isaiah is clear. For Isaiah had prophesied in the face of a military threat to Jerusalem, and his warnings had been fulfilled in the tragic events of 587. More important, there is a fundamental identity of religious perspective between the two—particularly with regard to the holiness and power of Yahweh and God's election of Israel. Second Isaiah can be regarded quite properly as a creative reinterpretation of the oracles of Isaiah of Jerusalem. The points previously put forward in favor of the unity of authorship are probably better understood as indicating a consciousness of continuity, of a standing within the authoritative tradition begun by Isaiah of Jerusalem and identified by his name.

Similarly with chapters 55–66. Only here, as in the case of the postexilic treatment of the Pentateuch, the earlier tradition seems to have become more fixed. So-called Third Isaiah is full of near or complete citations from the two earlier works, and the reworking of the tradition now seems to take the form of a sort of midrashic exegesis of texts. The malleability and flexibility of the tradition is not infinite in either character or time. Only what stands in direct line of continuity can be reckoned as part of that tradition. And the longer the period intervening between the original fountainhead of the tradition, the more the process of reworking it becomes interpretation of fixed texts and less the expansion of the texts themselves.

For all this Meade uses the helpful German word *Vergegenwärtigung,* "making present, contemporizing." This is a helpful key to the character of living tradition—its contemporaneity, its applicability to new and different situations, achieved by the reexpression of the earlier tradition or its emphases in new forms which demonstrate that relevance. In the case in point, whatever the dispute on points of detail, there would be widespread agreement that in canonical Isaiah we see the process of such living tradition—a tradition which was no less authoritative because it was being interpreted, or because the interpretation was itself becoming part of that tradition—a tradition which because it took its origin and essential character from the great figure of Isaiah of Jerusalem, continued to be thought of as *his,* without impropriety or deception.

(c) The Writings. The third section of the Old Testament canon proffers various different kinds of *Vergegenwärtigung.* For example, the two books of Chronicles. These are generally recognized to be in essence a revision of the earlier works that we know as Samuel and Kings. Some of the material has been taken over virtually unchanged; some modified, or replaced by an alternative version; sometimes old and new material have been meshed together; sometimes quite new material has been inserted. Here is another case of old tradition renewed, with the basic form maintained but the content elaborated, to give expression to a fresh perspective on the past.

A different example would be provided by the Psalms, since it is now clear from the finds at Qumran, and elsewhere, that the psalter was by no means thought of as closed. We know of at least five other psalms, three of them attributed to David, which were also used in the worship of Jewish communities at the time of Jesus. As we might expect, the reality of a living tradition was most vigorous in the practice of liturgy—old and new expressions of praise used together in the vitality of worship, just as today in our own worship. Of course we are quite some distance here from the problem of pseudepigraphy. I mention these instances simply to make the point that there is a consistent attitude clearly evident behind all this—a powerful interaction between older tradition and immediate experience of inspiration, with the same result of a tradition that can be elaborated and extended without any sense of disloyalty to or of abuse done to the older forms. This consistent breadth of attitude is of vital importance if we are to appreciate the milieu within which the issue of pseudonymity should be viewed.

The only other example I will cite is that of Ecclesiastes, or Qoheleth. Here the issue hangs principally on what are generally regarded as the two main redactions of what otherwise is the work of a single author. These come at the beginning and the end, the prologue (1:1-12) and the epilogue (12:8-14). The point is that the introduction seems intent to portray the author of Qoheleth as a king, and specifically Solomon. As in the case of the Wisdom of Solomon this identification would not be intended to mislead or to claim an authority for the work that it did not deserve. On the contrary, the identification is made because the redactor saw the sentiments of Qoheleth as a proper extension of the wisdom tradition begun by Solomon, a proper corrective of possible abuse of the wisdom tradition itself, but a corrective provided by and from within the wisdom tradition that bears the name of Solomon. And the community, in accepting Qoheleth into the canon, testifies not to its gullibility at being deceived on the question of authorship, but its acceptance of the redactor's claim: that Qoheleth is what the redactor claims, a legitimate expression of the Solomonic wisdom tradition.

The most interesting feature of the epilogue is the assertion of 12:11—"the sayings of the wise are sharp as goads, like nails driven home: they lead the assembled people, for they come from one shepherd." The meaning is not entirely clear, but clear enough for our purposes. Here is a claim to the unity of the tradition of wisdom, a claim that the sayings of Qoheleth, like all "the sayings of the wise" come from the "one shepherd."

What is particularly worthy of note in the case of Ecclesiastes is that the claim to stand in the authoritative tradition of Solomonic wisdom is made not for a redaction of some earlier wisdom writing, for some expanded and reworked version of an older book, but for an entirely new work. Here is a clear case of pseudonymity, if you like—the wisdom of Qoheleth put forward under the authority of Solomon. But if pseudonymity *is* the appropriate word we should note what it means—not any intention to deceive or success in so doing, but the claim to belong within the living tradition of Solomon's wisdom, even though a new and distinct literary work—a claim that the community of faith evidently accepted.

I have spent some time on the background of the Old Testament in order to build up a picture in some depth of the way in which authoritative tradition was regarded and the way in which it was handled. Hopefully enough has been said to make at least three points clear: (1) Authoritative tradition was not regarded as something fixed and static. It was living tradition, and as such was lived in and through, by means of elaboration and reworking, redaction and expansion. (2) The criterion for recognizing such reworking as acceptable, whether the criterion was explicit or implicit, was continuity and coherence of the newer expressions with the older. This criterion was flexible enough to allow quite new material under the old heading, even material with fresh emphases and distinctive characteristics, and even new books. (3) The claim that this newer material had the same authorship as the original material within the tradition was not intended to deceive and probably never did, at the time at least. Rather, it was a claim to belong to that tradition, to be a reexpression of the essential message of the original fountainhead of the tradition to meet the needs of a different day and situation. And as such it was probably accepted as bearing the same canonical authority.

This I would suggest is the proper and most illuminating background against which to attempt to make sense of the problem of pseudonymity in the New Testament.

4. The New Testament

It should cause little surprise that all that has been said so far coheres so well with the points and emphases of the earlier chapters. For it is precisely the same sense of a living tradition that lies behind Jesus' dispute with the Sadducees regarding the resurrection; in this, it will be recalled, he sides with the Pharisees. But also in his disputes with the Pharisees themselves. For though they recognized the need to interpret the sacred text, recognized that tradition was not something fixed and closed, their own interpretations were in danger of stifling that very tradition, by narrowing the legitimate range of interpretation too far, by preempting the possibility that the Spirit might prompt an obedience to the Torah which was significantly different from their own rulings. And Paul, no less than his fellow Pharisees, regarded his own exposition of scripture as wholly expressive of the main thrust of the Mosaic and prophetic tradition, even when it meant a radical revision of particular parts of that tradition.

And in chapter 2 we saw that just the same sort of process of *Vergegenwärtigung* is what makes the best sense of the Christian handling of the Jesus tradition itself. The same sense of a tradition which is like molten metal, not yet solidified into final shape, still able to be molded into different forms, still capable of having fresh material assimilated. To underline the point we can add a few more examples that may help to bring out the parallel with the Old Testament instances cited above.

One interesting parallel is between the Chronicler's handling of the Samuel-Kings material and Matthew and Luke's use of Mark. The parallel is so close because in both cases we have the earlier versions retained within the canon, as well as the later versions. In both instances this fact, that both earlier and later versions have been preserved, enables us to witness the process and character of the living tradition. The way in which it was passed down, added to, subtracted from, reminded, and redacted, yet still authoritative tradition, and in the case of the Gospels, still the gospel (singular) of Jesus Christ.

Another example is the tradition of the sending out of the Twelve by Jesus (Mark 6 pars.). Conservative scholars have long been perplexed by the puzzling variation of detail—what seems indeed to be outright contradiction between the Evangelists. "Only a staff and sandals," says Mark. "Nothing," says Matthew, "not even shoes or a staff" (Mark 6:8-9; Matt. 10:10). The most obvious explanation is not that one or the other has got it wrong, or that some subtle harmonization is necessary and probable. In the light of what we have seen above, it is much more natural to see here a further example of traditions being *used*. Jesus gave them these instructions not as an example of a particular mission carried out during his time in Galilee, and of no greater interest than that, but as instructions for mission, so they would be remembered and so used. And as the character and circumstances of the mission changed, as change they did, they would interpret and adapt that instruction accordingly. Not with any sense of cheating, or of accusing Jesus for being short-sighted, or anything like that. But simply with the recognition that the words appropriate for one kind of mission were less appropriate for another, and that the words of the commission could be adapted to reflect this fact and still express the *same* commission. So, in this case, Matthew's version seems to reflect the conditions of a limited mileage mission as was appropriate in the conditions of Galilee; whereas Mark's version seems to reflect the circumstances of the Gentile mission, where to venture forth without a staff and shoes would have been foolhardy. Here again, then, is a case where words can be altered without being unfaithful to the tradition or to the original speaker, simply because the tradition has that degree of flexibility and adaptability to changing circumstances, so that it retains its applicability and authority precisely by being changed!

Another minor example. Matthew's retelling of the parable of the royal wedding feast includes the improbable detail of the invited guests attacking and killing the servants sent to call them to the feast, and of the king's furious response in sending troops to kill them and set their town on fire (Matt. 22:6-7). It would be very hard to avoid the conclusion that this retelling reflects the events of 70 c.e., the destruction of Jerusalem and death of many of its inhabitants. Here is a straightforward case of a parable of Jesus retold with details added to increase the impact of the parable on a post–70 audience. The point is more or less the same—it is the same parable: Jesus can still be presented as its author without straining belief. But it has been developed and reworked. It is a piece of living tradition.

What we see in small degree in the case of the Synoptics we see in larger degree in John's Gospel—no essential difference in kind, but only in degree. Against the context of the Jewish tradition process and practice of *Vergegenwärtigung*, so clear in the Old Testament, what the Fourth Evangelist was doing makes perfect sense. For John, we might say, was simply doing what Deuteronomy did before him—presenting the founding tradition of his community in first-person sermon form as delivered by the authoritative founder and fountainhead of that tradition. In both cases a form of pseudonymity is involved. In neither case would it have been thought deceitful or improper. It was simply a way of expressing the continuity, continuing vitality, and fuller significance of the revelation which came through that person of normative authority. In other terms, John was simply doing what Second Isaiah had done before him—presenting a further exposition of the great prophet's message for the new situation of a later generation. Not words actually spoken by the one in whose name they were now given, but sufficiently continuous and coherent with them as to bear his name without impropriety or falsehood or likelihood to deceive. John's Gospel lies well within the bounds of the *Vergegenwärtigung* we saw attested in the Old Testament.

What, then, of the problem of pseudonymity as such in the New Testament. It will occasion no surprise if I say that I see in the process of living tradition sketched out above the key to the solution of this problem. Let me attempt to demonstrate my point with reference to the two best examples of this sort of pseudonymity in the New Testament—the Pastoral epistles and 2 Peter.

(a) The Pastorals. Here again there is no need to rehearse the arguments for and against the post-Pauline authorship of the Pastorals. It will serve my purpose sufficiently if pseudonymity is taken as a real possibility and the issue examined within the context of the present discussion. Suffice it to recall the clear differences of style as between the Pastorals and the undisputed Paulines; also the developed pattern of church order clearly reflected in the Pastorals, evidencing a degree of institutionalization beyond anything visible in the earlier Paulines.

Of the more conservative solutions, the most attractive and most plausible is the suggestion that Paul was dependent on different secretaries in writing his various letters. But on this occasion that suggestion does not appear to offer sufficient explanation, and in fact concedes more than most conservatives would consider wise. For the style of the undisputed Paulines is characteristically uniform, despite the use of secretaries; as is the style of the Pastorals. And the two groups are characteristically different from each other in style. To resolve this problem by attributing to the secretary or secretaries who penned the

Pastorals much greater freedom in transcribing what Paul had commissioned them to say provides only a partial resolution of the problem. Not only so, but this resolution of the problem has already gone more than halfway toward the solution offered by the recognition of the living quality of the tradition process. A secretary who creatively shapes the words of the living Paul into his own style and with his own emphases is little different from a disciple who works with the tradition stemming from the now dead Paul to reexpress it in his own style with the different emphases that the changed situation of his own time calls for. Both could be classified as examples of *Vergegenwärtigung*, of actualizing or contemporizing a particular stream of tradition.

In fact, however, against the background of the traditioning process examined above, there are several characteristics of the Pastorals that point more strongly toward a post-Pauline authorship than has usually been recognized; in particular the emphasis on tradition itself, and on the established or fixed character of the tradition—"the faith," "sound teaching," "that which has been entrusted," and so forth. And even more so the emphasis on the continuity of the teaching of the Pastorals themselves with the earlier tradition. The role of the church hierarchy is to preserve, cling to, protect the tradition. Timothy is to take care to pass on the teaching to trustworthy men, capable of teaching others also. It is precisely this emphasis on the continuity of tradition that is the mark of what we might now call legitimate or canonical pseudepigraphy. The claim to stand within, to be continuous with, part of the authoritative tradition—the claim of a second-generation disciple to belong to the authentic line of tradition that he has inherited from the past.

Equally striking is the depiction of Paul within the Pastorals. Using a word that occurs only in the Pastorals, Paul is described as the "prototype" of future disciples (1 Tim. 1:16) and his teaching likewise, "the sound teaching which you heard from me" (2 Tim. 1:13). Paul is the fountainhead of the Pastorals' tradition. Paul himself in his teaching is archetypal for the communities addressed. Moreover, the gospel with which he is identified was entrusted to him (1 Tim. 1:11; Titus 1:3). He is the prototype of the faithful teacher. All this underlines the continuity between Paul and his teaching on the one hand and the teaching of the Pastorals on the other. The writer of the Pastorals has deliberately patterned his teaching and responsibility as a teacher on Paul. The teaching given in the Pastorals is *Paul's*. The personal notes which are a feature of the letter are probably the last few notes that Paul was able to send out from his last imprisonment, woven round with older tradition reworked and reexpressed for the later situation reflected in the Pastorals to serve as the voice of the Pauline tradition for a new day.

Within the tradition of Jewish contemporizing of the authoritative tradition stemming from a revered figure this procedure would be wholly acceptable and unlikely to constitute any "problem of pseudonymity." So far as we can tell, assuming a date for the Pastorals in the last decade of the first century, give or take ten years or so, the presence of the Pastorals within the Pauline tradition went unremarked for a further two or three generations. It was only when the question of canonicity came formally to the agenda, and the chief criterion fixed on was that of apostolicity, that the assessment of the Pastorals probably changed. The older style of legitimate pseudepigraphy as understood within a Jewish context had probably been more and more lost sight of in the increasingly dominant Gentile church, and the criterion of canonicity required that the personal references in the Pastorals had to be understood as claims to authorship as such. And so the pattern became set that has dominated the understanding of the church since. But if I am right, it was not so in the beginning: the Pastorals made their first impact and took the first step toward formal canonicity by being acknowledged as appropriate and authentic reexpression of the Pauline heritage and tradition and not as the products of Paul's pen as such.

(b) 2 Peter. There is no need to elaborate the case of 2 Peter at length. If any document in the New Testament is pseudonymous it is this one. Its language and style is so very different from that of 1 Peter. It is clearly post-Pauline and reflects an anxiety over the delay of the parousia that would be unlikely were Peter himself still alive. And its difficulty in gaining acceptance into the canon points firmly to the same conclusion.

More to the point, however, the epistle reflects just the sort of emphases that we have now grown to expect within the Jewish traditioning process. A major reason for its being written is the danger of false interpretation of older revelation, particularly of scripture and of Paul (1:20; 3:15-16). In the face of false teachers and prophets (2:1) a stronger continuity and coherence with the older revelation is necessary. Hence the appeal back to 1 Peter; this is the second letter from Peter (3:1). Hence the reuse of the theme of 1 Peter 1:3-9 in 2 Peter 1:3-11. And hence the deliberate appeal back to the tradition of the transfiguration in 1:16-18 and the appeal to "the commands given by the Lord and Savior through your apostles" (3:2). Particularly interesting is 1:12-15. It asserts that the truth taught here is simply a reminder and memory refresher of what they already knew. But it also implies that this is Peter's last testament and that he will make provision for its teaching to be remembered after he is gone.

All this smacks strongly of the tradition of legitimate pseudonymity outlined above. Here is the appeal to authoritative tradition and the claim to be not only continuous with that tradition but the authentic voice and bearer of it. Within a Jewish context it was quite legitimate and acceptable to express this claim by using the name of the originator or fountainhead of that tradition. The test was whether the church would accept that claim: and the criterion would be not so much the inspiration of the actual author but the degree to which his writing could be regarded as the voice of the one named. In this case 2 Peter passed the test—but only just.

5. Conclusion

Canonical pseudepigraphy is best seen as an example of the Jewish understanding and practice of tradition as a living force. That practice consisted essentially in the reworking and contemporizing of authoritative tradition which stemmed from a recognized spokesman for God and channel of divine revelation. A later disciple standing within that tradition and intent to reexpress its message or to develop its emphases for a new day and situation saw himself as the mouthpiece of that tradition, speaking words congruent with the earlier revelation. He could present his message as the message of the originator of that stream of tradition, because in his eyes that is what it was. Actual use of the name of the original lawgiver, prophet, sage, scribe, or apostle was simply a literary device consistent with that practice. There was no intention to deceive, and almost certainly the final readers were not in fact deceived. Canonical pseudepigraphy was thus legitimate and ceases to be a problem.

"The living word" is thus a fitting expression for the vitality of the traditioning process within earliest Judaism and Christianity. The phrase makes it clear that revelation was conceived not as a static, once-for-all speaking of particular words which thereby immediately became fixed and petrified. The medium through which the revelation came was conceived of in a much more fluid way. The words and style and idiom could be reworked and indeed transformed into a different form, with enlarged scope and emphasis and adapted to changed circumstances.

In fact, our study enables us to distinguish two stages in this traditioning process: a first stage that consists in a reworking of the tradition itself, and a second stage at which the tradition has become largely fixed and the contemporizing process proceeds by interpretation of the authoritative text without altering the text as such. But in each case we see the same basic understanding of revelation and of the process by which revelation from the past can still speak to the present. In both stages we can speak quite properly and accurately of "the living word."

PART II

5. THE AUTHORITY OF SCRIPTURE ACCORDING TO SCRIPTURE

I. The Issue

1. WHAT IS THE ISSUE CONCERNING SCRIPTURE that seems to be dividing and confusing evangelicals today? It is not, I believe, the question of inspiration as such: of whether and how the Bible was inspired. No evangelical that I know of would wish to deny that the biblical writers were inspired by God in what they wrote, or to dispute the basic assertions of 2 Timothy 3:16 and 2 Peter 1:21. Nor is it, I believe, the question of authority as such: of whether the Bible is authoritative for Christians. All evangelicals are united in affirming that the Bible is the word of God unto salvation, the constitutional authority for the church's faith and life.

Where evangelicals begin to disagree is over the implications and corollaries of these basic affirmations of the Bible's inspiration and authority. When we begin to unpack these basic affirmations, how much more is involved in them? How much more is *necessarily* involved in them? The disagreement, it is worth noting right away, depends partly on theological considerations (what is the theological logic of affirming the inspiration of scripture?), and partly on apologetic and pastoral concerns (what can we not yield concerning the Bible's authority without endangering the whole faith, center as well as circumference?). In order to maintain these affirmations (inspiration and authority) with consistency of faith and logic, in order to safeguard these affirmations from being undermined or weakened—what more precisely must we define and defend? What does the assertion of the Bible's inspiration require us to affirm about the content of the Bible and of its constituent parts? What does the assertion of the Bible's authority require us to affirm about the continuing authority of any particular word or passage of scripture?

2. There was a time (in the seventeenth century) when the defenders of the Bible thought that the inspiration of the Bible could be understood only in terms of what we now call "the mechanical dictation theory," with the writers described as "living and writing pens."[1] There were even those at this period of scholastic Protestantism who found it necessary to maintain that the pointing of the Massoretic text of the Old Testament belonged to the original autographs;[2] and that the Greek of the New Testament must be pure, free of the vulgarisms of the spoken Greek of the time and of Hebraisms in construction, otherwise God's credit as an author would be compromised.[3] Thankfully I know of no evangelical today who would wish to pitch his first line of defence at such an indefensible position. Evangelicals today are united in believing that such a fuller definition is both unnecessary and unfounded.[4]

Nevertheless, evangelicals do still disagree on where that first line of defense should be pitched. In particular, for a hundred years now there has been disagreement among evangelicals on whether it can or should be pitched at the line called "inerrancy." A century ago, A. A. Hodge and B. B. Warfield were the most doughty proponents of the view that the line could be drawn nowhere else. Thus, for example, in 1881 they made the following claim:

> The historical faith of the Church has always been, that all the affirmations of Scripture of all kinds, whether of spiritual doctrine or duty, or of physical or historical fact, or of psychological or philosophical principle, are without any error, when the *ipsissima verba* of the original autographs are ascertained and interpreted in their natural and intended sense.[5]

In cordial disagreement was James Orr, another evangelical stalwart,[6] who evidently was just as strongly of the opinion that the "inerrancy" line of defense was no more defensible or worth trying to defend than the mechanical dictation theory of scholastic Protestantism.

> It is urged, for example, that unless we can demonstrate what is called the 'inerrancy' of the biblical record, down even to its minutest details, the whole edifice of belief in revealed religion falls to the ground. This, on the face of it, is a most suicidal position for any defender of revelation to take up.[7]

Thus was the range of disagreement within evangelical ranks on the question of inerrancy clearly outlined almost from the start.

For a lengthy period in the middle of this last hundred years, it looked as though the word *infallible* would provide a better ground of defense on which almost all evangelicals could unite. This was in part because the word *infallible* was more flexible than the word *inerrant*, a fact we should not ignore. On the one hand were those who interpreted it in terms of the classic Protestant formulation: "an infallible rule of faith and life."[8] On the other hand were those who consciously took their stand within the particular tradition of the great Princeton theologians and interpreted it as "infallible full stop." An example of the latter is E. J. Young:

> In all parts, in its very entirety, the Bible, if we are to accept its witness to itself, is utterly infallible. It is not only that each book given the name of Scripture is infallible but, more than that, the content of each such book is itself Scripture, the Word of God written and, hence, infallible, free entirely from the errors which adhere to mere human compositions. Not alone to moral and ethical truths, but to all statements of fact does this inspiration extend.[9]

But there were also those who would have preferred to echo the words of James Denney:

> The infallibility of the Scriptures is not a mere verbal inerrancy or historical accuracy, but an infallibility of power to save. The Word of God infallibly carries God's power to save men's souls. If a man submit his heart and mind to the Spirit of God speaking in it, he will infallibly become a new creature in Christ Jesus. That is the only kind of infallibility I believe in. For a mere verbal inerrancy I care not one straw. It is worth nothing to me; it would be worth nothing if it were there, and it is not.[10]

Unfortunately that period of relative calm and consensus has been broken. In the last few years those who see themselves as the heirs of Warfield have begun to insist that the line must be held at inerrancy. They sincerely believe that those evangelicals who do not hold to inerrancy are on the slippery slope which leads to unfaith, that inerrancy is only the first of a long line of dominoes whose fall will bring the whole line of Christian beliefs tumbling down. The storm broke in America with the publication of Harold Lindsell's book, *The Battle for the Bible* (Zondervan), in 1976, with its forthright insistence that only the Warfield position on scripture is valid and orthodox, and its fierce attack on those evangelicals and evangelical institutions who, in Lindsell's view, have apostatized by abandoning the inerrancy line—a particular case in point being Fuller Seminary where Lindsell had previously been vice president.[11]

The inerrancy wing of evangelicalism has continued to make the running in this renewed debate. In 1977 the International Council on Biblical Inerrancy (ICBI) was founded in North America, its objective being to provide a rallying point for evangelicals based on "a Bible that is true in whatever it touches," "not merely in matters of faith and practice but also in other matters such as statements relating to history and science."[12] Or as James Boice, ICBI's first chairman, puts it more concisely, "What Scripture says, God says—through human agents and without error."[13] One of the signs of the times is that someone of the stature of J. I. Packer feels it no longer enough to affirm the Bible's inspiration and authority, no longer enough to affirm even its infallibility. These have become "weasel words" through having some of their meaning rubbed off, so that "inerrancy" it has to be, despite the negative form of the word.[14]

3. The issues raised by these developments are serious and cannot be ignored. Are only those who affirm "inerrancy" to be permitted to rejoice in the description "evangelical"? Are those who think "inerrancy" a misguided and unhelpful word in this context—as indefensible a line of defense as Orr thought, as incapacitating a line of attack as Denney saw it—are they to be dubbed apostates and renegades, as grievous offenders against the holy majesty of God? Should "inerrancy" be the watchword for today, the banner under which all those who acknowledge the inspiration and authority of scripture unite?

How to answer such questions? At least we can agree that all evangelicals would want to give the first priority to listening to the voice of scripture itself. We may need to dispute with nonevangelicals as to whether in so doing we are arguing in a circle. With other evangelicals we can assume a common willingness to submit such issues to scripture.

But how to marshal the testimony of scripture? Here at once the differences begin to appear within the ranks of evangelicals. The standard Warfield approach is to appeal, not unnaturally, to the passages that contain explicit or implicit teaching on scripture as such. These are understood as requiring nothing short of the full inerrancy position. Other passages which may seem to contradict that conclusion, or to put it under strain, can usually be harmonized without overstraining the bounds of possibility, or if still intractable can be set aside until fuller illumination is given us. On the other hand, those less happy with the inerrancy line are less happy not because they wish to resist a clearly stated teaching of scripture, but because they do not think this in fact is what scripture teaches. They do not find the teaching passages pointing to such a thoroughgoing conclusion. To clarify what precisely they do teach about scripture's inspiration and authority, it is necessary to listen to the fuller testimony of scripture: necessary, that is, to observe not only what scripture teaches about scripture, but also how scripture uses scripture.

Since my brief is to expound the more "radical" evangelical position on this issue, the rest of this chapter will be devoted to exploring what I see to be (*a*) the weaknesses of the Warfield position, and (*b*) the strengths and implications of the alternative, also scriptural, also evangelical. As the title of the chapter indicates, I am concerned here above all with the *authority* of scripture: to ascertain what is involved in asserting scripture's authority, how its authority "works," and whether, in particular, inerrancy is a necessary condition of its authority.[15]

II. The Weakness of the Warfield Position

4. The passages that contain the strongest teaching about scripture are 2 Timothy 3:16 and 2 Peter 1:21 (already mentioned at the beginning), and, in addition, two Gospel passages, John 10:35 and Matthew 5:18.[16]

a. 2 Timothy 3:16

> All scripture is inspired (*theopneustos*) by God and profitable (*ōphelimos*) for teaching, for reproof, for correction, and for training in righteousness.

It is difficult to see how this verse requires inerrancy. The word *inspired* (*theopneustos*) is certainly a word rich in significance, which Warfield not unfairly translates "God-breathed,"[17] but the quality which it affirms of scripture is that of having been given by divine inspiration. There is no indication that the author wanted to be more precise than that. And the consequence he himself draws is that since it is God-breathed, therefore it is "profitable, useful, beneficial, advantageous"[18] in the matters of salvation (3:15), sanctification, and moral education (3:17). If anything, the most natural interpretation of the verse would seem to support the distinction that some evangelicals have urged between what scripture teaches concerning the believer's faith and life[19] and what it touches beyond that (scientific and historical detail).[20] At any rate it is hard to see how the verse can be used to justify extending the scope of biblical authority beyond that of "teaching, reproof, correction, and training in righteousness" (see further below, p. 77).

b. 2 Peter 1:20-21

> No prophecy of scripture is a matter of one's own (or the prophet's own) interpretation, because no prophecy ever came by the impulse of man, but men moved by the Holy Spirit spoke from God.

Here again the talk is of inspiration, and the metaphor is even more vigorous—of the prophecy as uttered by one borne along by the Spirit. But it says nothing more about the character of the prophecy, as to whether, for example, the words, descriptions or historical references used therein must therefore be error-free in all points of fact. Verse 20 probably draws attention to the dangers of subsequent interpretation (RSV, NEB, JB): the interpreter can mistake the meaning of the prophet, unless he is as dependent on the Spirit to understand the prophecy as the original author was in his writing. But some maintain that the reference is to the prophet's own interpretation (NIV): a thought perhaps parallel to that in 1 Peter 1:10-12.

c. John 10:35

> The scripture cannot be broken.

The context is Jesus' response to the charge that he was making himself God. Jesus replies by citing Psalm 82:6, "I said, You are gods," where those referred to were probably thought to be judges.[21] If men can be called "gods" (and scripture cannot be broken), how much more the Son of God. The parenthetical phrase is open to a strong interpretation. For example, Leon Morris:

> The term 'broken' is not defined. . . . But it is perfectly intelligible. It means that Scripture cannot be emptied of its force by being shown to be erroneous.[22]

But the point is not whether the psalmist was in error when he called judges "gods." It is rather that the psalmist's words cannot be without significance: that is, cannot be emptied of the significance they obviously contain, and which significance Jesus proceeds to draw out in the typical Jewish *a fortiori* or *a minori ad maius* argument. So the first half of Morris's last sentence catches the sense well ("scripture cannot be emptied of its force"), whereas the latter half ("by being shown to be erroneous") is his own corollary rather than that of Jesus or John.[23]

Warfield also makes much of the casual nature of the clause in Psalm 82:6:

In the Saviour's view the indefectible authority of Scripture attaches to the very form of expression of its most casual clauses. It belongs to Scripture through and through, down to its minutest particulars, that it is of indefectible authority.[24]

Whether that is an appropriate categorization of the original passage ("casual clause") may well be doubted, but in any case there is sufficient evidence that, in the first century c.e., Psalm 82 (including v. 6) was a focus of considerable interest, both among the rabbis and at Qumran: to whom did the description "God" and "gods" refer in verses 1 and 6?[25] No one doubted that the use of these words was significant; it was their reference that was uncertain. John therefore represents Jesus as drawing on a passage of contemporary interest whose force would be accepted (that men are called "gods"), and as building his argument on that significance in good rabbinic style.

d. Matthew 5:18

Truly, I say to you, till heaven and earth pass away, not an iota, not a dot, will pass from the law until all is accomplished [genētai].

One of the interesting and puzzling features of this saying is that the very strong middle clause ("not one iota . . . will pass from the law") is qualified by *two* temporal clauses ("until heaven and earth pass away" and "until all is accomplished"). It is clearly possible to take the first clause as asserting the law's *eternal* validity, as Boice does:

Jesus Christ not only assumed the Bible's (*sic*) authority; he taught it, going so far as to teach that it is entirely without error and is eternal, being the Word of God [Matt. 5:18 is then quoted].[26]

The problem which that interpretation leaves us is to explain how the early churches could nevertheless abandon various important requirements of the law (more than just iotas and dots): animal sacrifice, the distinction between clean and unclean foods, and the sabbath.

The last clause is more ambiguous: it could be interpreted as referring to the end of the age, and understood as a reaffirmation of the law's eternal validity—in which case the same problem arises. Alternatively, it could refer to the fulfillment of the law (and the Old Testament scriptures?) in the person and work of Christ; and the first clause could then be taken as a hyperbolic affirmation of the law's continuing force (cf. Luke 16:17).[27] But if that durability of the law was only until it had been fulfilled in Christ, then we can hardly say that either Jesus or Matthew thought of the Old Testament as of eternally binding authority. The answer is most probably somewhere in between: Matthew probably thinks of the law here as the law reinterpreted through the life and teaching of Jesus, and not just in verse 18 but throughout these four verses (5:17-20).[28] In which case, the force of the iota/dot affirmation has to be understood accordingly and cannot be taken as asserting the unconditional authority of the law.

Either way, it is the *authority* of the law that is in view here: the extent to which, and the way in which, its claim to complete authority still binds the believer. If that is what "without error" means in this context (of continuing binding authority), then Matthew 5:18 can be interpreted only doubtfully and improbably as an unqualified affirmation of the law's lack of error—an interpretation that leaves larger problems than it resolves. And if "without error" extends to points of history and science, then it need hardly be said that such a question lies not at all within the scope of the thought.

There is other biblical material that the followers of Warfield use to reinforce their stand on the inerrancy line, and some of it we will allude to later. But these four verses can justifiably be called the four corner pillars of the inerrancy stronghold. What a closer examination of them has revealed is the weakness rather than the strength of these four pillars (when treated as assertions of inerrancy). This weakness can be further clarified by reference to two key words: *intention* and *interpretation*.

5. The supporters of inerrancy have not paid sufficient heed to the question of the biblical author's *intention*.[29] To be sure, they recognize that the scriptural writer's intention must be taken into account,[30] but the point seems to serve primarily as a convenient explanation of a good deal of the phenomena of scripture that clashes with an unqualified assertion of inerrancy ("lack of modern technical precision, irregularities of grammer or spelling, observational descriptions of nature, the reporting of falsehoods, the use of hyperbole and round numbers, the topical arrangement of material, variant selections of material in parallel accounts, or the use of free citations").[31] Where it was not the author's intention to give precise details—so the argument runs, quite rightly—it is unjustified to count his imprecision as error.[32]

Unfortunately, however, the question of the author's intention too often ceases to have bearing beyond the resolution of "problem passages." In the case of the four pillar passages reviewed above, for example, it is a question often not really posed at all—or else answered far too casually. But what *was* the intention of each of the authors of these four passages? In each case the proponents of inerrancy tend simply to *assume* that the utterance embraces the thought of inerrancy. But (as we have seen) in no case can it be shown with any probability that such was the author's intention. In particular, the conclusion that 2 Timothy 3:16 draws from the "God-breathed" character of scripture is its value for doctrinal and ethical instruction, which hardly amounts to an assertion or assumption of scripture's lack of error.[33]

In point of fact, the conclusion drawn by the proponents of inerrancy (that these passages teach inerrancy) is not an exegetical conclusion at all. It is a dogmatic deduction drawn from their concept of God. "God's character demands inerrancy. . . . If every utterance in the Bible is from God and if God is a God of truth . . . then the Bible must be wholly truthful or inerrant."[34] But here again the question of divine *intention* has been totally ignored. What, after all, if it was *not* God's intention to preserve the writers of scripture from the sort of scientific and historical inaccuracy, to admit the presence of which in the Bible would be a slight on the divine honor (in view of the ICBI)?[35] What if God's rule of faith and life never was intended to be confused with, or depend on, the possibility of harmonizing the variant accounts, for example, of Judas's death (Matt. 27:3-8; Acts 1:18-19)? What if it was God's intention that, for example, sayings of the exalted Christ through an inspired prophet or interpreter should be given a place in the tradition of Jesus' teachings and accorded the same authority?[36] Such questions *cannot* be answered (or dismissed) simply on the basis of a dogmatic premise. They are real and legitimate questions, and can only be answered, if answers can be achieved, by means of exegesis.

Consider two more cases that illustrate well the importance of taking the question of divine intention more seriously and some of the wider ramifications: the historicity of Jesus' utterances in the Fourth Gospel, and the acceptability of pseudonymous letters within the New Testament. Here, too, we must ask, in the first case: What if it never was the Fourth Evangelist's intention that the extended discourses of the Fourth Gospel should be understood as uttered by Jesus during his ministry on earth? What if it was quite clearly understood, by author and first readers alike, that these were sermons or meditations on some particular saying or episode or facet of Jesus' ministry? Reference to the repeated phrase "Jesus said," and its equivalents, cannot be assumed to settle the matter, as any preacher who has elaborated a Gospel incident in order to make it more vivid or to bring out its point more clearly for his hearers must acknowledge. What the intention of the author or inspiring Spirit was on this point cannot be prejudged.[37] Such an issue can only be settled, if at all, by exegesis: by an exegesis that gives sufficient attention to historical context of meaning and genre; an exegesis that in this case must take proper account of the differences between John and the Synoptics, and of the midrashic character of the Johannine discourses.[38] And if the exegesis points to the answer that the Johannine discourses *are* sermons or meditations on particular words or events from Jesus' life, then the most probable conclusion is that this is precisely what John intended them to be. With such a conclusion, it should be noted, the inspiration and authority of John as inspired scripture is in no way threatened, but only properly understood; whereas the attempt to insist that John must have intended his readers to understand that the historical Jesus said every word while on earth detracts from the authority of John as scripture by making it teach something the author probably never intended.

Likewise on the issue of pseudonymity: What if pseudepigraphy was at least in some instances in the first century c.e. a recognized and acceptable form of literature? What if, for example, a disciple of Paul wrote one of the New Testament letters in the name of Paul, and the letter was received in the same spirit by the addressees? Here, too, the issue cannot be assumed to be settled by appeal to the opening words of a disputed letter, without reference to the wider historical context of literary practice and form.[39] B. M. Metzger, in his valuable review of this evidence, at one point cites Tertullian's comment that "it is allowable that that which disciples publish should be regarded as their master's work."[40] He subsequently concludes quite fairly:

> Since the use of the literary form of pseudepigraphy need not be regarded as necessarily involving fraudulent intent, it cannot be argued that the character of inspiration excludes the possibility of pseudepigraphy among the canonical writings.[41]

In both these instances the question of intention has not been given sufficient scope, and the inerrancy line has been drawn much too restrictively. By insisting on a particular understanding of the text which pays too little attention to a properly historical exegesis, the authority of scripture has been more abused than defended.

The fact is, then, that once the question of intention is given wider scope (as above), the inerrancy line ceases to have the firmness and solidity that its proponents assume when they insist on building their defense on it. For not only does it have to be relaxed to allow for all sorts of inexactitudes and casualness (as above, p. 76, and n.31, below), but it has *always* to be subordinated to the issue of intended meaning. And each time exegesis points to the conclusion that an author's intended meaning does not depend on the inerrancy or otherwise of "whatever he touches,"[42] then the inevitable corollary is that the inerrancy claim has missed the point. In other words, when the question of divine intention in scripture is taken seriously, the idea of inerrancy at best becomes more problematic and obscure than helpful. To say that a biblical author is true and reliable in the meaning he intends is a statement which makes good sense. To insist that he is more than that—inerrant in all he says—confuses more than clarifies, and, worse still, directs attention as often as not away from the force of the biblical statement on to subordinate issues of factual detail.[43]

6. The other key word is *interpretation:* a word that opens up what is really another facet of the same broader issue. Interpretation is more demanding than exegesis. Exegesis I take to be the task of trying to understand the biblical writing in its original meaning, within its own terms, within its own context.[44] Interpretation, on the other hand, can be defined, for the moment, as the task of trying to translate that meaning into the language, thought-forms, and idioms of the interpreter's day, as far as possible without adding to or subtracting from that original meaning. No one doubts that interpretation is necessary. We cannot expect all Christians to operate directly out of the Hebrew, Aramaic, and Greek in which the Bible was originally written. But as soon as we say translation, we are caught up in interpretation, and when translation becomes exposition, then interpretation is the name of the game.

The point is that interpretation inevitably involves *uncertainty*. Interpretation is the art of weighing probability against possibility. Again and again we cannot be certain as to what the biblical author intended to say and teach, and must settle for the most probable interpretation. We have seen this already in the case of the four pillar passages examined above. The same uncertainty affects even the most central elements in New Testament teaching. What, after all, did Jesus mean by "the kingdom of God"? The fairly broad consensus on this one has been recently called in sharp question by Bruce Chilton.[45] What does Paul mean by justification through faith? Here, too, the Protestant consensus has similarly been called in question by the work of Krister Stendahl and Ed Sanders.[46] Is the *Living Bible* justified in its interpretative translation of John 1:1, "Before anything else existed, there was Christ with God"? I for one take leave to doubt it.[47]

Of course, in most cases we can be sufficiently confident of the substance of the sense intended—of the author's main emphasis. There is no doubt, for example, that the Bible consistently presents God as Creator, even if the "technical details" remain unclear. Again, there is no doubt that the New Testament consistently teaches that the resurrection of Jesus is something which happened to Jesus and not simply to his disciples, even though there remains uncertainty as to whether we are talking about a physical resurrection (Luke 24:39) or of his resurrection as a spiritual body (1 Cor. 15:44-50). And in its overall instruction "unto salvation" (2 Tim. 3:15), the message of the Bible is quite clear enough and consistent, even when emphases differ in different contexts.[48] The trouble is that the assertion of inerrancy wants to say more, and to be meaningful needs to be able to claim more. To be "sufficiently confident of the substance of the sense intended, of the author's main emphasis" is not enough. It is inerrancy that is being asserted, not merely authority. It is inerrancy in point of detail, not merely authority of the main point of teaching (even if, it would appear, the author only *intended* to teach that one main point, to instruct unto salvation; see the discussion above, pp. 76ff.).

To cry "inerrancy" on all that the Bible touches, when we have to live with such uncertainty, is to promote a kind of double-think that cannot be healthy. Here it seems to me that Denney's point gains force. The authority of scripture is not the kind that essentially depends on rational argument and logical demonstration of detailed inerrancy; it is rather a power that grasps the hearer, so that conscience, mind, and will cry out, "This is the word of God." Was it not just such a contrast Paul had in mind when he reminded the Corinthians that "my speech and my message were not in plausible words of wisdom, but in demonstration of the Spirit and power" (1 Cor. 2:4)?[49]

When we move beyond particular texts to larger patterns and beliefs more broadly based in scripture, the question of interpretation becomes even more important. Of course, central affirmations and insights of faith, consistently expressed throughout scripture, become more firmly established: the one God's redemptive love, human pride and selfish grasping, and so forth. But beyond such essentials, the simple fact is that *different* schemes and systems of faith and practice can be drawn from scripture and claim legitimate grounding in scripture. Here the important principle of interpretation, the perspicuity of scripture, must be handled with great self-critical circumspection, otherwise it can quickly degenerate into little more than a confidence trick. For what it usually boils down to, in application, is the rule of thumb whereby I interpret the unclear passages of scripture to conform to the clear passages. What I can too easily forget, or conveniently ignore, is that what is clear to me may not be clear to you, and what is unclear to me may be quite obvious to you. Consequently the *same* hermeneutical principle quickly leads to *different* patterns of faith and life. Why is it, for example, that almost all Christians have abandoned the sabbath as their holy day? The awkward answer is that they have conformed the very *clear* teaching of Exodus 2:8-11 to what is at best an *implication* drawn from the New Testament. Another awkward example: Reformed tradition (including not least Princeton theology) has developed a form of worship that gives pride of place to the sermon, where the model of the Christian preacher, as like as not, is the Old Testament prophet. Yet the same tradition has managed to ignore (or discount) almost completely what is after all the most clear guidance in the New Testament on what should take place in Christian worship (1 Cor. 14:26).[50]

The fact is, like it or not, that we each one individually, and as part of a particular tradition, work with what amounts to a canon within the canon in order to justify the distinctive emphases of that tradition. For example: for the Lutheran it is Paul's teaching on justification through faith to which everything else is conformed; for the Pentecostal it is the pneumatology of Acts and 1 Corinthians 12–14 that is the "clear" which enables one to interpret the "unclear."[51] Indeed, *all* Christians must work with a canon within the canon, otherwise we would not be Christians. For we all interpret the Old Testament in the light of the revelation of Jesus Christ. We can only justify the abandoning of clear scriptural commands—for example, regarding the sabbath and sacrifices—by appealing to our canon within the canon. Whether we call it the principle of progressive revelation or not, the fact remains that we allow one scripture to reduce the force of another, to set aside another. But notice what this means. If we take the point about interpretation seriously—the inevitable necessity of interpretation and the character of interpretation—we *cannot* simply affirm "What the Bible says, God says" as meaning that each word of scripture is of continuing and irreversible authority, calling forth from us unquestioning obedience. In which case inerrancy, in the sense of indefectible authority, becomes a concept requiring still more qualification and causing still more confusion. And if we take seriously the diversity of legitimate interpretations, we cannot simply assert that problems will be resolved by harmonizing[52] without justifying the point of view from which we engage in the harmonizing; without justifying the exegetical clarity of the "clear" to accord with which we interpret the "unclear"; without justifying the canon within the canon by which we in effect render the rest of the canon of only deuterocanonical authority. But as soon as we recognize and admit that, at least in some instances, we have to choose *between* scriptures, the blanket assertion of inerrancy becomes inappropriate and indefensible.

In particular, the dogma of inerrancy is itself a particular interpretation of particular scriptural passages, an interpretation which, as we have already seen, is by no means self-evident. The Warfield line of Princeton theology is itself a particular tradition within evangelical Christianity that is by no means clear to other evangelicals, let alone to other Christians.[53] To insist on this tradition as the only legitimate way of understanding the New Testament is to ignore the hermeneutical process altogether. It ignores the fact that the inerrancy line is built on at best doubtful exegetical foundations. It ignores the hermeneutical uncertainty as to the divine intention in not a few passages of scripture.[54] It ignores the fact that we all in effect ignore the teaching of many passages of scripture because we find others more clear or more conducive.[55] In short, it seems to me to be a very dangerous kind of unself-critical blinkeredness that makes it possible for some Christians to take an interpretation of scripture whose hermeneutical justification from within scripture is weaker than other interpretations, to exalt it above all other alternative views of scripture, and to use it to deny validity to those others, even when they have at least as strong an exegetical base.

7. It will be clear by now that I have grave reservations about the legitimacy of the inerrancy position as an interpretation of scripture—both of scripture in its teaching on scripture and of scripture as a whole—and a deep disquiet at the attempt of the ICBI to persuade all evangelicals that the inerrancy line is the only sound line for the defense of scripture's inspiration and authority. I fully recognize that for the proponents of inerrancy there are even bigger issues at stake—no less than the honor and trustworthiness of God.[56] I respect that concern, even when I believe they have jumped too quickly from "God says" to "without error," and have missed out the absolutely crucial intermediate questions—How has he said? With respect to what? With what intention?—questions whose answers in terms of exegesis and interpretation point up the inaccuracy and inadequacy of "inerrancy" as a scriptural concept applicable to scripture.[57]

I, too, think that the issues go beyond the confines of debate over hermeneutical principles and procedures. At three points in particular I believe the proponents of inerrancy are in considerable spiritual peril and are putting the faith of their disciples seriously at risk—I would not be so bold were it not that the issues are so grave.

a. In all seriousness, I fear that the ICBI, in its position on scripture, cannot escape the charge of Pharisaic *legalism*. The Pharisees believed that the Torah must be clarified by their oral tradition. The oral law, they sincerely believed, was simply an explanation of the written law, and therefore of equal force. By means of their hermeneutical techniques, they were able to develop a tradition that made a consistent whole of the teaching of the law and the prophets. But Jesus criticized the Pharisees severely because their traditions were actually nullifying the clear teaching of scripture—which, of course, they had incorporated into their systematized tradition, but with lesser force (Mark 7:9-13). From the criticisms leveled earlier against the inerrancy line, it will be apparent that it, too, is a tradition: a tradition based more on a systematized dogma than on scripture itself; a tradition that ignores or harmonizes into conformity too much in scripture which points away from inerrancy. Speaking personally, it is the harmonizing expedients of the proponents of inerrancy[58] that have reminded me most strongly of the rabbinic casuistry which drew such outspoken condemnation from Jesus. It is possible, is it not, as Paul warned us (Rom. 7:6; 2 Cor. 3:6, 14-17), to be so concerned for the letter of scripture that we actually miss what the Spirit seeks to say to us through it; to stifle the life of the Spirit by concentrating on the incidental forms through which he speaks? That is the danger that I fear the ICBI is courting.

b. The second point is linked with the first. It is the fear that the heirs of Princeton theology are in grave danger of *bibliolatry.*[59] By asserting of the Bible an indefectible authority, they are attributing to it an authority proper *only* to God the Father, Son, and Holy Spirit. If we say the biblical authors wrote without error, we attribute to their writing what we otherwise recognize to be true only of Christ. We do for the Bible what Roman Catholic dogma has done for Mary the mother of Jesus; and if the charge of Mariolatry is appropriate against Catholic dogma, then the charge of bibliolatry is no less appropriate against the inerrancy dogma. We cannot argue for a precise analogy between the divine and human in Christ (effecting sinlessness) and the divine and human in scripture (effecting inerrancy) without making the Bible worthy of the same honor as Christ—and that is bibliolatry.[60]

c. The third charge is even more serious, since it involves the spiritual health of others. It is that the inerrancy line is *pastorally disastrous.* Integral to the inerrancy position is the all-or-nothing argument, the slippery-slope mentality, the repeated reasoning that if we cannot trust the Bible in all, we cannot trust it at all.[61] That may be an argument which appeals to the over-simplifications of spiritual infancy; but it is hardly an appropriate expression of the spiritual maturity defined by Paul as the enabling to discern the things that really matter, to approve what is essential (Phil. 1:10).[62] To make, for example, Jesus' teaching on love of God and love of neighbor dependent on the historicity of the fact that Jesus cursed the fig tree on the day after the cleansing of the temple (Matt. 21:12-19)—or was it the same day (Mark 11:12-15)?—is neither discriminating nor brave. In my experience of teaching theology, the student who is most at risk as regards faith is precisely the one who has been previously instructed in this logic. When such a student finds that some such peripheral matters cannot be harmonized without doing some exegetical violence to the text, he or she is forced by this logic to abandon all. The worst thing about the slippery-slope imagery is that it is a self-fulfilling prophecy in far too many cases. And the fault, be it noted, lies not with those who seek to train the student in exegesis, to develop his or her theological awareness and expertise, to enable him or her to discriminate between the primary and the secondary, and to handle the big questions confronting faith in today's world. The fault lies rather with those who have taught the student that it is all or nothing. And even those who cling firmly to the top of the slope—what a burden of (subconscious) fear they carry: fear of finding even one error in the biblical record, fear of what the archaeologist's spade might turn up, fear of engaging in open-ended discussion, fear of asking searching questions in case the answer does not fit into the system. The top of that slippery slope looks to me too much like that state of spiritual immaturity which Paul was delighted to have left behind, where the spirit of slavery to fear and bondage to the letter is more noticeable than the liberty and life of the Spirit of sonship (Rom. 8:14f.; 2 Cor. 3:6, 17; Gal. 4:1-7). After all, the Pharisees were as convinced as the ICBI that their understanding and elaboration of the law was the only way to remain faithful to scripture.

In short, if I had to sum up my criticism of the Warfield position it would be that it is exegetically improbable, hermeneutically defective, theologically dangerous, and educationally disastrous.

III. According to Scripture

8. What then is the alternative to inerrancy? Not, of course, an assumption of wholesale error or complete untrustworthiness. That is the alternative suggested by the "all-or-nothing" slippery-slope argument—appropriate perhaps when the discussion has to be simplified to the level of a lower-school debating society, but *not* at the level of exegesis and interpretation. So what is implied in the assertion of the Bible's inspiration and authority? What does that assertion say about the continuing authority of any particular passage in its intended meaning?

How can we answer this question? The biblical passages that express or imply a doctrine of inspired scriptural authority take us so far, as we have seen ("inspired and therefore profitable," etc.). The trouble is that on their own they are not sufficiently explicit for our purposes. What then? What is too often forgotten in such discussions is that in scripture we have not only passages that teach an "in principle" view of scriptural authority, but also passages where scripture is actually used—where scripture functioned as authority in practice. Here obviously is our best hope of a clearer answer to our question: an examination of how scripture is actually handled by and within scripture. If we assume a consistency of inspiration, and a consistency in the divine will expressed through inspiration, then this presumably will be reflected in the inspired writer's attitude to, and use of, earlier inspired writings. Thus we will learn how scripture worked as scripture; how its authority was actually perceived and regarded by scripture. Thus we will learn what the biblical writers themselves meant when they elsewhere asserted scripture's inspiration and authority.[63] In other words, a properly critical method of hermeneutics need not be imposed on scripture,[64] but can be derived from scripture itself. Scripture can indeed show us how to interpret scripture.

This procedure, it should be noted, will avoid the weakness of Warfield's famous essay, "'It says': 'Scripture says': 'God says'."[65] Warfield points quite properly to the fact that these phrases can be used interchangeably in the New Testament—scriptural passages being attributed to *God* where God was not represented in that passage as the actual speaker (Matt. 19:4f.; Acts 13:34), or attributed to *scripture* where the original was actually a message from God (Rom. 9:17; Gal. 3:8). He also notes, not unfairly, that in some instances the formula is used in the present tense ("says," not "said"), the thought being of scripture as "the ever-present and ever-speaking Word of God" (e.g., Acts 13:35; Rom. 9:17; Heb. 3:7).[66] The weakness of Warfield's study is that he focuses exclusively on the formula introducing the scriptural quotation. But the question for us is, What was the precise force of that formula? How did the scripture quoted actually function as authority—as word of God? And this question can be answered only by looking at the quotations themselves, and at how they were handled by the New Testament writers in question. To build a case simply on the introductory formulae is to run the risk of unjustified generalizations—and Warfield is certainly vulnerable to that criticism.

For example, it is not enough simply to quote the formula "God said" in Matthew 19:4f., for the whole point of that passage is that one scripture is being used to interpret (and in some sense to discount?) another, as we shall see (below, p. 89). In other words, the function of the passage cited as authoritative scripture is more complex than the simple appeal to the introductory formula allows. Similarly, the introductory formula of Galatians 3:8 should not be used as the basis of a wider generalization regarding the authority of the scriptural promise to Abraham, without taking cognizance of the way Paul interprets the other strand of the same promise[67] a few verses later. For, as is well known, in Galatians 3:16 Paul interprets the promise to Abraham and his descendants ("seed," collective singular) as fulfilled in Christ ("seed," single individual). In other words, he adapts the clear reference of the original and gives the scripture a different sense from that which was obviously intended in the original.[68] That, of course, is not to say his interpretation was without justification. It was an interpretation which by the canons of that time would have been wholly acceptable,[69] and from the Christian perspective was wholly on target. The point is that the scripture which is recognized as authoritative is *not* the scripture in its original and originally intended and understood meaning. The authoritative scripture is scripture interpreted, scripture understood in a sense that constituted a significant variation or development or departure or difference from the original sense.[70]

Such examples strongly suggest that Warfield's conclusions from his study of the formulae introducing Old Testament quotations must be received with a good deal more caution than, say, the International Council on Biblical Inerrancy would acknowledge.[71] These formulae certainly show that at least these scriptures quoted were regarded as having continuing authority. But is it right to generalize from these particular instances and conclude that every sentence in the Old Testament was regarded by Jesus and the New Testament authors as having the same continuing authority? And even if the answer to that question was yes (but see below, pp. 89f.), it would still leave unanswered the question, How did that authority function? Was the authoritative utterance that meaning of the scripture as established by grammatico-historical investigation (then Paul is to be censured in Gal. 3:16)? And if the answer is "No, not always," then the issue of interpretation and the canons of interpretation is back on the agenda with reinforced significance.

Our task, then, is to explore the way in which scripture actually uses scripture. As we observe how the authority of scripture was understood by Jesus and his first followers, how the authority of the Old Testament actually functioned in the New Testament, we should hopefully gain a clearer grasp of how the inspiration and authority of scripture should be received and expressed today. We will look first at Jesus' attitude to, and use of, scripture; and then at the earliest churches' attitude to, and use of, scripture. Inevitably it will be a too sketchy treatment, but sufficient, I trust, to achieve a positive and properly scriptural formulation of our theme, "The Authority of Scripture according to Scripture."

9. Jesus' attitude to and use of scripture. It cannot be disputed that Jesus regarded the writings of the Old Testament as inspired and authoritative.[72] We need only to think of a passage like Mark 12:35ff. ("David, inspired by the Holy Spirit, declares") and the repeated "it is written" (e.g., Mark 11:17 pars.; 14:21 pars.; Matt. 11:10/Luke 7:27). On more than one occasion he met queries and disputatious questions by referring to scripture (Mark 10:18f. pars.; 12:24-27 pars.; 12:29-31 pars.).[73] He clearly applied at least some passages of the Old Testament to himself, and drew his understanding of his mission from them—most noticeably Isaiah 61:1f. (Luke 4:18f.; Matt. 5:3f./ Luke 6:20f.; Matt. 11:5/Luke 7:22),[74] and probably at least also the vision of Daniel 7:13f.[75] But once again we must ask, How did this authority work for Jesus? Was every passage of the then scriptures of equal authority and of equally binding authority—inerrant in that sense? To gain a clearer picture we should also consider the following passages.

a. The first is Jesus' use of Isaiah 61:1f. I have just pointed out that if any passage of the Old Testament informed Jesus as to his mission, it was this one. But at once we have to note a striking feature of his use of that passage, explicitly in Luke 4:18f. and implicitly in the other references: specifically, his use of it stopped short in the middle of a sentence—"to proclaim the year of the Lord's favor"—whereas Isaiah continues "and the day of vengeance of our God." Indeed, if we can take it that the very next clauses ("to comfort all who mourn . . .") influenced Jesus' formulation of the beatitudes (Matt. 5:4/ Luke 6:20b), it would appear that Jesus deliberately set aside or ignored the single phrase about the day of vengeance. This is borne out by his reply to the disciples of the Baptist in Matthew 11:5/Luke 7:22. Where the Baptist had clearly expected a fire-dispensing figure of judgment (Matt. 3:7-12/Luke 3:7-9, 15-17), Jesus evidently saw his mission in different terms.[76] Thus, in his reply to the Baptist he alluded deliberately to three Isaianic passages, all three of which, as Jeremias has pointed out, contain warning of judgment as well as promise of blessing (Isa. 29:18-20; 35:4-6; 61:1-2).[77] But Jesus picked out only the promise of blessing.

How was it that Jesus could be so selective in his use of Isaiah? There was nothing in Isaiah itself which even suggested that two separate pictures were in view, or that a time scale was intended for the warning different from that of the promise—particularly in Isaiah 61:2, where the threat of vengeance is an integral part of the one prophecy. We cannot say, therefore, that Jesus simply set himself under the authority of the Old Testament, or that all parts and words of these scriptures were of equal, and equally binding, authority. Evidently he approached these prophecies in a way, or from a perspective, or with an insight, that enabled him, or made it necessary for him, to interpret these passages somewhat selectively. Was it that other scriptures gave him the clue on how to read these Isaiah passages? Then the same point arises: What was it about these other scriptures that provided the authoritative interpretation of the Isaiah passages? Why, for example, did he not conversely take the Baptist's preaching as confirmation that it was the judgmental strand of these scriptures which should inform his mission? We still have to explain a certain degree of picking or choosing whereby one scripture, or one part of a single scripture, was found to be more authoritative for Jesus' understanding of his mission at that point than another. Was it his own conviction as to what God's will was for his mission—a conviction derived from his intimacy with the Father, and only partly drawn from, or informed by, scripture? If so, then we cannot say that scripture was Jesus' sole authority. And since it was his own immediate knowledge of God's will which enabled him to see that some passages or parts of scripture were more relevant to his mission than others, again we are forced to deny that all scripture was of equal, and of equally binding, authority for him.

Consequently we cannot conclude that the authority of scripture for Jesus was simply a matter of being obedient to the words of scripture in their grammatico-historical sense. The authority of scripture for Jesus was a more complex interaction of finding and being found by particular scriptures, of personal conviction and knowledge of God's will—partly informed from scripture and partly informing his understanding of scripture and his understanding of its particular relevance to him and his mission. This complexity of the hermeneutical process in the matter of Jesus' self-understanding must not be ignored or oversimplified.

b. Consider, second, three passages where Jesus had something to say about the relevance and authority of Old Testament scriptures on particular issues: Matthew 5:38-39, Mark 7, and Mark 10:2-12.

Matthew 5:38-39. "You have heard that it was said, 'An eye for an eye and a tooth for a tooth.' But I say to you, 'Do not resist one who is evil. But if anyone strikes you on the right cheek, turn to him the other also . . .'" Jesus refers here explicitly to an Old Testament principle of retribution, as expressed in Exodus 21:24, Leviticus 24:20, and Deuteronomy 19:21. And it is difficult to avoid the straightforward conclusion that Jesus was thereby abrogating part of the Mosaic law.[78] I would prefer to express the point more carefully. Jesus does not deny that this was an inspired word from God when it was given. We can quite fairly argue, indeed, that Jesus recognized the purpose of the original legislation—to limit and restrict the destructiveness of private revenge and family feud[79]—and that his own words were intended as an extension of the same healthy trend. On the other hand, it is of doubtful validity to argue that Jesus' words implied a distinction between the public morality of the law court (where the *lex talionis* legislation was still valid) and the private morality of personal relations (to which Jesus' words were solely directed).[80] There is no evidence of such a dichotomy in Jesus' own mission, either his life or his teaching, and no indication that such a distinction was intended or would even make sense in the illustrations used in Matthew 5:38-42. More likely, Jesus was saying simply that this rule of the Torah is not to serve as the rule of life of those who belong to, or look for, the kingdom. In other words, here we have scriptures that Jesus did *not* regard as giving authoritative guidance for the situation he was addressing. He did not dispute that they were the word of God for their own time. He did in effect deny that they were the word of God for his time. These were authoritative words, but their authority was *relative* to the particular historical period for which God intended them. In the new situation introduced by Jesus' ministry they were no longer of the same relevance, no longer of the same authority.

Mark 7:1-23. The context is the discussion about ritual cleanliness, where the principal object of attack was clearly the Pharisaic multiplication of rules governing ritual purity.[81] But in the course of this attack, Jesus formulated a very important principle. "There is nothing outside a man which by going into him can defile him; but the things which come out of a man are what defile him" (7:15); "whatever goes into a man from outside cannot defile him . . . what comes out of a man is what defiles a man" (7:18, 20). As stated, this principle does not mention any specific Old Testament regulation. But, as stated, it nevertheless undermines the whole distinction between clean and unclean foods—a distinction clearly promulgated in the Torah (Lev. 11:1-23; Deut. 14:3-21), and an absolutely fundamental ruling for the Pharisees upon which they were even then building their whole elaborate system of *halakhoth* (see n.81, below). He who denies so unequivocally that food can make a man "unclean" can hardly be said to regard the Torah's ruling on clean and unclean foods as of continuing and binding authority. On the contrary, the clear implication is that that law no longer has relevance—is no longer to have authority for his disciples—what Mark so clearly saw when he highlighted the point by adding the note to 7:19, "Thus he declared all foods clean"; which is the same as saying, "Thus he repealed the law classifying some foods as unclean and declared it void for his disciples."[82]

Mark 10:2-12. The striking feature of this passage for us is that Jesus seems to play off one Old Testament passage against another; or rather, he uses one Old Testament passage to determine the relevance of another. One was the Deuteronomic permission of divorce (Deut. 24:1-4) whereby the husband could put away his wife by writing a certificate of divorce (Mark 10:4). The other was the creation narrative's institution of marriage (Gen. 2:24), legitimating the man leaving his parents to unite in one flesh with his wife (Mark 10:7f.). The implication which Jesus drew from the latter, at least as we have it in Mark, is that the oneness of marriage is something God-given and that man should not tamper with it (10:8f.). As further explained in 10:11f., it is hard to dispute that Jesus was denying the validity of divorce altogether: "Whoever divorces his wife and marries another commits adultery against her." That seems to allow of no exception—if it was intended to, Mark has been astonishingly careless.[83] In other words, it is difficult to escape the conclusion that Jesus was once again denying the continuing authority of a particular Mosaic ruling: no situation is envisaged where a certificate of divorce would constitute a separation of what God had joined and so validate a second marriage.[84]

Of course, it is true that Jesus does not dispute the divine origin of the Deuteronomic law—it would be a highly questionable argument to press the distinction between "Moses commanded you" and the "he [God] said" of the Matthean parallel (Matt. 19:4f.). And of course we need to say no more than that Jesus regarded the Mosaic permission of divorce as a divinely given law appropriate to its times ("for the hardness of your hearts") but no longer appropriate for the people of the kingdom.[85] But once again the key point for us is that Jesus treated a particular scripture as no longer of authority for his followers. He did not deny that Deuteronomy 24:1f. was a word of God to Israel. But he did clearly imply that it was a word to a particular situation, a word whose authority was contextually conditioned, a word whose authority was relative for the time for which it was spoken, a word that could be interpreted only with reference to these conditioning factors. Even as scripture, it did not have an absolute authority, an indefectible authority—certainly not the same continuing authority as Genesis 2:24. Even as scripture, it was no longer the living word of God for Jesus' followers.

In each case, then, we can see that Jesus did not regard the Old Testament text in question as having an absolute, infallible (= unrefusable) authority.[86] Rather, he understood these texts in their relation and relevance to the historical situations to which they were originally spoken. He did *not* deny that these scriptures were the word of God to these situations. He *did* say or imply that they were no longer God's word to the situation he had brought about. In other words, their authority as word of God was relative to the particular situation to which they were addressed, for which they were intended to be the word of God. This recognition of the historical relativity of at least some scriptures must indicate an important hermeneutical principle that can in no way be overthrown or set aside by simple appeals to introductory formulae or by sweeping generalizations drawn from 2 Timothy 3:16.

10. The earliest churches' attitude to and use of scripture. We have already noted the New Testament passages that demonstrate most clearly early Christianity's affirmation of the Old Testament's inspiration and authority. If someone should point out that 2 Timothy 3:16 and 2 Peter 1:21 most probably belong to the later parts of the New Testament, that would not alter the overall judgment. The very frequency with which Old Testament passages are cited and echoed throughout the New Testament shows that 2 Timothy 3:16 and 2 Peter 1:21 are not expressing a view that only emerged after the first generation of Christians had already left the stage. On the contrary, the claim that scripture has been fulfilled is as important for the early speeches in Acts, and for Paul (note particularly Romans 9–11), as it is for Matthew and John. And a glance at a Nestle Greek text shows that on almost every page (apart from the Johannine epistles) there are direct scriptural references (indicated by heavier type).[87] But, once again, the fact that the New Testament writers believed the Old Testament writings to be inspired and authoritative is not the issue. The key question is once again, How did the New Testament writers actually use the Old Testament? How did the authority of the Old Testament actually function in practice? To help us find the answer, we should observe three features.

a. The first is the point, already made, that within the earliest churches we soon find important elements in the Old Testament law being abandoned: circumcision and the sabbath law, the law requiring a distinction between clean and unclean foods, and the practice of animal sacrifice. These developments are so well known that we hardly need to pause to document them: the refusal of Paul to allow Gentile converts to be circumcised (particularly Gal. 2:3-5), even though he claimed that they were heirs of Abraham (Galatians 3) and shared the faith and righteousness whose sign and seal in Abraham's case was circumcision (Rom. 4:11); the way in which the new weekly festival of the Christian Sunday soon superseded the Jewish festival of the sabbath in the Pauline churches at least (1 Cor. 16:2; Acts 20:7).[88] As for the law on clean and unclean foods, whatever we make of Mark 7 (above, p. 88), it is quite clear that the Gentile mission involved a complete abandonment of such distinctions more or less from the first (particularly Acts 10:10-16; Rom. 14:20).[89] And the letter to the Hebrews is a powerful exposition of the Christian belief that the old law was obsolete, and in particular that the law of sacrifice was abolished (particularly Heb. 8:13; 10:9).

We should not underestimate the significance of these developments. These were among the most cherished features of Israel's faith and life, and it was the challenge to them in the second century B.C.E., which had led to the Maccabean revolt (see, e.g., 1 Macc. 1:41-50, 62f.). These were clearly enunciated rules in scripture, unequivocal commands of God. Their continuing, binding authority on the earliest Christians was at first simply taken for granted, as Peter's reaction to the vision in Joppa well shows: "I have never eaten anything that is common or unclean" (Acts 10:14). And yet they were abandoned. As soon as the "how" of Gentile conversions and acceptance became an issue, so soon were these cherished requirements of scripture questioned and quickly abandoned, outside Palestine at any rate. Why? Because in these issues a greater revelatory authority was attached to the vision of Peter, the conviction of Paul, and what was recognized as the manifest work of the Spirit (e.g., Acts 10:44-48; Gal. 3:2-5). In the light of their own (inspired) understanding of what God was doing in their own time, they were willing to take an astounding step—to set aside the authority of many scriptures and the traditions of a thousand years! In this light they saw the fulfillment of Jeremiah 31:31-34 taking place in their own ranks, and interpreted it as rendering obsolete the old covenant (2 Cor. 3:3-6; Heb. 10:11-18). In this light Mark, at least, understood Jesus' words about true cleanliness as an abrogation of the law distinguishing clean and unclean foods (Mark 7:19). Here, at any rate, whole tracts of scripture in their obvious and intended sense were regarded as no longer of binding authority, no longer a word of God that could be disregarded only at the greatest spiritual peril.

b. The scripture that the New Testament writers regarded as of continuing authority was scripture *interpreted.* We have seen this already in the case of Galatians 3:16 (above, pp. 85f.). Two other passages in Paul illustrate the same point equally well: Romans 1:17 and 10:6-10. In Romans 1:17 Paul quotes from Habakkuk 2:4; but his quotation is significantly different from either the Hebrew or the LXX.

Habakkuk 2:4, "the righteous shall live by *his* faith/faithfulness";

LXX, "He that is righteous shall live by *my* faith" (i.e., probably, God's faithfulness);

Romans 1:17, "he that is righteous by faith shall live."

Most commentators agree that "by faith" is intended by Paul to go with "he that is righteous,"[90] as the rest of the letter certainly implies (Rom. 3:26, 30; 4:16; 5:1; 9:30, 32; 10:6). In which case, the scripture that provides Paul with his text in Romans is a scripture interpreted—interpreted in a way acceptable to his own Jewish contemporaries, but in a sense different from that most probably intended by Habakkuk.

Even more striking is his use of Deuteronomy 30:11-14 in Romans 10:6-10. For where Deuteronomy speaks of the law as something close to hand and heart, and so relatively easy to keep, Paul transforms the meaning into a reference to Christ and the gospel. Again it is obvious from parallels in Baruch 3:29f. and Targum Neofiti that this sort of interpretation was quite acceptable for Paul's own day and purpose.[91] But once again it is clear that the authoritative scripture is scripture interpreted, and interpreted in a sense significantly different from the original: what Deuteronomy referred to the law as such, Paul referred to (the law fulfilled in) Christ and the gospel.[92]

Here again the principle of interpretation seems to be not to reexpress and apply the meaning intended by the original author, but to understand and interpret scripture in the light of the revelation of Jesus Christ. On the other hand, it must be stressed that this did not involve a wholesale abandoning of, or disregard for, the Old Testament scriptures. It was important for these New Testament authors that they could show, by using acceptable canons of interpretation, that scripture had been fulfilled in Christ and in the gospel. The point is this: that the authoritative word of God for them was *not* scripture *tout simple; nor* was it their own immediate perception of the will and purpose of God. The authoritative word of God was heard through *the interaction of both,* through the coming together of revelation from their past and revelation in their present. If I may repeat the point for the sake of clarity— their interpretation of a particular scripture did not have to accord with the originally intended meaning of that scripture. But it had to be an acceptable interpretation of that scripture, and to accord more immediately with other scriptures (like Gen. 15:6 and Jer. 31:31-34). Likewise, their perception of God's will was often immediate, through the Spirit, and not simply through the Old Testament scriptures as though the Spirit could not speak directly (cf., e.g., Gal. 1:12 with 1 Cor. 15:3f.; Gal. 2:2; 5:16, 18, 25); though, at the same time, their overall perception of God's will was informed by scripture and had to be shown to be conformable to scripture. It was the fact that the revelation of Jesus Christ and the revelation of scripture could marry and did marry so fittingly which made (and still makes) it possible for Christianity to claim to be the proper heir of the Old Testament. But it was this marriage which was for the first Christians the authoritative word of God.

c. A third observation concerns the evident freedom the New Testament writers exercised in their choice or adaptation of the form of the authoritative text quoted. It is possible that Paul, for example, knew variant forms of several texts, and chose to quote the form most appropriate for his rendering (as a modern preacher may choose between RSV, NEB, JB, NIV, etc.). Cases in point may be Romans 10:6-8 (above, p. 92), Ephesians 4:8,[93] and possibly Romans 1:17 (above, p. 92). The point would then be that Paul's aim in such citations was not to uncover and use the originally intended meaning, but to use the version which made his own interpretation most acceptable and which, to be sure, had perhaps sparked off his interpretation.[94] The authoritative text was an already modified text: that is, a text already altered to give a different sense from that of the original. Here we may simply recall in addition that the LXX itself, the authoritative scriptures for all Greek-speaking Christians in the early days of Christianity, was in part at least a tendentious translation of the Hebrew, incorporating alterations designed to improve (i.e., change, for the better) the sense of the original.[95] Other Old Testament citations that differ from all known texts of the Old Testament are best explained as deliberate adaptations to demonstrate a closer "fit" between the prophecy and its fulfillment. The best examples here are Matthew 2:23, where the scripture cited does not exist as such, but was probably formed by a combination of Judges 13:5 and Isaiah 11:1; and Matthew 27:9-10, where the details have clearly (and awkwardly) been modified to fit more precisely the tradition of Judas's fate.[96] Here again it is evident that the authoritative scripture for Matthew was not a text in its original meaning, as determined by grammatico-historical exegesis, but the text in a form that can be seen (without resorting to unacceptable modification) to express most clearly the Christian understanding of it.

In all these cases, it should again be stressed, the choice of text was not arbitrary, the emendation was not arbitrary, and the interpretation was by no means completely divorced from the original intention of the author (as was the case, for example, in the allegorizing of Philo). Nevertheless, the texts used were often significantly different in sense from the original—whether the difference had been introduced by earlier translations and versions, or by the New Testament writers themselves in furthering their own interpretation.[97] This willingness to use variant versions, and readiness to adapt the text oneself, must be put in the balance and weighed together with passages like Matthew

5:18 and John 10:35. For it certainly indicates that the New Testament authors were not concerned with the iota and dot level of a text in the way that Princeton theology so readily assumes. On the contrary, their concern for the deeper meaning revealed in a text by the light of the revelation of Christ made them often sit loose precisely to such iotas and dots.[98]

d. One further observation may be appropriate. It is that the New Testament writers appear to have treated the Jesus-tradition with something of the same combination of respect and freedom. We can see this, for example, in the case of two of the passages already discussed above (pp. 88–90): Mark 7:1-23 and Mark 10:2-12. The point is that Matthew, in his use of Mark,[99] seems to soften the sharpness of both passages. He omits not only Mark's interpretative addition in Mark 7:19 ("Thus he declared all foods clean"), but also the element in the saying itself that provided strongest justification for Mark's interpretation. That is to say, whereas in Mark Jesus affirmed twice that what goes into a man *cannot* defile him (7:15, "there is nothing outside a man which by going into him can defile him"; 7:18, "whatever goes into a man from outside cannot defile him"), in Matthew the first saying is softened (Matt. 15:11, "not what goes into the mouth defiles a man, but what comes out of the mouth . . .") and its repetition omitted (Matt. 15:17). It is difficult to avoid the conclusion that Matthew was less than happy with the suggestion that Jesus' words amounted to an abrogation of the law on clean and unclean foods—an implication not hard to recognize within the Markan form of the saying, as Mark himself shows, but one less easy to argue for once Matthew had done his editing. Such editing can fairly be said to be concerned with the main thrust of the passage at the expense of some of its iotas and dots.

Similarly, it is now widely recognized[100] that Matthew's modification of Mark 10:2 transforms a general question about divorce and sets it within the rabbinic debate between the schools of Hillel and Shammai: Mark 10:2, "Can a man divorce his wife?"; Matthew 19:3, "Can a man divorce his wife *for any cause?*" The Matthean formulation goes on to show Jesus rejecting the then dominant Hillelite position (divorce permissible for any cause) and advocating the more rigorous position of Shammai (divorce possible only in cases of unchastity). That is to say, the ideal promulgated by Jesus in Mark (denying the possibility of a valid divorce—see above, pp. 89f.) is softened by its application to the particular situation of Matthew's time, and understood, and so rendered, as supporting the stricter of the two current options. Once again, be it noted, it is the adapted form of Jesus' saying that serves as the authoritative utterance of Jesus. A similar willingness to apply Jesus' original words in a more flexible way is evident in 1 Corinthians 7:10-15.[101]

If we have understood correctly what Matthew was doing, then it is clear that Matthew interpreted the sayings of Jesus in a way which made them speak more directly to the situation in which Jewish Christians found themselves in the second half of the first century. It was with the teaching of Jesus that he was concerned; it was that which had authority for him (cf. 1 Cor. 7:10). There is no suggestion that he would even have thought of creating or inventing sayings *de novo* and putting them in Jesus' mouth. Nor, if his treatments of these sayings is characteristic, did he attempt to alter the meaning of Jesus' sayings in an arbitrary or dramatic way. But neither can we say that he treated these sayings as unyielding dogma whose words (including iotas and dots) could not on any account be altered. Rather, we see a concern to show the words of Jesus speaking to his own time and to the issues of his own time. And where we might have felt it more proper to leave the saying in its original form and to add our interpretative gloss after it, it was evidently quite an acceptable procedure in Matthew's time to *incorporate the interpretation into the saying itself* by modifying the form of the saying. Not surprisingly, since this is precisely how he and other interpreters of his time (including Qumran and other New Testament writers) evidently handled the Old Testament, as we have seen (above, p. 89).[102] At this point, the gap between the Synoptics' handling of the Jesus-tradition and John's handling of the Jesus-tradition is not so wide as is sometimes asserted.[103]

11. The significance of all that has been said under section III can be summed up in the key phrase, *historical relativity.* What we have seen again and again in the attitude of Jesus, and of the first Christians, to scripture is their recognition and assertion of its authority, but recognition also of the fact that that authority is relative. To understand the word of God properly, it had to be related to the historical situation to which these words of God were first spoken, and related also to the situation of the interpreter. Let me try to elaborate a little on these two sides of the hermeneutical circle.

This recognition of historical relativity with respect to original context was obviously one of the hermeneutical principles that determined Jesus' and the first Christians' interpretation of the law. The fact cannot be denied that the words of various scriptures, enunciating specific laws, were seen as having authority for the time preceding Jesus, but as no longer authoritative in their originally intended sense. It was not a matter of saying, for example, that the intention of the laws on clean and unclean foods or divorce had always been simply and solely to point to their fulfillment in Christ—that would have been to deny their authority in the time before Christ. It was rather that their authority was recognized as being relevant to, and relative to, the time of the old covenant. To affirm that the laws on sacrifice, circumcision, sabbath, and so forth were the word of God only and always in the sense, and with the force, with which Christianity understood them, is in fact to deny that the Torah was the word of God before Christ came. Even a doctrine of progressive revelation cannot escape this corollary, if it affirms that now the only acceptable interpretation of the law is that given by the New Testament. For it still implies that scriptural injunctions were once the word of God in a sense which Christians no longer recognize as authoritative. If, for example, the sabbath law is to be interpreted in a sense other than its obvious sense, and if the Christian interpretation is the only proper interpretation, then in effect we deny that the Fourth Commandment ever was the word of God prior to the resurrection of Jesus. And since most Christians do not in fact observe the Fourth Commandment, that in effect amounts to a complete denial of the Fourth Commandment's authority as word of God (in other than some very spiritualized sense). To assert the *historical relativity* of God's word in the Fourth Commandment is surely preferable to affirming that it *never* was God's word (as understood for centuries) and still is not!

If recognition of relativity with respect to original context is as it were the more negative side of the hermeneutical circle, the recognition of relativity with respect to the interpreter's context is the more positive side of the same circle. The authoritative word of God for Jesus was that understanding of scripture which emerged from the interaction of particular scriptures with his own consciousness of sonship and sense of mission. The one did not ride roughshod over the other; each informed the other, each interpreted the other. The result was, however, an interpretation of some scriptures that involved pronouncing them as no longer of binding authority on his followers, and of others an interpretation that involved affirming the immediate relevance (and so authority) of one part but not of another. Likewise, the revelation given immediately to Peter and to Paul led them to judge various scriptures to be no longer a word of God whose authority still bound them. The revelation did not come through scripture in these cases, but its meaning was not a complete departure from scripture. Here again, it was the interaction of particular scriptures (like Jer. 31:31-34) with their own consciousness of being led by God's Spirit that provided the hermeneutical key. The point is that the result was the same as in the case of Jesus: the rendering of some scriptures in a sense somewhat different from the original, and the affirmation that other scriptures were no longer of binding authority on Christians. Such scriptures had fulfilled their role as word of God in their obvious sense; now that sense had been transcended by the fuller revelation of Christ and absorbed into it, with the effect that their obvious meaning was no longer relevant to, and so no longer of authority for, believers.

We saw this same interplay of historical relativities in the way Matthew quoted both the Old Testament and sayings of Jesus—quoted in a way that incorporated his interpretation of them into the words quoted. A good case in point is his handling of Jesus' words on divorce. Here again we see an interpretation that recognized the context of Jesus' original utterance, but which recognized also that these words had a different force when applied to Matthew's context. What we see, in fact, is Matthew softening the ideal expressed originally by Jesus, in the very same way that Deuteronomy 24:1f. softened in practice the principle enunciated in Genesis 2:24. In both cases the word that God actually spoke (through Deut. 24:1f., through Matt. 19:9) was a word which took account of the circumstances being addressed—making allowance for the hardness of men's hearts. In the same way Paul interpreted the same command of the Lord (that the wife should not separate from her husband) in a way that took account of the particular circumstances he was addressing (1 Cor. 7:10-15). No more than the words of the Old Testament were the words of Jesus, unyielding dogma to be observed to the letter whatever the circumstances, but principles whose statement and application could vary in the light of the circumstances. In other words, we might say that the New Testament writers recognized that hearing and understanding the word of God in scripture and in the Jesus-tradition involved the two-sided process of recognizing the original inspiration behind a particular saying but also of interpreting that saying in dependence upon the same Spirit (following 2 Peter 1:20f. in its more probable sense; see above, p. 74).[104]

It must be stressed that this recognition of the historical relativity of the word of God does not diminish its authority as word of God. Precisely to the contrary, it sets scripture free to function as word of God in the way intended. If we insist, with the logic of the inerrancy school, that scripture must always say precisely the same thing in every historical context, then we muzzle scripture: we filter the word of God through a systematizing and harmonizing process that filters out much that God would say to particular situations, and lets through a message that soon becomes predictably repetitive, whatever the scripture consulted. Why should it be so hard to accept that God speaks different words to different situations (because different situations require different words)? In Jesus Christ, God committed God's word to all the relativities of historical existence in first-century Palestine. Paul did not hesitate to express the gospel in different terms in different contexts, terms that no doubt would sound contradictory if they were abstracted from these contexts into some system and harmony which paid no heed to these contexts (1 Cor. 9:20f.)—hence the apparent conflict between Paul and James (cf. Rom. 3:28, "justified by faith apart from works"; James 2:26, "faith without works is dead"). Mark did not hesitate to press the implication of Jesus' words about true cleanliness with a view presumably to the Gentile mission (Mark 7:19), whereas Matthew softened the force of the same words, since he had the Jewish mission in view (Matt. 15:17). If we ignore such differentiation of the word of God in and to different situations, we rob scripture of its power to speak to different situations. It is only when we properly recognize the historical relativity of scripture that our ears can be properly attuned to hear the authoritative word that God speaks to us in the words of scripture here and now.

IV. Toward an Evangelical Hermeneutic

12. We may conclude by drawing together some of our findings, by reflecting further on them, and by highlighting their implications for our own understanding of, and response to, the authority of scripture in the present. Two basic assertions provide the starting point for an evangelical hermeneutic.

a. An evangelical hermeneutic starts, as this chapter started, from the assertion of the inspiration and authority of scripture. That starting point has been validated from scripture, since Jesus and the New Testament writers clearly taught and based their teaching on the inspiration and authority of the Old Testament scriptures. It is true that many evangelicals want to go further and to demand a much more precise definition of scripture's inspiration and authority as the starting point; in particular, a definition spelled out in terms of inerrancy: that is, a definition of scripture as consisting of statements whose freedom from error gives them an indefectible authority. It must be stated quite firmly, however, that such a definition is *not* validated from scripture: while the New Testament passages that teach or imply a doctrine of scripture certainly affirm its inspiration and authority, it cannot be shown with any probability that the intention of their authors was to teach inerrancy. On the contrary, to assume such inerrancy as the starting point for an evangelical hermeneutic is to go beyond scripture, to out-scripture scripture.[105] That is another way of saying that this inerrancy signpost points not to a scriptural hermeneutic but, rather, to the legalism of the Pharisees and the bibliolatry of scholastic Protestantism. It is precisely because some evangelicals pitch their starting point too *high,* that the only way to progress in knowledge of God and of God's truth for some of their disciples is *down* what they regard as the "slippery slope"—a slippery slope that has been created more by their elevation of their interpretation of scripture *above* scripture (human tradition above the word of God) than by anything else.

b. An evangelical hermeneutic starts from the assumption that the New Testament attitude to, and use of, scripture provides a pattern and norm for all subsequent Christian attitude to, and use of, scripture. By this I do *not* meant that Christians in the twenty-first century should reproduce the hermeneutical *techniques* of the first century—as we have seen, these techniques were themselves also relative to their time and are often unacceptable for modern exegesis. What I *do* mean is that Christians should show the same *respect* for scripture in their attitude to, and use of, scripture as that shown by the first Christians, as that demonstrated by their first-century hermeneutical techniques when we see them within their historical context. *Nor* do I mean that Christians today can necessarily treat the scriptures (New as well as Old Testament) with the same sovereign freedom exercised by Jesus and Paul. There is a certain once-for-allness in the impact made by the revelation of Christ upon the status and authority of the Old Testament—the only scripture for Jesus and the first Christians. Nevertheless, that being said, the way in which Jesus and the first Christians handled the authoritative word from God in their historical contexts does give us guidelines for our handling of scripture in the present.

This latter point is so fundamental that we must pause to clarify it before we move on.[106] The simplest way to do so is to subdivide the point about historical relativity (above, para. 11) into two subcategories, which we may designate "covenant relativity" and "cultural relativity."

Most of the points at which the revelation of the Old Testament was abrogated are examples of *covenant relativity*. They were abrogated because they belonged to the old covenant: sacrifice, circumcision, clean and unclean. They had been superseded by the new covenant, the revelation through Christ, the revelation of Christ. Here the twenty-first-century Christian has a norm and pattern for his or her own handling of the Old Testament: he or she must read the Old Testament in the light of the fuller revelation of Christ—the New Testament witness to Christ serves as the primary norm by which all other revelation is to be understood.[107] It is this recognition of the covenant relativity of so much of the Old Testament that makes inevitable a certain choosing between scriptures (above, pp. 86f.), which means unavoidably that the New Testament functions as a canon within the canon by which to measure and interpret the rest of the canon—the Old Testament (above, pp. 80f.).[108] But clearly the same cannot be said of the New Testament. We cannot treat the scriptures of the new covenant as Jesus and the first Christians treated the scriptures of the old covenant. There has been a once-for-all shift in the movement of salvation-history, and the revelation of Christ which brought about that shift becomes the yardstick by which we judge everything that claims revelatory authority both before and *after* that shift took place. The church of the new covenant may follow Jesus' footsteps and declare many rulings of the Old Testament no longer relevant and binding because they belong to the old covenant. But such considerations can never weaken or detract from the authority of the New Testament, since that provides the primary norm by which all other authority claims are to be judged—the charter of the new covenant itself.[109]

On the other hand, several of the rulings of the Old Testament were declared abrogated not so much because they were covenant-relative, but primarily because they were *culture-relative*. This would apply to the Mosaic ruling about divorce, and the *lex talionis* (eye for an eye, tooth for a tooth), both examples of what some would classify as the moral law as distinct from the ceremonial law (above, pp. 88–90). Here, too, Jesus' handling of the Old Testament scriptures can serve as a model and norm for our own response to the Old Testament. But at this point the similarity between covenant relativity and culture relativity ceases. For the consideration of culture relativity has to be a factor in our response to the New Testament as well as the Old Testament. The validation for this claim can be seen in the way Matthew and Paul adapt Jesus' words about divorce to the situations of their time, or the way in which James denounces as inappropriate in his context a slogan highly appropriate in Paul's (above, p. 97). Culture relativity applies not only to Old Testament regulations, but to traditions and sayings *within* the New Testament itself. Just so, we must recognize that what was word of God in and to a culture and time very different from ours (New Testament as well as Old Testament) may well no longer be the word of God to our culture and time. In such cases, the normative force of the scripture will lie more in *how* God spoke to their situation and context than in *what* God said.[110]

In short, whereas in terms of covenant relativity the New Testament's use of the Old Testament provides us a norm and pattern only for our handling of the Old Testament, in terms of culture relativity, scripture's use of scripture provides us a norm and pattern for our handling of New Testament as well as Old.

c. If these are the basic presuppositions of an evangelical hermeneutic, then the first step in an evangelical hermeneutic is to discover what was being said in the passage under study. *The primary task of exegesis must be to uncover the historical sense of the text:* what it was that the writer intended his readers to hear and understand. To assert the inspiration of that scripture is to assert primarily that the text thus understood was the authoritative word of God to these readers. The more clearly we can uncover the historical context of that text—by whom it was written, to whom it was written, to what situation it was addressed—the more clearly we will hear it as it was intended to be heard, the more clearly we will hear it with its original force and authority. That is to say, recognition of the historical conditionedness of a text (written for a particular purpose to a particular historical situation) means also recognition of its historical conditionedness as word of God (it was God's word to that situation).

But that also means that the reference of a text may be so closely tied in to that original situation for which it was written, that it cannot have the same reference and meaning outside that situation, or abstracted from that situation. In particular, it would be unwise to assume that a word spoken to Israel at some stage in its history before Christ must have the same reference and relevance or force for us today. On the contrary, we should accept that there will be texts which cannot function for us as word of God in the sense in which they were written (because of their covenant conditionedness, or culture conditionedness, or both). We can affirm of such a text that it is God's word in the sense that what it says, God *said*. We can affirm of such a text that it played a constitutive role in God's purpose for Israel and the world, in the history of salvation (that is why it was preserved). What God said to God's people at a particular stage in their development remains of crucial value for our understanding of that development, as a development planned and shaped by God. But if we want to say, in addition, that what it says God *says*, in the sense that that word (interpreted to conform with some other scripture) is still of binding authority on our faith and conscience, to be neglected only at grave spiritual peril, then we must recognize that in so doing it is functioning as word of God in a sense different from its originally intended sense.

d. The second stage is to recognize that God still speaks through scripture; that throughout the Christian era believers (and unbelievers) have experienced scripture as God's Word addressed to them, convicting and converting, breaking down and building up, comforting and commissioning, tutoring and challenging. This includes, of course, scriptures understood in their intended sense, parables of Jesus, exhortations of Paul, and so forth. But it includes also scriptures where the word that is heard is at some remove from the sense originally intended—as when C. T. Studd heard Psalm 2:8 as a word of God addressed to *him*,'" without any sense of impropriety in applying a messianic prophecy to someone other than the son of David. Here we must recognize that a scripture *can* function as word of God with a sense or application different from that intended. Here we must recognize that a word spoken with one force to a particular historical situation can still function as word of God with a different force in a different situation. To recognize this is simply to confess faith in the Spirit, as the living power of God still abroad, in the church and in the believer—to confess faith in the interpreter Spirit whose work it is precisely to bring home that scripture as a word of God directly to the soul.

What is important for evangelicals is the exegetical recognition that there is plenty of precedent for such a hermeneutic in scripture itself, precisely in the sort of passages and instances examined above in section III. The levitical regulations governing ritual cleanliness can still be heard as God's command to spiritual cleanliness, but no longer as an attitude of heart that should accompany the ritual ablution, rather as a spiritual act that renders the ritual act unnecessary, despite Leviticus.[112] The call for circumcision was clearly heard by Paul and the others in the Gentile mission as a call for the circumcision of the heart; but now no longer seen as complementing the circumcision of the flesh as in Deuteronomy and Jeremiah, rather as replacing the circumcision of the flesh. So, too, Matthew's softening of the words of Jesus regarding true cleanliness and divorce should not be regarded as a denial that the Torah ever was the word of God, or as a denial that Mark's version was the word of God; rather as a *de facto* recognition that God speaks with different force to different times (old and new covenant) and to different situations (Mark to Gentile Christians, Matthew to Jewish Christians). It is only by recognizing this diversity of the word of God (its historical relativity, different words to different times) that evangelicals can effectively shut the door to legalism and bibliolatry, for it is precisely recognition of this diversity that removes the necessity of imposing a dogmatic uniformity on such differences, which saves us from a casuistic harmonization. It is precisely recognition of this diversity that exalts the Spirit above the Bible, that prevents us from shutting the Spirit up in the book, that opens us to the freedom of the Spirit rather than constricting us to the narrowness of the letter.

e. It is of absolutely crucial importance that these two steps are not taken in isolation from each other. In a proper hermeneutic—a properly scriptural hermeneutic—the two are closely conjoined, two sides of one and the same coin (to change the metaphor). As soon as the two come apart—are treated in isolation—we have lost the word of God. If, on the one hand, we confine the hermeneutical task to discovering the original intention and meaning of a text, we run the serious risk of relegating the word of God to a remote past, where all our textual and exegetical skill can only uncover what the word of God was, where the Word of God is shut up in the letter. If, on the other hand, we ignore the original intention and message of a text and seek to understand it differently, or listen for the voice of God speaking through it without regard to the author's intention and meaning, we run the equally serious risk of courting a spirit of enthusiasm, of opening the door to an uncontrolled prophetism, of abandoning the word of God for the inspiration of the moment. It is only the interaction of a strictly historical exegesis with a prophetic openness to the Spirit now, where each acts as stimulus and check to the other, which can count as a truly scriptural hermeneutic.

It is such a hermeneutic that we saw at work in the New Testament use of (Old Testament) scripture. Generalizing from these particular instances, we can say that there will be some scriptures which speak with more or less the same force in the twenty-first century as when they were first written (the human condition addressed being basically the same); that there will be others whose authoritative message has to be understood from a different context or perspective, which qualifies the original sense in some significant but not sweeping way (men's hearts still being hard);[113] that there will be some texts where we see the original scripture as expressing a principle in a way which is no longer necessary or possible for us, but which lays upon us the task of expressing the same principle in a different way (the same word of God coming to diverse expression in diverse situations);[114] that there will be others where the particular text can have continuing authoritative meaning only within a much broader framework and not as an individual unit on its own (individual commandments within a law understood from the perspective of its fulfillment in Christ). This two-sided hermeneutical process may often function in a very simple, even unconscious way, in the believer's reading of scripture. But it should not be simplified, and certainly cannot be reduced to a set of rules applicable to every text which will ensure that the interpreter has unfailing and automatic access to the word of God. There is a certain elusiveness in the word of God in its relation to any text, and in those texts that are closely tied to a particular historical context now very different from our own, the interaction between scriptural text and word of God can be very subtle.[115] This is why the interpreter can never depend simply upon lexicon and commentary, but must work in constant dependence on the Spirit who gave the text being studied.

The character of the hermeneutical process, and its bearing upon the question of authority in particular, may become a little clearer if we make a distinction between normative authority and directive authority. The Bible—that is, primarily the New Testament—functions as a *normative* authority, a definition of what Christianity is and should be, a yardstick by which to test all subsequent definitions of Christianity, all other claims to revelatory authority. But for *directive* authority, in order to learn what to do in any particular situation (the kind of theological, ethical, ecumenical, political, etc. questions facing individuals, churches, and denominations today), we must look to the Spirit of God, whether the Spirit speaks through or apart from the Bible. Since the Spirit *speaks* now presumably with the same character as the Spirit *spoke* previously, the New Testament will provide a check on any word or policy claiming directive authority today. But since, also presumably, the Spirit speaks to particular situations, and since our situations are usually different in significant degree from those of the New Testament, we cannot depend solely on the normative authority of scripture but must depend on the directive authority of the Spirit revealing the mind of God here and now. It is in this interaction between the Spirit's inspiration then, and the mind of Christ now, that the authoritative word of God is to be heard speaking to particular situations today.

f. When the hermeneutical process is thus understood and followed through, it becomes increasingly clear that the traditional evangelical dichotomy between scripture, reason, and tradition as the source and measure of revelatory authority has often been too sharply drawn.[116] For, as we have now seen, the authoritative word of God in scripture is not so objective that it can always be found by grammatico-historical technique designed to uncover the original meaning of a text. As soon as we utter the word *interpretation*, we recognize the interpreter's involvement in the hermeneutical process: his or her own historical relativity that conditions his or her capacity to understand the original text, his or her own verbal and cultural frame of reference, his or her own tradition of what is the "clear" teaching of scripture, his or her own experience of God's grace (or lack of it). The hermeneutical process is a dialectic, an interaction between the text in all its historical relativity and the interpreter in all his or her historical relativity. In other words, scripture and reason are not two clearly distinct elements that can be neatly separated and opposed to each other. To pretend otherwise is disingenuous.[117] If we take Jesus and Paul (to mention no others) as our models here, then we cannot but speak of an understanding of scripture as the authoritative word of God that comes about through an interplay between the inspired text and the (still) inspiring Spirit.

I might simply add that, at the end of the day, we cannot neatly separate off the other factor usually set over against scripture and reason at this point—church, or tradition. For church and tradition are also inevitably bound up in the hermeneutical process. Protestants, for all their protest against the authority attributed to Catholic tradition, for all their individualism, are just as dependent on their own tradition in their her understanding of scripture as any other Christians—the less they are conscious of the way their tradition has shaped their standpoint and understanding, the more firmly bound they are within that tradition.[118] And the evangelical of all people should take seriously Paul's understanding of the church as the body of Christ, where grace is experienced through mutual interdependence, and a right understanding of the prophetic word is a matter of corporate discernment. The person who always relies on one's own hermeneutic alone will inevitably confuse the word of God with one's own aspirations and predispositions as often as not. One needs the check not only of historical exegesis, but also of the mind of the faithful. The hermeneutical process is in fact a three-sided process; authority is a stool balanced on three legs, not just two, far less just one.

g. To sum up: We can give the Bible too much honor; we can exalt the letter above the Spirit. And that, in my judgment, I have to say with sorrow, is what the proponents of Princeton theology are doing. They have read their inerrancy dogma *into* the teaching of Jesus and of the New Testament. But in fact their position with regard to scripture is closer to that of the Pharisees condemned by Jesus, and of the Judaizers attacked by Paul. Inerrancy is a less than scriptural teaching, because its proponents cannot show that the biblical authors intended to teach it; even in the pillar passages (above, pp. 73–6) such a meaning has to be pressed upon the words rather than read out by grammatico-historical exegesis. The more scriptural way, derived from scripture itself, recognizes the historical relativity of the word of God, recognizes the need to engage in the interpretative process, recognizes that the Spirit may speak a word through the words of some Bible passages that is not wholly in accord with its originally intended meaning.

Thus, to engage in the hermeneutical process is to leave the comfortable securities of a systematized exegesis that harmonizes everything into a legalistic conformity. It allows greater diversity, leaves more questions open, lets faith be faith in face of greater uncertainties. Not, let it be stressed, that we are talking here of "those things which are necessary to be known, believed, and observed, for salvation," which are clearly and consistently taught throughout the New Testament. Indeed, the more timeless the truth, the clearer and more consistent the teaching on it in scripture. But not a few words of scriptural teaching were more conditioned to situation and context-addressed—a properly scriptural exegesis has to acknowledge that—and a properly historical exegesis will usually be able to determine the extent of the contextual conditioning. Consequently, in many secondary matters of belief and conduct, what we mean by "the infallible rule of faith and life" is not scripture *per se,* scripture in its grammatico-historical sense as such, but *the Spirit speaking through scripture as understood by the faithful.* And this is just as it should be, for it was as an authority functioning in this way that Jesus, Paul, and the other New Testament writers honored the Old Testament. Such, in a word, is the authority of scripture according to scripture.

✳✳✳

Letter to Professor R. Nicole

Professor R. Nicole
Gordon-Conwell Theological Seminary

Dear Dr. Nicole,

It was kind of you to send me a copy of your article, "The Inspiration and Authority of Scripture: Prof. Dunn versus Warfield," which you are submitting to *Churchman* in response to my earlier piece. It is an act of courtesy that is insufficiently practiced in the circles within which we move and I have greatly appreciated it. Although I am under considerable pressure in my new post (having only now been able to move house from Nottingham to Durham, while I'm still learning the ropes), I do feel the matters you raise are of such importance that I have tried to squeeze in time to reply.

There are various points where I felt your criticisms were unnecessary, which smacked somewhat of point-scoring, and there were also quite a number of other sections of your response in which I felt you had missed my point or not taken its full force.

But the chief value of your response for me was that it helped bring into sharper focus several key points on which our disagreement really turns. These are the fulcrum points on which I suggest further discussion should focus. Indeed, I would strongly recommend that if the evangelical constituency wants to take this present debate forward in a positive form in which the unadulterated affirmation of the divine is spirit (rather than retreating into the carping, point-scoring, sniping-from-fixed-positions arguments that too often dominate), it is precisely on the following points that it should concentrate.

1. How *valid* is the proposition that inerrancy is *the necessary implication* of scripture being God's word?: God is without error; therefore God's spoken word is without error; therefore the Bible is without error. In your words: "Inerrancy is simply bound to take" (*Churchman* 97, p. 209). I note how often you appealed, in effect or explicitly, to this key principle, what I shall call briefly "the inerrancy proposition." But is it so secure as you seem to think? For myself the inerrancy proposition is too simplistic: it is compelling on neither logical, nor theological nor scriptural grounds.

a. We cannot exclude on *a priori* grounds the possibility or probability that the limitation which God imposes upon God's word by speaking it through the limitations of human mind and voice extend to the sort of detail which inerrantists feel so sensitive about ("all scripture touches").

b. The proposition cannot stand without reference to the question of intention. Which is sounder—to say that God ensured that the meaning God intended was clearly enough expressed in what was written, or to say that God's perfection extends to every aspect of the spoken or written words which God inspired? The latter is nearer the logic of the inerrantists, but even they do not press their primary proposition so far (divine perfection has not extended to grammar and syntax!). The former would seem to me the sounder proposition—one that can be maintained fully without pressing for the inerrancy position, *and* without damaging the honor of God.

c. The inerrancy proposition cannot be posed without asking the *exegetical* question: *How* has God spoken in the event? If scripture is God's word, what does scripture show us about the way God's word actually was spoken? I remain of the firm opinion that the inerrancy position only *appears* to respect the text of scripture; it does not, however, *properly* subordinate itself to the text, that is, by letting the text speak for itself, by acknowledging the priority of exegesis over the *a priori* logic of the inerrancy proposition, or the priority of exegesis in determining the scope of biblical statements about inspiration in the event of scripture itself.

There is surely space here for a proper debate, where we examine the meaning and propriety even of basic axioms without feeling threatened by it all. I hope you will agree.

2. The issue of *how* one determines the *extent* to which the logic of the inerrancy proposition *must be qualified.* Inerrantists seem willing to recognize several qualifications: (*a*) diversity of interpretation is acceptable in such areas as baptism and the second coming—we cannot achieve agreed certainty on what God's will is, even on such important elements in New Testament teaching; (*b*) the perfection of scripture ("the absolute character of revealed truth" is your phrase) does not extend to such features as imprecise quotations, rounded numbers, grammatical irregularities; (*c*) the historical relativity of various scriptural instructions (which you acknowledge in your comment on 1 Cor. 14:26), and the covenant relativity of much of the Old Testament law, particularly the regulations in Leviticus.

The question to be debated is this: How do these qualifications emerge? How can their validity be tested and demonstrated? The answer surely is, by studying scripture itself. *It is the recognition of what scripture actually consists of which makes such qualifications of the inerrancy proposition necessary.* But once you grant this methodological principle (the character of scripture determining the meaning of our definition of scripture as God's word), you must surely also recognize that my position emerges from an application of that same principle. What needs to be debated is, why inerrantists stop at the qualifications listed in ICBI's Article XIII, and why the status of scripture as God's word should be threatened if we recognize the further qualification that scriptural writers were not always concerned with the historical accuracy of details in all that scripture touches. The need for *some* qualification of the inerrancy proposition is evidently not in dispute. So a crucial area for clarification in further discussion is, how we determine the extent of legitimate qualifications.

3. The significance of the fact that Jesus and/or the first Christians *abandoned* some key prescriptions in the law, *set aside* clearly formulated scriptural instructions. In what proper sense, for instance, can we speak of the law of clean and unclean foods as having "perennial validity" (*Churchman* 97, p. 204)? It is certainly no longer binding for Christians, and so no longer valid as an expression of God's will for today in what was its most obviously intended meaning. If you reply that it is still authoritative in that it was fulfilled in Christ, then I have to ask: In what sense can we speak of the law of clean and unclean foods as "literally 'fulfilled' in Jesus Christ" (*Churchman* 98, p. 13)? My historical and covenant-relativity point has the merit at least of recognizing the full word-of-God force of such a prescription as such, up until it was abrogated for Christians. And you may not like my talk of a "canon within the canon," specifically, the revelation of Jesus Christ. But you really do operate with it yourself. How could we call the commands of Genesis 17:9-14 "provisional" on any other grounds, or abandon the clear command regarding the sabbath without *any* explicit New Testament justification? Just how all this bears upon our doctrine of scripture does need clarification in the current debate.

4. *The problem posed by any historical method in the study of scripture.* How legitimate is it to demand "*proven* error"? In historical reconstruction we can only deal in probabilities; you recognize this to the extent that you acknowledge that your interpretation of a passage like 2 Timothy 3:16 can only claim acceptance as "most probable." The demand that "errors" be "proven" is inconsistent with this. And it is precisely this demand that sets up the tension for many students when they are instructed in the techniques of historical study. Please note, I do not refer here to the "historical-critical method" as such, but to *any* historical method. The ramifications of historical study on this issue need further exploration: both the tension the demand for proven error sets up for anyone concerned with the study of history at a scholarly level; and the pastoral problem of the evangelical student who is asked to deal with historical difficulties in scripture using a different methodology, often resulting in a kind of intellectual schizophrenia.

5. *Do inerrantists take with sufficient seriousness even the most basic exegetical findings,* particularly with regard to the Synoptic Gospels? I refer here not to any particular theory of the relation between these Gospels, on which there is dispute, but to the fact of *literary dependence* between the material within these

Gospels when that material was already in Greek, on which there is no dispute as far as I am aware. Where literary dependence at the level of the tradition in Greek is so clear, the sort of harmonizations that depend on postulating several incidents/sayings rather than different versions of the one incident/saying become increasingly improbable. Insistence on such harmonizations is one of the ways in which the character and text of scripture is not taken with sufficient seriousness. More important, it is one of the factors that cause greatest stress to students from an inerrancy background, when they find that the most self-evident character of the text is being ignored and denied as a way of escaping a "difficulty" or "error."

I hope you will agree that these are all points worthy and deserving of further discussion, and that you will encourage such discussion. Perhaps you will be willing also to support the suggestion that a moratorium be called on evangelical infighting on the issue of scripture until such time as these issues have been properly ventilated in appropriate forums.

With greetings and all good wishes,

Yours sincerely,

James D. G. Dunn
University of Durham
5 October 83

6. LEVELS OF CANONICAL AUTHORITY

I

IN 1970 A VOLUME APPEARED, edited by Ernst Käsemann, under the title *The New Testament as Canon*.[1] It consisted of a collection of published material spanning the preceding thirty years, with Käsemann's own critique of each item at the end. The range of discussion showed clearly that the subject matter is one which in the second half of the twentieth century still provokes lively debate. The old questions first asked in the early centuries are still on the agenda: By what process and on what grounds did the New Testament documents come to be regarded as canonical and as together constituting a closed canon?[2] Should we today, in the light of our modern (we would like to claim) fuller knowledge of these documents, reassess those old decisions and redraw the content and boundary of the canon afresh? Some would ask, more radically, not just whether *this* canon is necessary, but whether *any* canon is necessary. Does Christianity need a canon in the first place? The old debate between Protestants and Catholics on the relation of scripture and tradition also still rumbles on, revitalized not least by the Protestant exegetical recognition that New Testament writers themselves set considerable store on tradition, and that the Gospels in particular are a deposit of church traditions about Jesus: Is then the New Testament itself simply a selection of various developing traditions frozen in writing at particular points in their development as they were set down in response to particular needs?[3]

In addition there are more modern questions, particularly the two most sharply posed in the past generation by Käsemann himself: the problem of the diversity among the writings contained within the New Testament canon,[4] and the related issue of whether it is necessary to speak in terms of canon *within* the canon.[5] Does the canon in fact provide a foundation of the church's unity? Or is it rather the case, as Käsemann claims, that the canon "provides the basis for the multiplicity of the confessions," that the canon indeed legitimizes "all sects and false teaching"?[6] And given such diversity, do we not need some means of evaluating these various possibilities, a criterion by which to judge these claims to canonical authentication, a canon within the canon? Whether it be, for example, "justification by faith," as Käsemann, true to his Lutheran heritage, insists,[7] or "the earliest traditions of the Christian witness . . . 'the Jesus-kerygma,'" as others would argue.[8]

In the years since Käsemann's volume was published, however, the most vigorous debate on canonical questions has hardly touched the New Testament or New Testament scholarship. The debate in which the names of B. S. Childs and J. A. Sanders figure most prominently has focused almost exclusively on the Old Testament,[9] Childs with his initial call for an Old Testament exegesis oriented primarily with reference to the "canonical context" of a text and not its precanonical history,[10] and Sanders with his call for a "canonical criticism" which recognizes that a text functioned as authoritative "scripture" at different stages of its development and to different historical communities.[11] As a *Neutestamentler* and Christian I must confess that I find it somewhat surprising (and just a little disturbing) that there has not been more interaction at this point between Old Testament and New Testament specialists (at least so far as I have been aware). Childs in his *Introduction* and Sanders give the New Testament only passing attention, even though it is *prima facie* obvious that a canonical interpretation or criticism of the Old Testament as *Jewish* scripture will be different from a canonical interpretation or criticism of it as the *Old* Testament part of the *Christian* canon. Particularly if the demand is to respect the canonical context, then it is not enough simply to assert that the Christians took over the Jewish canon (even if we leave aside the question of whether it was the Hebrew Bible or the LXX they treated "wholistically"), or merely to describe the New Testament's use of the Old.[12] There are crucial questions that cannot be avoided: How does the Old Testament stand or function as canon in the light of the New Testament and of the new revelation to which the New Testament lays claim and bears witness?[13] Can the same case be made for "canonical criticism" or for respect for "canonical context" in the case of the New Testament? And how does the answer to this question affect the theses of Sanders and Childs with regard to the Old Testament?[14]

At the same time *Neutestamentlers* with concerns in this area cannot escape an equivalent criticism. For they too have been largely content to confine themselves to various aspects of the New Testament's use of the Old, either to illuminate particular New Testament texts or to trace hermeneutical patterns or to examine various hermeneutical techniques.[15] Bolder attempts to gain a more systematic view of the relation of the two Testaments—in terms particularly of typology, the motif of promise-fulfillment, or salvation-history[16]—have not only tended inevitably to impose a New Testament perspective on the Old but have also to greater or less degree failed to take sufficient account of the diversity within the Old Testament.[17] And even those who insist on the need to continue speaking in terms of a biblical theology have been content in effect to follow the older models, though in a more modest version that takes at least some account of the conclusions and uncertainties of a critically historical exegesis—what may be loosely described as a biblical theology that consists in tracing thematic links and continuities.[18] In neither case is there any real coming to terms with the kind of questions discussed by Childs and Sanders and posed by them for biblical hermeneutics as a whole.

It is of course wholly understandable that there should be a divergence of interest and motivation at this point between *Alttestamentlers* and *Neutestamentlers*. Childs's concern for the canonical context is a natural reaction to the overwhelming complexities of tracing a tradition-history that extends over hundreds of years. The New Testament exegete is faced with nothing so daunting in his or her tradition-history analysis. In most of the letters we can take the present text as sufficiently close to what was originally written and so can speak of an "original author" and inquire directly into his intention in writing the letter. And even when we turn to the complexities of Gospel criticism we are dealing with a process of development that lasted at most a few decades, and a process that we can often trace with greater confidence since we have two or even three versions of the same tradition. Moreover, where the great salvation-history events on which Israel saw itself founded as a nation lie far back at the beginning of that long process of tradition (the exodus and the Sinai covenant), so that "God's saving acts" become as much a problem for historical exegesis as a key to biblical theology, the equivalent events on which Christianity is founded (the "Christ-event") lie within one generation of the earliest New Testament documents, and many at least of the Gospel traditions take us back into the Christ-event itself and give us a contemporaneity with Jesus of Nazareth that the student of Israel's origins can never hope to enjoy. In some ways most frustrating of all is the *Alttestamentler's* difficulty in determining which texts it is that he should be endeavoring to work from—the Masoretic text, which was not finally stabilized until well into the Christian era, one or another of the divergent texts that seem to have been current at the time of Jesus, the text of the LXX, or the Samaritan text, or some original autograph, or what? Can he speak of a normative or canonical text without specifying to whom, where, and when?[19] Whereas the *Neutestamentler* can be confident that apart from a few significant textual variants he is dealing with the text more or less as it left Matthew, Mark, Luke, and so on. It is just these differences between the New Testament and the Old and different possibilities and tasks confronting Old and New Testament exegesis which make it all the more imperative that discussions on the canon and on the canonical relation of Jewish scriptures to Old Testament to New Testament, and on the canonical authority of their constituent documents do not continue in isolation from one another.

The issue I wish to focus on in the present chapter is that of *canonical authority*. Both Sanders and Childs are saying something of which *Neutestamentlers* need to be reminded—the fact that the documents we are dealing with did in fact exercise a crucially significant influence in shaping the self-understanding of Christian churches from the first. But what do we mean by "canonical authority" and how did the biblical writings function as "canonical authorities"? When and how did they exercise that function? Is canonical authority a timeless attribute or always circumscribed by reference to particular historical contexts, attributable only to the complete document or also to its parts independently of the whole, attributable only to a document as part of the whole canon or also to the document independently of the whole? Does "canonical authority" mean that all canonical documents must be heard to speak with one voice, or can they disagree and conflict and still be recognized as canonically authoritative? And what does "canonical authority" say regarding the possibility of continuing revelation in the present? Not least the Christian must ask, Does canonical authority adhere to the Hebrew Bible as such or to the LXX as such or to either or both only when juxtaposed with the New Testament within the Christian Bible? These are the sort of questions that lie behind the following discussion and which hopefully will gain some clarification in the process.

II

In what ways then can we properly speak of the Bible, as a whole or in its constituent elements, functioning canonically? If there is anything in the view that present-day hermenuetics must respect the canonical character of a text, what is this canonical force of the text which commentators must keep in mind? The answer given to this question will depend in part on the definition of "canon" used. But it would be fairest to at least begin with a broader definition as Sanders encourages us to do—"canon" as referring to any formulation(s) or writing(s) that a community of faith treats as its rule of faith, as constitutive or normative for its self-understanding. In which case it becomes possible to distinguish no less than *four broad levels of canonical authority*, each level with different levels contained within it.[20]

(a) Tradition-history level. Tradition-history analysis in both Old and New Testaments has revealed that behind the present form of a text there often lie several stages of that text's prehistory, both oral and written. In the case of the Old Testament, we may for example distinguish within the Pentateuch units like the Song of Moses in Exodus 15, or "the Book of the Covenant" (Exodus 21–23), or the credo in Deuteronomy 26:5-9, as well as the different redactional stages of J and E, the Deuteronomist and Priestly writer, the Hexateuch or Tetrateuch and the Torah (Pentateuch). In the case of the prophets we are accustomed now to attempts to distinguish an earliest stage of particular (brief) prophetic oracles, from early groupings and elaborations by their disciples, from the fuller written text with its possible further redactions. In the case of the Synoptic Gospels we can think of various sayings of Jesus put into particular forms and grouped in different ways before being gathered into the fuller sources used by our present Evangelists. Or again, New Testament criticism is now well accustomed to thinking in terms of pre-Pauline formulae, kerygmatic, credal and liturgical, lying behind Paul's letters and used by Paul often with redactional additions (e.g., Rom. 1:3-4; 1 Cor. 15:3-8; Phil. 2:6-11).[21]

The point is, and in this I follow Sanders completely, that *at each of these levels the traditions in question functioned as constitutive and normative for the self-understanding of the communities which used them.* From the very fact that these traditions were preserved in recognizable form we can fairly conclude that at each stage these statements or fuller writings were heard as the word of God by the community of faith to which they were addressed, or which treasured or made use of them. We know that there were gatherings from ancient times at which the "saving deeds" of the Lord were recited (Sanders refers particularly to 1 Sam. 12:7-8)[22]—it is *prima facie* fitting to associate these early units of the Pentateuch with such occasions, or particular psalms like Psalms 105 and 106.[23] The Josianic reformation based on the impact and authority of the rediscovered book of Deuteronomy is one of the basic postulates in Old Testament scholarship. Most clearly of all, the authoritative weight of "the words of the law" under the reform of Ezra, four centuries before Christ, is clearly attested in Nehemiah 8. As for the prophets, it is sufficiently clear that from the earliest stages the utterances were treasured as the word of God, even if at first only among a relatively small group of disciples, and were preserved and written up because they continued to speak with the force of divine authority. Likewise in the New Testament. Jesus' words were heard by his first disciples as words of unsurpassed authority, were preserved and used because of their continuing authority and relevance. At no stage prior to the present form of the Gospels would they have been regarded as less than divinely authoritative, an assessment that naturally would include whatever editing and redacting took place in each case. So, too, in the epistles: even in cases like the individual words *abba* and *maranatha* we can be sure that they were preserved into the Greek-speaking churches precisely because they were fundamentally constitutive of each church's self-understanding and faith.

Whether or not we wish to use the *term* "canonical authority" to describe the functioning of these various tradition-history levels underlying our present texts is a matter of secondary importance. The fact is that these writings, at each stage of their prehistory, exercised the sort of influence and were held in the sort of regard which Christians have thought proper to attribute only to scripture; they were seen as normative and determinative of the life and faith of the communities at each stage in a way that can properly be described as canonical. Not least of importance is it to recognize that such traditions were utilized by the biblical authors precisely because they were *already* functioning as word of God in one or more communities of faith: as "canonical authority" was not a status *first* accorded to the Old Testament books by Ezra and Jamnia or to the New Testament books by the church of the second and third centuries, but a recognition of status already demonstrated, so "word of God" was not an attribute first attached to these older traditions by virtue of the biblical writers' use of them, rather the biblical writers' use of them is a testimony to the power with which these traditional forms and materials had already proved themselves to be word of God.[24]

(b) Final author or final composition level. At this level we think primarily of the individual books of the Old and New Testaments, where the task of exegesis is to uncover the meaning intended when the material was finally put into its present shape, that is, into the form in which it has endured since that time. So, for example, with the Pentateuch, any reconstruction of the work of J or E or P is better seen as part of the Pentateuch's tradition-history and exegesis at this level should be directed toward uncovering the function and meaning of these traditions in their present form and position within the Pentateuch.[25] Or in the case of the Synoptic Gospels, the source usually called "Q" should be regarded as part of Matthew's and Luke's tradition-history, since we cannot reconstruct the source as a whole with sufficient confidence (however coherently particular "Q" material hangs together), and exegesis at this level should be oriented toward uncovering the meaning intended by Matthew and Luke in their use of this material.

Here, in fact, we are talking about Childs's concept of the "canonical shape" or "final form" of a biblical writing.[26] The main differences are, first, that

I would want to focus attention on the editorial/literary final form whereas Child argues more for the *textual* final form stabilized by the end of the first century c.e.,[27] and second, that I would want to speak of a final composition level also with respect to any work which is now only part of a larger whole within the Bible but which originally stood on its own as an independent work and which can still be recognized as a coherent composition whose form has remained substantially unmodified by its incorporation into the larger whole. In the Old Testament I am thinking particularly of Deuteronomy and the work of Second Isaiah (40–55).[28] In the New Testament a case in point might be the elements of 2 Corinthians: if it can be demonstrated that, for example, chapters 8 and 9 were originally composed by Paul as independent letters,[29] exegesis at this level can ask *both* what was the meaning and purpose of chapters 8 and 9 as independent entities, *and* what was their meaning and purpose within the final form of 2 Corinthians. In both these Old and New Testament examples we have to reckon with at least two levels of "final author"—on one level the Deuteronomist, Second Isaiah, and Paul, on the other the force of these works as incorporated within the larger wholes of the Pentateuch, Isaiah 1–66, and 2 Corinthians, respectively.

It is at this level that we see one of the clearest differences between the canons of Old and New Testaments and between the challenges that they pose to the students of each. In the case of the New Testament we can speak very meaningfully of a "final author," or indeed of an "original author," since in the majority of cases the document as we have it is still substantially what was written or dictated by the evangelist or letter writer; the "canonical shape" was given by "Matthew," by Luke, by Paul, and so on; in the case of the letters in particular the meaning intended when the words were first composed is the meaning preserved by the final form. But in the Old Testament there is regularly a considerable gap between first utterance and final form, not least in the case of the prophets, so that again and again there is plenty of scope for argument about whether a final redactor whose editorial work may have been quite limited should be regarded as the "final author" or whether the substantially similar penultimate edition should be taken as "final." There are probably exceptions in both Testaments. In the New Testament, for example, the concept of a "final author" runs into some difficulty in the case of the Fourth Gospel; from this aspect, in other words, the Fourth Gospel is closer in character to the majority of the Old Testament prophetic books than any other New Testament document. That is to say, we cannot confidently remove a final redactorial layer from the Gospel (except probably John 21) so as to uncover a sufficiently agreed earlier form whose coherence would enable us to designate it as "final composition" instead of or alongside the canonical John.[30] Whereas in the Old Testament "final author" might be a more meaningful concept in relation to Ezekiel. That is to say, it is at least arguable that the bulk of Ezekiel is sufficiently close to what emanated from Ezekiel himself, that it was Ezekiel who impressed the most coherent "shape" on the canonical material,[31] and that consequently we can speak of Ezekiel himself as a final author.[32] Nevertheless, these exceptions apart, the contrast between Old and New Testaments remains: in the case of the Old Testament the complexities of disentangling levels of composition and redaction in most cases are such that it is advisable to direct exegesis in the first instance to the final composition level, the canonical shape, and to regard the earlier levels, including that of the eponymous prophet, as levels of tradition-history; whereas in the case of the New Testament original author (per se) and final author are usually one and the same, and exegesis of the canonical shape can inquire into the historical context of Matthew or 1 Corinthians from the first.

At the level of the final author or final composition it can simply be assumed that *the form put on the material at that level was so decisive and endured so successfully precisely because in that form it made a lasting and continuing impact.* In each case the document was recognized to have normative authority in that form, so that substantial redaction either was thought unnecessary or did not find favor in the community of faith, and even if its material was substantially reused by a later author (Mark by Matthew, Jude by 2 Peter), it itself was still treasured and preserved in the form put upon it by the final hand. At this level, even more clearly than in the former, we can recognize writings functioning as the word of God, exercising a formative and normative influence on communities of faith, doing the job of "canon."

(c) Canonical level. By canonical level I mean the level provided by the canon itself. At this level the primary context of an individual document is the larger group of documents to which it belongs and which together have been declared or are being treated as a canon of scripture. It is the level where the meaning that carries canonical authority is the meaning of the individual writing as seen within the context of the whole canon (Childs's "canonical context"). If at the level of "final composition" individual passages of a particular book have to be interpreted only as incorporated within that final composition, so to work at the canonical level means interpreting individual books as part of the complete canon. It could well be argued that only this level properly warrants the attribution "canonical authority," since *from very early centuries of the common era it is only as a part of a canon of scripture that individual biblical documents have functioned as authority for faith and life.*

At this level questions of historical context, whether of original author or of final composition, become more distant and less significant; it is the authority that the document had at the stage of formal canonization which counts for more. At this level law has to be held in tension with prophecy; a particular Gospel becomes important as one of the four Gospels. At this level we can handle Ecclesiastes more easily in the light of the rest of the Hebrew scriptures; the polemical Paul of the major Pauline epistles becomes a more amenable figure when these epistles are set within the frame of Acts and the Pastorals as provided by the larger canonical context. At this level we can ignore the obscure fumblings of the early Jewish speculation about life after death and speak of the Judeo-Christian, the canonical teaching on the subject. At this level indeed the ideal of a *biblical theology* becomes meaningful for the first time and can be pursued with some hope of success and in a way not possible at the earlier levels[33]—precisely because we can abstract from the questions of historical context of each writing, precisely because we are working at the level of the Bible as such.

Yet here too we must use the plural "levels," and speak of *different* levels, simply because the larger group of writings within which the individual document is seen to belong has differed in scope, depending on what historical period and what community of faith is in view. For most Jews the Pentateuch would have had primary canonical status more or less from Ezra onward, even when the prophets were also already regarded as scripture. In diaspora Judaism the greater extent of the LXX gave scope for wider hermeneutical possibilities, as both Philo and the Hellenistic Christians demonstrate. The canon of the Hebrew Bible is obviously not the same as the canon of the Christian Bible, despite the synonymity of Hebrew Bible with Protestant Old Testament. And we need only mention the further diversities of Catholic and Coptic and Ethiopic canons. We cannot therefore avoid the necessity of reckoning with different levels of canonical authority even in this narrower sense of the term. For example, the canonical significance and authority of Leviticus will be different depending on whether the canonical context is seen as the Pentateuch, the Hebrew Bible, the LXX, or the Christian Bible.

In more general terms, so long as the concept of canon as *closed* canon has not yet been reached, so long as communities of faith are open to the possibility of including new writings within their collections of authoritative scripture, the canonical level will be a rather shifting base for interpretation. Here again we cannot ignore the strains that are brought into the discussion as soon as *Alttestamentler* and *Neutestamentler* attempt to take account of each other's perspective on the question. It is all very well for Childs to settle on the Hebrew text of the Old Testament toward the end of the first century c.e. as the primary canonical text (above, n.27). But the *Neutestamentler* cannot ignore the fact that for most New Testament authors the LXX was the determinative (should we not say canonical) form of the Jewish scriptures,[34] nor can he or she ignore the fact that at that very period the process of moving toward a New Testament canon was only just beginning. The canonical level, far from freeing hermeneutics for a truly biblical theology, may in the end tie the interpreter more firmly to the theology of the Jamnian and post-Jamnian rabbis or of the Greek and Latin Fathers than he or she at first realized.[35]

(d) Ecclesiastical level.[36] We must mark off this further level for the simple reason that churches have in fact always distinguished what the Bible *means* from what it *meant,* that dogmatic theology, not least in the creeds and confessions it has produced, has always gone beyond biblical theology in content as well as in structure and aim. If we allow any sort of *sensus plenior* hermeneutic[37] to apply to New Testament as well as Old, if we allow any possibility of fresh revelation through scripture, if we allow that God can speak through the words of the Bible with a meaning having existential authority different from the text's historical meaning, then we must distinguish an ecclesiastical level of canonical authority from the level authorized by the canon as such. As Pharisee and rabbi saw the need for an oral tradition to interpret the written Torah to the different circumstances of later ages, with the consequence, for example, that the traditions relating to ritual purity went far beyond what was envisaged even at the canonical level of the Torah, so catholic Christianity developed its oral traditions in order to validate a role for Mary far beyond what could be achieved by exegesis of scripture and to claim a normativeness for the threefold order of ministry and for apostolic succession far beyond anything that could be justified from scripture. In all periods of Judeo-Christian history, at least from the first wisdom writers onward, contemporary philosophies and social patterns have been used to find in canonical literature meanings that none of the previous levels would have recognized, meanings that nevertheless were claimed to bear canonical authority.[38]

Here, too, it is patently obvious that we have to speak of different levels (plural) of canonical authority. The diversity within the canon has allowed significantly different patterns of theology to emerge. The process of achieving a canonical meaning of scripture can begin at several different points, different "unclear" scriptures can be interpreted by different "clear" scriptures, with the inevitable result that *different and even contradictory theologies and ecclesiologies can all claim canonical authority.* History has certainly proved that Käsemann's thesis is well founded—the canon has been the basis as much for Christianity's diversity of denomination as for its unity.

It is clear then that the term "canonical authority" can be used with sufficient meaningfulness and validity at all four levels outlined above. *As a matter of historical fact each biblical text can be shown to have different levels of meaning and significance,* in some cases stretching back before the meaning of the final composition, in some cases stretching forward beyond its meaning within the canonical context, in some cases stretching both ways, but at every level exercising an authority recognized as normative by the community that treasured the text.

III

Out of these basic observations about the different levels of canonical authority arise various other considerations.

(a) For the sake of analysis I have distinguished four different levels. But it should be stressed that each level cannot usually be sharply or clearly marked off from the next—as has already been obvious in some of the previous discussion. Hence the difficulty of distinguishing tradition-history from final composition from redaction in most of the prophets or in the case of the Fourth Gospel. Hence the need to recognize that some of our material was already functioning at a canonical level (the law and the prophets) even before some of our other material was written (the New Testament); or the nicer problem of deciding between different canonical forms—which is the final composition and which the canonical form in the cases of Daniel and Ezra, the Hebrew and Aramaic versions (Hebrew Bible) or the Greek version (LXX)? Hence, too, the problem of determining whether a particular ecclesiology (such as the doctrine of the threefold ministry) or a particular doctrine of the atonement is derived properly speaking from the canonical level of authority or rather from the ecclesiastical level. In fact, what we actually see is a considerable continuity between all these different levels, or more precisely, a considerable continuity of form, content, and meaning in a text as it is passed from one historical community context to the next. We are witnessing, in other words, *the continuity of living tradition.*[39] To this extent S. Sandmel's much quoted dictum carries weight: "Canon is an incident, and no more than that."[40]

We can of course recognize particular moments within this continuity; it is not a wholly even flow of tradition. The writing down of oral traditions would have been one.[41] The relative stabilization in the text of the final author/ composition is another.[42] Above all, the concept of a *closed* canon enables us to distinguish the ecclesiastical levels from what went before, however diverse the actual content of the closed canon, the texts in use and the subsequent hermeneutical methods and results. But none of these stages can be treated as absolutes. The freezing of tradition in particular forms that retained normative authority beyond the immediate context certainly lifts these forms above the complete relativization of a constantly changing, never settled tradition. But even so the freezing process is not a freezing of the whole stream of tradition into a final unmovable, unchangeable block. It is more like a freezing that results in a relatively stable ice floe being carried down the still-moving stream. So the Chronicler can rework the already stabilized and authoritative traditions of the former prophets, and both blocks of material are retained in the canon.[43] Matthew can reword the already stabilized and authoritative traditions of Mark, and both attain canonical authority (whereas "Q" is more like an ice floe that disintegrated and was reabsorbed in different-sized pieces into larger floes). The *de facto* canonical authority of some creedal statements or church orders is in effect a reworking of the supposedly more weighty canonical authority of the scriptures. To recognize different levels of canonical authority, therefore, is to recognize not just the continuity of living tradition but the elements within that living tradition which attained greater fixity of form.

(b) In recognizing the continuity between the different canonical levels we are not thinking in terms of a river of tradition that follows a completely straight path, as though each stage flowed from what went before in complete harmony with it, as though each stage led directly into the next in a straightforward progressive development. Rather, we are confronted with a river that twists and turns, sometimes apparently doubling back on itself, where there is discontinuity as well as continuity in the tradition. Or perhaps more accurately, we are often confronted with different streams of tradition whose courses sometimes diverge quite markedly. For example, if Sanders is correct, the separation of the Pentateuch from the former prophets marks a significantly different self-understanding of Judah from that contained in the early recitals, in the Hexateuch or in Isaiah of Jerusalem—the period of Moses, of the exodus, Sinai and the wilderness wanderings is separated from the conquest of Canaan, the establishment of Jerusalem as the unified capital, the Davidic succession, and is given a normative authority that markedly qualifies the significance of the later periods.[44] Similarly, Matthew and James not only differ from Mark and Paul in their expression of Christianity's relation to the law, but do so by deliberately diverting and, indeed, reversing particular tendencies in Mark and Paul.[45] Or again, the ecclesiology of Acts and the Pastorals constitutes some sort of qualification of the ecclesiology of the early letters of the Pauline corpus.[46] Most striking of all, of course, the New Testament in effect decanonizes much of the Old Testament law for Christians, abolishing as it does not least the fundamental Mosaic distinction between clean and unclean foods, so that the Pentateuch can never function as canon for a Christian with the same effect as it does for a Jew. This can all be summed up as *the diversity of canonical authority*, the diversity between traditions used and evaluated in different ways at different periods of their canonical history.

All this involves the recognition that God was heard to speak differently at different periods. Often one generation heard the same tradition as the word of God in a sense different from that heard by preceding generations; or a new word of revelatory authority gained recognition even though it qualified an older word of revelatory authority. Whatever unity we may legitimately detect running through all the levels of canonical authority— unity of salvation-history, continuity of faith in the one God, and so on— the element of diversity is equally if not more important in any attempt to achieve a canonical hermeneutic. Not least in importance is the fact that even when an earlier tradition was qualified or superseded, it was often evidently retained; this retention attests as much to the canonical authority already attributed to the earlier tradition as to the revelatory authority that caused it to be reassessed. To retain such a tradition even when literally "out of date" (continuity of Davidic succession, imminence of the parousia) shows that the communities of faith both recognized the diversity of canonical authority and *canonized* it. Moreover, by retaining a tradition even when qualified by their own perception of God's will, they made it possible for their own and future generations both to understand that perception and to *correct* it where necessary. To recognize the different levels of canonical authority and their diversity is to accept that God may well speak differently from one generation to another, one historical situation to another, is to accept a larger canon than simply what speaks to my generation or situation, is to accept the possibility of my perception of God's will being corrected in turn by others.

(c) We can thus see more clearly what it was that has given certain texts normative authority. It was not simply the fact that they were inspired, far less simply that they claimed to be inspired. We can be quite certain that there were many inspired utterances that did not attain to any level of canonical authority—prophecies that were never retained, words and deeds of Jesus that have been forgotten (cf. John 21:25). We know of documents that were apparently no different in kind from those which achieved canonical status— source documents, lost letters of Paul, as well as those normally described as apocryphal or pseudepigraphal, and so on—many of them claiming an inspiration no different from that of prophet or apostle;[47] yet they either were never regarded as authoritative or achieved only a limited sway, limited both temporally and geographically. However much inspiration is to be regarded as a necessary qualification for a text to become canonical, it is clearly not a sufficient condition.[48]

What marked off some materials as possessed of canonical authority from others was both *their inspiration* and *particular communities' recognition of that inspiration*.[49] It was those ancient recitals of Israel's election, the various prophecies, the traditions of Jesus, and so forth, which in the event were heard as words of divine revelation, with which we have to deal at the various levels—texts that informed and shaped the self-understanding of successive communities of faith, which were treasured for that reason, and which in this way exercised normative authority even before they were formally recognized as scripture. Other texts, even inspired texts, do not enter our consideration because either they were never heard as words of God at all, or heard as God's word in such a limited way that they never secured a lasting place in the wider consciousness of any community. Both inspiration and recognition of inspiration therefore are equally crucial in any definition of canonical authority.

A further corollary to the recognition of various levels of canonical authority and of the continuity between them is that it becomes impossible to attribute a particular degree of inspiration to any one level, to distinguish, say, the final composition level as qualitatively distinct in inspiration from any of the others. If anyone was "more inspired" than others it would presumably have been Moses who "talked with God" and Jesus who alone "knows the Father." Yet we only have their revelations at one or more remove, through the inspiration of lesser men—do we have to say through the qualitatively lesser inspiration of lesser men? Or again, is the inspiration which recognized the canon and framed the creeds qualitatively different from that of the final authors of the scriptures? The fact is that none of the earlier forms would have survived and been treasured had they not been seen to carry authority as word of God, that is, to be inspired, by the communities which treasured them. At each level of canonical authority we are dealing with texts whose inspiration was taken for granted, whose inspiration was attested by the impact of their revelatory authority.

(d) Furthermore, we can also see more clearly that the whole process discussed in section II involves *a continuing interaction between what had already been accorded canonical authority and new revelation.*[50] The effective authority of canon did not depend on the belief that there had been a once-for-all burst of revelation over a short piece of time—Moses as sole and final author of the Pentateuch, the LXX as the identical translation of the seventy-two working independently, or whatever. The very fact that we have had to talk of the continuity of living tradition involves the recognition that what constituted established revelation was again and again being expanded by new revelation. The very fact that we have had to talk of the diversity of canonical authority involves the recognition that at not a few points in the whole process established revelation was adjudged to have been qualified by new revelation.

This we might note is one of the most significant differences between the situations confronting us today and, say, Christian Jews of the first century, the difference caused by closure of the canon. In the first century, believers could hold firmly to the idea of already normative writings while treating other writings in such a similar way that they became recognized as canonical too, whereas Christians today have been conditioned by the centuries-old presupposition that the canon is firmly closed. The difference is not so great as that bold contrast might imply. For as already pointed out (IId), our hermeneutical methods and dogmatic syntheses drawn from canonical material have again and again become a *de facto* modification of the Bible's effective canonical function. Nevertheless, there is a difference between a mind-set open to the possibility of a fresh word from God that should be accorded canonical authority, and one that understands the functioning of canonical authority simply in terms of expounding or interpreting the word of God from previous centuries. If we are to appreciate how canonical authority functioned all through the most formative period of Judaism and Christianity we must give weight to this interaction between old word and new word of God—something that is all the more important if the functioning of canonical authority during this period is itself to have any kind of canonical weight in our own evaluation of canonical authority.

The point is that a concept of canonical authority which recognizes that the process of canonization is not complete is bound to be *more flexible* than one which begins from the assertion that the canon is closed. Any community of faith which begins from the recognition that the authoritative word of God in a particular instance involves the interaction of accepted canon and proffered new revelation will inevitably be much more sensitive and circumspect in its judgment as to the will of God—the authority of canon will neither be appealed to nor applied in a wooden or mechanical way, "scripture" is less likely to become "letter." How else can a community of faith decide between a Jeremiah who claims a new word of God and a Hananiah who appeals to the older certainties (Jeremiah 28)? How else was it possible for the first Christians to accept a revelation claimed by Peter or Paul that the gospel should go to Gentiles without requiring circumcision (despite Gen. 17:9-14), that the law of clean and unclean foods was no longer binding (despite Lev. 11:1-23; Deut. 14:3-21)? For a faith that professes belief in the Holy Spirit the perception and exercise of canonical authority can never rest solely on the assertion "The Bible says."

(e) It follows that we have to allow also for *the historical relativity of canonical authority*—the recognition that the *de facto* authority of canonical texts is not some idealized postulate suspended from heaven and never actually interacting with historical reality. Canonical authority in practice is what God was heard to say in this or that particular situation, usually by direct appeal to what had been already recognized as canonical, but

sufficiently often also by appeal to what was perceived as a new word from God that qualified the old, which made it necessary to read some canonical text differently *because* the historical context was different. Thus, the exile forced the Judaeans to hear the same older promises afresh and with different meaning; the advent of Christ caused more and more Christians to hear the same Torah but with different significance; in the different situation of his Hellenistic Jewish context Matthew presented the Jesus-tradition differently from Mark writing with a view to the Gentile mission; the institutionalized church justified an order of priesthood despite obvious lack of justification within the New Testament. It is only by recognizing that God was heard to speak differently in different historical contexts that we can cope with the growth and *development* of canonical texts (IIIa) or the *diversity* within that development and subsequently enshrined within the canon (IIIb).[51] It is only by recognizing that an immediacy of revelation in a particular situation could be accorded normative authority over against the hitherto regulative canonical authority, because it spoke to that situation in a way that the older canonical authority did not, that we can make canonical sense of the fact of different levels of canonical authority (II).[52]

What this means in practice is that *we cannot ask after the canonical authority of any text at any level without having regard to the historical context of that level.*[53] The exegete of any text who wants to take the issue of canonical authority seriously will be concerned to reconstruct the historical context of each level.[54] By having due regard for the differences and diversity of historical contexts he or she will find some canonical guidance on how to cope with the differences and diversity of canonical authority, on how to relate canonical documents to the different situations of one's own day. In this way he or she will hope to hear afresh the word of God as it came to different generations and situations. In this way he or she will come to see how canonical authority actually functioned in practice. In this way he or she will be able to feed valuable material to systematic theologians in their inquiry into how God speaks *now* and how revelation in the present is to be related to what has been canonized as the revelation of the past.[55]

IV

All this poses more sharply the issue of whether within all these different levels of canonical authority there is one level that should be regarded as possessing primacy of canonical authority, as normative—normative for the exegete, or for contemporary faith, or indeed for all time and all issues. Given the continuity between these different levels, the continuity of living tradition (IIIa), is the very idea of canon wholly relativized—or can we treat one level as more regulative than the others? Given the diversity between these levels, the diversity of and within our present canons (IIIb), can we in fact locate a canon within the canon, can we isolate a primary criterion of canonicity by which to judge all claims to canonical authority, as Käsemann has urged? Given that immediate perception of God's will in a particular situation, whether designated as revelation or not, can be appealed to as a reason for qualifying or even setting aside the most obvious meaning of a canonical text, what means have we for "testing the spirits," for discerning the false prophecy that ought to be rejected as against the genuine insight into God's will which can legitimately claim its own weight of "canonical authority"?[56] If the freezing of tradition in any particular form is so incidental in the living flow of tradition, so contingent on the peculiarities of particular historical circumstances, so open to qualification and correction subsequently, can we give any weight to the idea of canon as a rule for faith and life of lasting significance? Can we regard any level of canonical authority as having more than passing significance?

(a) If we ask these questions first with respect to *the task of exegesis,* I believe a clear answer can be given. In exegesis, whatever the level of the text's history and meaning that is being investigated, *the level of the final composition* (final author, canonical form) *has to be regarded as normative*—normative in the sense of exercising a *control* over or check on the lines of investigation and any hypotheses or results that emerge.[57] It has to be the level of the final composition for the simple reason that as a rule we gain a clearer grasp of the meaning and function of any particular text at that level than at any other. Especially when we are dealing with a text of several (or many) chapters in length we can gain a clearer picture of the characteristic features, motifs, and concerns at the level of the final composition than is possible at any other level. In a word, at the level of the final composition we have the best hope of ascertaining the intended *meaning* of the text within its most durative context. In contrast, any attempt to penetrate back to one or other of the tradition-history levels is bound to be more speculative, both as to the form of the text and as to its function and meaning. Likewise, the more coherent the text as a unified composition the clearer its meaning and function is likely to be, whereas the diversities within a larger canon are bound to make its significance at the canonical level less clear. *It is this handle on a text's meaning that the relative coherence of the final composition level provides which makes it both possible and necessary for this level to serve as control over our exegesis at other levels.*

All this does *not* mean, of course, that it is only the final composition level which should be subjected to investigation. On the contrary, investigation of other levels, particularly of course the tradition-history levels, will often throw more light on the meaning of the final composition. It does mean however that all attempts to inquire into a text's tradition-history have to make sufficient sense of that text's function and meaning at the level of the final composition; the more difficult it is to explain the transition from a hypothesized earlier form and meaning to the form and meaning of the final composition, the less likely is that hypothesis to be correct; and vice versa— the more light the hypothesized tradition-history of a text sheds on that text's meaning at the final composition level, the more likely is that hypothesis to be correct. So, too, any exegesis directed to the canonical level of a text, its function and meaning within the canon, will have to explain how that function and meaning developed from the function and meaning provided by the final composition, for the greater the divergence of the canonical meaning from that given by the final composition the more ambiguous within the diversity of the canon that canonical meaning is liable to be. In every case the clearer "known" is the level of the final composition, which consequently can and must provide a control and check over investigations into the less clear "unknowns" of the other levels.

As will be obvious from the earlier discussion (IIb) the case argued here is much more easily justified with regard to the bulk of the New Testament writings where we can usually speak with confidence both of final author (or original author) and of the meaning he intended. So, for example, I am arguing that in terms of exegesis the meaning intended by Matthew at any point in his Gospel must be the starting point for and check on investigations into the pre-Matthean history of the tradition, and any hypothesis regarding that tradition-history must include a sufficient explanation of how Matthew used it as he did. So, too, with Paul the primary exegetical task must be to explain Paul's letters as far as possible in their own terms, and so far as exegesis of Paul is concerned the question of how they square with the Acts of the Apostles (or with the Pastorals) is a secondary issue; moreover, any hypothesis regarding the canonical Paul must "fit" individually with the exegetical results of the Pauline epistles, Acts, and the Pastorals respectively. The normative level as the control level is the level of the final author.

However, I would like to argue for the same principle of exegetical control with regard to the Old Testament documents as well. And here in effect I side with Childs by appealing to the control provided by the "canonical shape" of an Old Testament book as a check on the inevitably more speculative reconstructions of the levels of tradition-history, to the canonical shape of Amos or Micah as a control on attempts to reconstruct the original form and force of Amos's and Micah's prophetic utterances, to the canonical shape of the Pentateuch as a check on any attempt to reconstruct the form of J or E or the redactional editing of P. Any hypothesis regarding the historical Amos or the historical Micah or regarding J or E or P must include within it a sufficient explanation of the present canonical shapes of Amos, Micah, and the Pentateuch. In addition, I would wish to appeal to the final composition form of Deuteronomy or Second Isaiah or to the Hebrew texts of Jeremiah and Kings as checks and controls on any assessment of their meaning within the Hebrew Bible, or the LXX, or the Christian Bible.

In short, so far as the task of exegesis of both Old and New Testaments is concerned the level of final composition must be regarded as primary and normative in relation to all other levels.

(b) What then about the canon in the sense of rule for faith and life? Can any of the different levels of canonical authority be given priority over the rest as defining more authoritatively what the faith is, as more regulative for Christianity's self-understanding than any other, as providing a more adequate test for any further claims to prophetic inspiration or revelatory authority? A case can be made for each of the four levels already distinguished, but once again I would wish to argue that the final composition level must carry greatest weight.

The *ecclesiastical level* is in fact the level that in practice carries greatest influence. This remains the force of Käsemann's assertion that the canon legitimizes different denominations and teachings. Every branch of the church, every theological tradition in practice operates with its own canon, its own selection of legitimizing texts, its own patterns of interpretation as much read into the text as read out of it. Not the canonical texts per se but the interpretation of the canonical texts becomes the starting point for all ecumenical dialogue, and it is the insistence on the authority of these diverse patterns, not any diversity regarding the authority of the canon itself, that repeatedly proves the stumbling block in ecumenical discussions. Yet no one would actually seek to justify this level as the primary canonical level; even in Roman Catholic circles scripture per se still has primacy, is normative for the subsequent tradition, even when the tradition is understood as an interpretation of scripture.[58] So whatever the actual practice of canonical authority, for all branches of Christianity the *theology* of the canon, at least in theory, puts the weight on the canonical level rather than the ecclesiastical level.

The *canonical level* certainly has the most impressive *prima facie* claim to be the normative level for faith and life.[59] In terms of the canon the canonical level is the real watershed. Prior to the recognition of just these and not other documents as canonical the range of texts that could be regarded as canonical was open. The content of the canon, as well as the text form and possible interpretations of these texts, was still fluid. Particularly in the first century c.e. the canon of Jewish scripture was still open, and for Christians, including Christian Jews, the possibility of the range of canonical documents being extended could hardly be ignored (even if it was not put in just these terms).

But since then, and certainly for the past eighteen centuries or so, there has been no real possibility for the vast majority of Jews and Christians of further documents being included within their canons. Whatever the inspiration claimed for subsequent creedal statements, for particular mystics or works of devotion, whatever disagreement about Old Testament apocrypha or the canonical status of documents like James or Revelation, there has been more or less universal accord for all these centuries that the canon or canons of holy scripture are now fixed. In that sense these canons of scripture have in fact exercised a normative authority over both Jewish and Christian communities for centuries which would certainly seem to give them first claim to primacy in terms of normative authority.

On the other hand, we cannot ignore the fact that this has been a theoretical primacy, that in practice, as already noted, the real canon is some pattern of interpretation imposed upon the canonical writings. Moreover, this diversity of interpretation simply reinforces the fact of diversity *within* the canon itself—a diversity that an exegesis directed to the historical context of each writing is bound to confirm. Consequently we either have to accept the fact that the canon as now constituted actually canonizes diversity, and a greater diversity than most seem willing to contemplate—and this will force us back to the final composition level as we attempt to clarify the precise scope of the diversity. Or if we want a more unified picture of faith and life to emerge from the canon, we will have to accept the necessity of selecting or importing some organizing concept or of imposing some arbitrary pattern on the diversity—which effectively drives us back to the ecclesiastical level. The point is that *the canon does not of itself provide any single unifying key*. There is nothing in the Jewish canon that requires the interpreter to see in Jesus the unifying factor,[60] nothing in the New Testament to say whether Mark's or Matthew's presentation of Jesus' attitude to the law is normative. In fact, the canon as canon cannot provide sufficient control on the potential vagaries of interpretation claiming canonical authority. The stronger any claim that the canon as such offers a single unifying pattern, the more sure we can be that it is a pattern abstracted without due regard for a properly historical exegesis or for the diversity of ecclesiastical traditions which all claim authentication from the canon.[61]

It is the *final composition level* that once again in the event gives greatest promise of providing a normative control.[62] However the message of any document may have been qualified by its being included within a larger canon, the crucial fact remains that it was this document which was preserved in this form because it was heard as God's word addressed to the community of God's people. It was the impact of this message in this form that resulted eventually in its being formally canonized. So the primary canonical force of any canonical writing is not the force it had at the time it was declared canonical, but the force that initially lifted it out of the run of everyday communication, caused it to be cherished and preserved until question of formal canonical status arose.[63] Moreover, it is this primary canonical force on which properly critical historical exegesis can shed most light. For particularly with New Testament writings we can usually discern the historical life-setting of a document with some broad detail by means of historical-critical exegesis, both the situation addressed and the meaningfulness of the address to that situation, so that we are enabled to hear with some clarity how the word of God worked, how the author spoke to particular situations and how he would have been heard in these situations. And even with Old Testament writings the meaning of any text at or within the final composition is always liable to be clearer than its meaning at any other level, so that we can usually hear that text in its force as the word of God at that level more clearly and more definitively than at any other level. It is the handle on this level of canonical authority that exegesis affords us which once again makes it possible for this level to provide the norm, the test, and check on the more ambiguous results both of the diversity of the canonical level and of the speculative investigations of the tradition-history levels. The charge that to focus attention on the meaning intended at the original author or final composition level results in "a fragmentizing exegesis" because it treats the biblical writers "as isolated individuals"[64] misses the point that the historical context of the final composition and of the community's recognition of its canonical authority cannot be "isolated" from Israel's history of faith, and the point that God was heard to speak in different ways to different situations in history so that *removal of the text from that context prevents us hearing that text with the force which gave it its determinative canonical shape—just as setting it within that context enables us to delimit its canonical authority more precisely.*

What then of the *tradition-history level?* Here particularly the *Neutestamentler* is in a different position from the *Alttestamentler.* However much the *Alttestamentler* may want to hear the word of God as it was heard at each level of tradition-history, a desirable objective as I have argued, the process of unraveling the tradition-history may be so complex and speculative that he or she has to eschew any attempt to recover the historical Abraham, that he or she has to labor inordinately to uncover the teaching of the historical Moses and has to strain unbearably to hear it with the ears of the first Israelites, though he or she may entertain higher hopes with regard to the historical Isaiah of Jerusalem.[65] But the Christian *Neutestamentler cannot* be content merely to hear Jesus as delivered to us by Matthew or Mark or Luke or John. It is not simply that historical exegesis points to the conclusion that each has slanted and/or developed the Jesus-tradition in his own way. More important for him is the Christian assertion of Jesus' significance. If

Jesus is indeed the Word of God incarnate, then he has a normativeness for faith that is unequaled and certainly unsurpassed by scripture. If we are indeed to think in terms of a canon within a canon, where else should we look but Christ himself? After all, it was the revelation of Christ that constituted the first Christians' canon, in the light of which they interpreted the Old Testament (not least as *Old* Testament), by means of which they evaluated its continuing significance. And ideally we in turn should like to be able to check the gospel of Matthew or of Paul or of John or of James against the message and canonical authority of Jesus himself. So the Christian scholar cannot but want to get back as far as possible to the historical context of Jesus' *own* ministry and proclamation, to hear it in its own terms, to hear how the (for him or her) most authoritative actions and utterances of all time spoke to particular situations and produced the faith of the first disciples.

Yet in the end the same difficulty confronts the *Neutestamentler* as confronts the *Alttestamentler,* by no means so complex a difficulty, but one which must make him or her properly cautious about any reconstruction of particular contexts and situations in the life of Jesus. However much the Christian *Neutestamentler* might want to check for example Matthew's Jesus against the historical Jesus, it is never quite so simple as that. One cannot simply assume that the Markan or reconstructed "Q" source of any text is closer to the message of the historical Jesus; and even when one can mark out a characteristic or fairly distinctive Matthean motif one cannot take it for granted that this a redactional addition to the tradition which moves away from the message of the historical Jesus. Again and again it will be the case that the more Matthew is said to have diverged from the teaching of the historical Jesus the more speculative will be the reconstruction of that original teaching, so that it must be the level of Matthew which provides the norm and check. That is by no means to deny that a word of Jesus at the level of the tradition-history behind Matthew may well speak to present-day hearing of faith with greater force than Matthew's version, but inevitably *the control against the danger of an imaginative reconstruction of the level of the historical Jesus* (as in the nineteenth-century Lives of Jesus) *must be the canonical form of the Gospels themselves.* Moreover, it is at least arguable that the chief impact of Christ for faith was the impact of the whole Christ-event, and particular sayings and actions of the historical Jesus only gain and only gained their full impact within the context of the Christ-event. It was actually the first Christians' memory of Christ and their appreciation of his life, death, and resurrection that determined for them the meaning of the Old Testament. So arguably the real canon within the canon is not Christ as such but the remembered Christ, the *geschichtliche Christus,* Jesus as he was presented to enquirers and young Christians in the years following his death and resurrection.

The value of uncovering the different tradition-history levels then is not that they provide a canonical authority distinct from or independent of the final author. Rather, *the value of tradition-history investigation is that it enables us to recognize more clearly the relativity of the final composition level,* the degree to which earlier tradition has been shaped so as to function as the word of God to different or new situations confronting particular communities of faith at particular periods in history. This recognition of the limitation of the canonical authority of the final author level is not to subtract from or diminish the canonical authority of the text; rather, *it allows the text to be heard with its full force* as addressed to a particular context within history.

To sum up then, investigation of all the levels of canonical authority must be important both for exegesis and particularly for faith. People of faith will always want to hear how Isaiah or Jeremiah spoke to their day, and Christians will certainly want to hear Jesus for themselves, always recognizing that God may speak God's earlier word with renewed power. Naturally also people of faith will want to look for some organizing principles in biblical theology or to some system of dogmatic theology that provides a framework for a fuller understanding of their faith. But in terms of a check and control on meanings that are heard as coming from particular texts, the final composition level provides the best norm. Especially where someone within the community of faith is open to the possibility of new revelation, or hears unusual meanings from a particular text, or offers strange systems of theology, the need for some check and norm becomes increasingly important; the community of faith that may have to judge the significance or respond to the challenge offered by such claims to speak with prescriptive authority will need some norm. The more clearly the historical context of each level of canonical authority can be reconstructed, the more valuable it will be as such a check, for they will then be able to see how God's word was heard and how it functioned in previous situations like theirs. And as the level of final composition is the one that usually provides the clearest meaning at this point, so it will also provide the clearest example of how canonical authority functioned at particular periods in the history of faith. As a rule, therefore, the level of final author, final composition is best able to provide the norm and check that the community of faith needs.

V

There are of course other issues that have only been touched on in the preceding discussion, and though I have concentrated on the theme of canonical authority the treatment is still only sketchy; in particular, all the while I have been conscious of my lack of familiarity with current Old Testament research.

But despite its limitations the discussion does seem to point up some useful and some familiar, but all I hope valuable, conclusions.

(a) We have seen something of *the importance of canonical authority* as a factor both in exegesis and in faith. The epic of Gilgamesh, the Chronicles of the Kings of Judah, the letter of Aristeas, the "Q" source, the epistle of Barnabas—none of them carry the same weight as the biblical texts, simply because in the history of Judeo-Christian faith they never have carried that sort of weight, that level of canonical authority. As illustration we need simply note the fact that all World Council of Churches papers on faith and order matters start from the recognition of a need to justify themselves at some level of canonical authority of the biblical texts. Above all, for the Christian the New Testament provides a normative definition of what Christianity is, a definition that inevitably must control to greater or less degree all subsequent definitions and expositions. Too often, however, the importance of canonical authority has gone unrecognized, or has been exercised uncritically, or the appeal to canonical authority has itself been insufficiently controlled by a historical awareness of how canonical authority has functioned in the past and can function today. A more careful analysis of what canonical authority actually has been and is has thus become increasingly desirable.

(b) The identification of *four different levels of canonical authority* may help to clarify some of the confusion and even resolve some of the difficulties that have confronted biblical scholars since J. P. Gabler first distinguished biblical theology—in particular, the relation between exegesis and interpretation, and between biblical theology as a purely descriptive exercise and biblical theology as a way of doing theology today, not to mention the ambiguities of Childs's "canonical process," "canonical shapes" and "canonical context." By distinguishing the level of final composition from, on the one hand, the tradition-history level, and on the other, the canonical level (the proper domain of biblical theology) and the ecclesiastical level (the proper domain of dogmatic theology), particular issues as they affect individual texts become clearer and a greater refinement of analysis becomes possible. More important, *the recognition that the texts in question functioned as canonical authority makes possible a much more positive interaction between a properly historical exegesis and faith seeking instruction than many scholars over the past century have thought possible.*[66] The point is, that once we recognize the dimension of the canonical authority of a text, and recognize that this text exercised its canonical force at different historical levels, then the elucidation of that dimension, of that force becomes a legitimate object of critical enquiry. The concern of faith does not need to distance itself as a concern from the concern of critically historical description. For faith will want, with the historian, to illuminate as sharply as possible the actual canonical authority of a text at whatever

level. Without denying for a moment the conflict that can arise between a properly critical historical methodology and a faith which seeks to be open to the *Vergegenwärtigung* of a text as the word of God, the very fact that the historical functioning of a text as canonical authority is the subject matter of investigation allows a positive interaction of self-critical faith and historical analysis which can be very beneficial to both.

(c) In particular, we have been able to see *how canonical authority functioned*—not only by highlighting the four different levels of canonical authority, and the continuity between them, but by showing how again and again the hearing of the word of God involved an *interaction of canonical tradition, immediate perception of the will of God, and community recognition.* The implication is that Christians today will not be able to hear the word of God as it was heard in these situations of the past unless we take into account *the historical context* of that word. Moreover, there will be many instances where it will become evident, on exegetical grounds, that the text which was heard as God's word was so closely tied to the particular context that *its prescriptive authority will be limited to that context* (so many would judge to be the case not only with regard to the Old Testament laws on clean and unclean food but also with regard to the New Testament restrictions on women's participation in the worship and order of the church). That is to say, the canonical authority of any text at any level is not independent of the historical context at each level. So, too, faith's hearing of the word of God today will inevitably involve the same interaction, with the community of faith prayerfully considering both its canonical precedents and any claim to a prophetic perception of God's will in relation to whatever issue requires a decision.

(d) Moreover, we have seen good reason to pick out *the level of final composition* as the one that provides *the clearest norm both for exegesis and for faith.* This will be a more *limited* canonical authority than has often been asserted for the Bible—precisely because it does not claim or depend on certain access to the historical level of the exodus or of the historical Jesus, precisely because it takes seriously the historical context of the final author or composition, takes seriously the inspiration of the Spirit at that level speaking a word of God in a form that made clear and lasting impact on faith. But precisely because it is the *clearest* norm it will be able to provide a crucial check against the dangers both of over-speculative exegesis in the task of hearing the word of God from the past and of false prophecy in the task of hearing the word of God in the present. Not least of the importance of focusing particular attention on this level is that it is the level on which the great bulk of believers can most easily work and where meaning can be most easily demonstrated—so that it provides a united basis for the wider community of faith, more so than the complex tradition-history investigations of the scholar

or the diverse patterns of biblical and dogmatic theology. At the level of final composition we can recognize most clearly the force of a text's canonical authority and so enable it to function most forcefully as norm, as canon for us today.

(e) One of the most striking features that has come to the fore repeatedly in this analysis is the differences between the Old Testament and the New Testament in this area of discussion, not least the difference made to the functioning of each as canonical authority by having to take account of the other's canonical authority. It is not simply that the issue is so much more complex in the case of the Old Testament (length of the tradition-history process, difficulty of defining "final author," etc.). It is also the fact that the canonical force of an Old Testament text at the final composition level will often be different from its significance when read in the light of Christ and the New Testament. It is the fact that a New Testament author will often be able to claim canonical backing from the Old Testament only by using hermeneutical techniques (as in Gal. 3:16) which, however legitimate in his own day, can hardly claim the same weight today—the fact, in other words, that the New Testament canonizes interpretations of Old Testament texts that an exegesis directed to the final composition level of these texts would find hard to justify. Likewise the salvation-history and other patterns read in the Old Testament by biblical and dogmatic theologians are equally arbitrary at the canonical level of the Old Testament itself, equally predetermined by the Christian assessment of the significance of Jesus of Nazareth. However, the Christian, including the Christian *Alttestamentler*, has no choice: he or she must affirm the exegetically arbitrary axiom of his or her faith, that the advent of Christ has set the historical contexts of all earlier canonical texts in an epoch that is passed (Old Testament), and that the New Testament that bears the most definitive witness to Christ and to the revelatory significance of the Christ-event has therefore a weight of canonical authority which the Old Testament texts as such cannot fully share. In other words, the Christian has no choice but to affirm that Christ is the norm of all norms, that the New Testament is the canon within the canon of the Christian Bible.

In short, to recognize the historical fact of a text's canonical authority, the different levels of canonical authority, and the normativeness of the final composition level within the four, as well as of the New Testament within the Christian Bible, is both to inform and liberate our hearing of scripture as the word of God and to make it more meaningful and more possible for scripture to continue exercising its proper role as canonical authority.[67]

7. GOD'S WORD IN HUMAN SPEECH: THE PRICE OF CERTAINTY

A FUNDAMENTAL FEATURE OF "FUNDAMENTALISM" is the desire for and claim to certainty. This desire for certainty may indeed be the psychological root of all fundamentalism—I would not pretend to be able to pronounce on that issue—but the claim to certainty seems to be a feature common to all fundamentalisms. It is because the truth claimed by the fundamentalist is certain that this truth can be, must be so unyieldingly fought for and its detractors so resolutely resisted.[1]

In the fundamentalisms of the three great monotheistic religions, this claim to certainty focuses particularly on the scriptures of each, on the Torah and its concomitant *halakah*, on the Christian Bible, and on the Qur'an. The desire for certainty is satisfied with the conviction that God has revealed God's truth in a wholly correct, infallible, and inerrant way. There are, of course, other features of "fundamentalism," but it is this claim to certainty focused in scripture on which I wish to concentrate. And since my own main exposure to fundamentalism has been to Christian fundamentalism I will have to take my examples from the claim to certainty focused in the Christian Bible.

Most of what follows will be a critique of this desire for and claim to certainty. So I shall begin by offering a brief sketch of what the claim to certainty involves and of its positive features.

I

The desire for certainty is in some ways admirable in its motivation. It wants clarity because it wants commitment. How can we really be committed to a cause if we do not know what it is we are committed to? The desire is for certainty, because *un*certainty undermines commitment. The desire is for a firm rock in a sea of otherwise constant change, for a truth unchanging in the face of so-called progress with its seemingly endless confusion. The assumption is that God would surely not want God's children to be tossed about by storms of doubt or lost in the mists of uncertainty.

The focus is on scripture precisely because written formulations hold out promise of such certainty—certainty of historical fact, certainty of cultic and ethical prescription, certainty of theological proposition. Not least of fundamentalism's appeal is this claim to honor scripture and give it due place as the definition and prime determinant of the religion to which it bears testimony. The assumption is that God the Absolute has revealed the divine self absolutely. Failure to honor God's chosen means of self-revelation is failure to honor God. For the fundamentalist such a failure properly to acknowledge scripture is itself a kind of blasphemy.

At its heart this desire for certainty is the desire for certainty of salvation. Once again, the assumption is that the loving God would not wish God's children to lack such assurance. In a conversation between the Archbishop of York and Cardinal Joseph Ratzinger (now Pope Benedict XVI) in 1983, the archbishop tried to suggest that the *magisterium* is better seen as an *approximation* to the truth and not as identical with it. To which the cardinal eventually replied: "Unless God has revealed himself to us in determinate, stateable propositions, then salvation is at risk."[2] Whatever one may think of the statement itself, the evangelistic and pastoral concern that it expresses is clear and its positive features should be acknowledged.

At the heart of the claim to certainty also is the conviction that God's truth is all of a piece. Those familiar with Protestant fundamentalism will be familiar with its "all or nothing" stance, the "seamless robe" picture of religious truth. But the point is equally found from the pen of a self-professed Muslim fundamentalist:[3]

> If a book can be fallible in its claims about astronomy and biology, there is no reason why it should be infallible in its pronouncements on religious doctrine.... For all Muslims, as for pre-Enlightenment Christians, faith should be an "all or nothing" affair. The reason is as decisive as it is simple. One cannot properly endorse the authoritative integrity of a partly infallible scripture.

Christian fundamentalism in particular thus sees itself in sharp antithesis to all woolly liberalism, all mushy modernism, all half-truths that undermine the one true faith, the endless compromises that only dilute and weaken God's truth as revealed in God's Word. Perhaps even more familiar in Protestant fundamentalist apologetic is the threatening image of the "slippery slope": to begin to question minor matters of the biblical testimony is to set one's foot on the top of a slippery slope down which one then slides with irrevocable finality to the total loss of faith at the foot of the slope. You may begin by questioning the literal account of the six days of creation, or the rule that women should wear a hair covering in church, but then you soon find yourself advocating abortion and homosexual marriage or denying the Virgin birth and the deity of Christ, and the end is complete moral relativism and total skepticism.[4]

The attraction of such arguments should not be underestimated, nor the enticing strength of the dogmatic or moral absolute. In a period marked by social, ideological, and political *un*certainity, the appeal of such fundamentalist certainty is obvious. In the context of the Western intellectual tradition it should cause no surprise that fundamentalism is the polar opposite of postmodernism; just as in the postcommunist world the clear-cut certainties of monoreligious nationalism seems for so many to be the most attractive alternative to multicultural, pluralistic internationalism or federalism.

The trouble is, however, that this desire for certainty confuses confidence of faith with certainity of knowledge. The danger is that a legitimate desire for confidence becomes an illegitimate lust for certainty—the danger being that a lust for certainty actually undermines faith. Far from being an affirmation of the scriptural testimony, such a claim to certainty constitutes an abuse of scripture. This is the substance of my critique of Christian fundamentalism, which I will now attempt to elaborate. But it may apply *mutatis mutandis* to all religious fundamentalisms.

II

Why is a desire for certainty illegitimate? Why is the claim to certainty an abuse of scripture? For the simple reason that in matters of religion and faith in particular such certainty is just not possible. Therefore, to lay claim to such certainty is to lay claim to a false certainty. And a false certainty is a far greater threat to the spirit and truth of religion, since the zeal of a false certainty is religion perverted and become demonic. Indeed, an almost inevitable corollary of the claim to certainty is that those who dispute it can be dismissed as blind or willfully perverse, whose lives become of little moment in the scales of eternity and whose deaths may even be thought to advance the cause of truth. But such a claim to certainty cannot be sustained.

(a) For one thing, human speech is simply inadequate to express divine reality. When God expresses the divine self or God's will in human terms, a degree of ambiguity and uncertainty is inevitable and unavoidable. For words are rarely precision instruments, except when used as rigorously controlled technical terms, that is, in narrow specialisms or in legal documents; and even then the control often slips. But for communication in language such as used by Moses or prophet or sage or apostle, the words used, however much inspired by God's Spirit, are imprecise instruments. The God who is beyond human sight and comprehension is also beyond human speech. God can be expressed no more adequately in the images of human language than God can be represented in images of wood or stone. This is an insight deep at the heart of the three monotheistic faiths. Even Moses was permitted to see only the "afterglow" of God's glory (Exod. 33:23). Even Ezekiel in the archetypal vision of merkabah mysticism was permitted to see only "a likeness as the appearance of a man" (Ezek. 1:26). And revelation of God's will as a revelation of the divine self shares the same constraints. All talk of God, however inspired, is bound to be tentative in at least some measure. To claim any more is to make the icon of a verbal image into an idol. In the last analysis, therefore, fundamentalism is a form of idolatry.

The point can be illustrated even in the most technical language used in Christian theology to speak of God, particularly in the patristic distinction between the "eternal generation" of the Son and the "procession" of the Spirit. No one, no matter how sophisticated theologically, can explain what the difference between "generation" and "procession" amounts to. These words are simply heuristic markers to indicate *that* there is a distinction, without pretending to indicate *what* it is.

But even the most common and basic Christian language shares the same basic defect. It is axiomatic for Christians that Jesus is "the Son of God." But what does that mean? It cannot be taken literally—that God literally impregnated a woman; the virginal conception narratives make a point of avoiding such a portrayal. Despite that, the Mormons, or so I believe, do take the language literally—believing that God had or has a wife as such. But Christian theology has always recognized that such language—God as Father, Jesus as God's Son—has to be understood analogically. It has been persisted with, come to be axiomatic for Christians, not because it is literally correct, not even because it is a perfect analogy, but because it has proved to be the most satisfactory and most durable way of indicating the character of the relation between Jesus and God. But even the best analogy is never wholly adequate.

To take a different example: Paul in speaking of the experience of salvation uses a whole kaleidoscope of metaphors—metaphors drawn from life, from athletic contests, from business and commerce, from medicine, from horticulture, and so on. The richness and diversity of the reality he was trying to express evidently could not be contained within a single metaphor. That, however, has not stopped many Christians from exalting one of these metaphors into the status of a technical term—regeneration, justification, salvation itself—and from subordinating all the rest to that one. The danger then emerges of squeezing all that rich diversity of experience through a narrowing and constrictive filter of a rigidly defined process—the danger of transforming a living metaphor into a dead mathematical formula.

In short, religion cannot express its basic beliefs without metaphor, but such speech must be allowed to remain as metaphor and not be forced to do service as legal formula. When the icon ceases to be a window through which one looks, when the icon becomes that on which one focuses, then the icon has become the idol.

(b) A second reason why certainty is impossible is that everything written in the Bible has an inescapable degree of particularity, of contingency. This, of course, is simply a further aspect of the basic point just made, but its importance calls for special mention.

The fact is that every word of the Bible was written at a particular time, in the language of the time, every formulation reflects and embodies the usage and idiom of its time, every claim or affirmation or petition reflects in one degree or other the convictions and values, the social and cultural world of their time. In a word, everything in the Jewish and Christian scriptures is context related, and much of it is context specific. Consequently, the meaning of most biblical texts is dependent in some degree or other on the context in and for which they were written. This is not at all to deny that the scriptures contain older material, or that their final, canonical form is often the product of a lengthy tradition process. Nor is it to affirm that all scriptures are context dependent in the same measure; in particular, most of the wisdom teaching both in the Writings and in the New Testament has a timelessness that minimizes its context dependence. Nevertheless, time and again throughout the scriptures the significance to be read from a text is so context specific that to ignore that context is to abuse the text. The appropriate image in this case is perhaps that of the plant rooted in its native soil by countless roots and tendrils, so that to remove it from that soil and attempt to transplant it elsewhere is likely to leave it weak and sickly if not dead.

The problem for fundamentalism at this point is obvious. Any text whose reference and relevance outside its native context is uncertain speaks with an uncertain voice. It cannot satisfy the lust for certainty. The danger for fundamentalism at this point is that again and again it will want to make an absolute out of a particular, a universal out of a specific. And if that cannot be done so simply the temptation for individual fundamentalists will be to find an apostle or prophet or rabbi or mullah who will tell them authoritatively which texts can be treated as absolutes and how to explain those texts which cannot. In fundamentalism the perspicacity of scripture soon becomes unconditional dependence on the authoritative ruling of the particular sect's guru.

In Christian theology the problem is well illustrated by the Christian attitude to many of the regulations in the Torah. Christians from earliest days have not observed the laws of clean and unclean, despite their clear enunciation in Leviticus and Deuteronomy. Despite the emphatic words of Genesis 17 on circumcision as an "everlasting covenant," Christians early on followed Paul in making it a point of principle to set aside the explicit scriptural teaching on the subject. And this despite continuing to claim the Tanakh as their scriptures. How could they do this? They could only do so consistently on the ground that such teaching was context related—for Israel, for a period, but not for all worshipers of God or for all time. Of course, the destruction of the Temple in 70 c.e. forced continuing Judaism to a somewhat similar conclusion so far as Temple sacrifices are concerned, and Halakah itself is the response to changing conditions and contexts. But Christians went much further. They even concluded that the sabbath was no longer to be the Christian holy day, despite the absence of any explicit ruling on the point within the Christian scriptures. Here we might say Seventh Day Adventists have followed a more consistent hermeneutic. But the basic point remains the same: that Christians can justify their treatment of Torah only by regarding such regulations of the Mosaic law as context conditioned; with the context now changed the word-of-God meaning and force of these regulations is not the same. Christian fundamentalists may respond by spiritualizing such texts, but that itself is an acknowledgment that their "plain meaning" is context dependent and their reference outside that context a matter of uncertainty.

Within the Christian scriptures themselves Christian fundamentalists find similar problems with the Pauline instructions regarding the participation of women in worship. Most would acknowledge a degree of cultural conditionedness in the ruling that a woman should only pray or prophesy with her head covered (1 Cor. 11:2-16). But they are generally loathe to allow similar considerations to qualify the force of the ruling three chapters later that women/wives should keep silence in church (1 Cor. 14:34-35), or of the similar ruling in 1 Timothy 2:11-12 forbidding a woman to teach or to have authority over a man/her husband. Here the price of certainty is the absolutizing of a social order whose degree of context dependency is recognized as uncertain.

Christology throws up another example. The claim that Jesus is Messiah is, of course, fundamental to Christianity. But it is actually doubtful whether Jesus himself ever fully accepted the title "Messiah" for himself. If so, this would probably be because, in part at least, the popular idea of the royal Messiah, Son of David, was of a military ruler who would free Israel from foreign domination (as in *Pss. Sol.* 17). That is what (Davidic) Messiah meant for most people. But Jesus himself seems to have shied away from such a role; that is to say, he probably rejected the only understanding of royal messiahship which was then current. And when Christians thereafter affirmed that Jesus nevertheless *was* Messiah, they could only do so by transforming the concept of Davidic Messiah in the light of Jesus' passion and by drawing on scriptures hitherto not regarded as messianic (cf., e.g., Luke 24:26-27). In other words, the whole Christian claim for the messiahship of Jesus, including Jesus' own attitude to the claim, makes sense only if "Messiah" is *not* treated as an absolute, only if its context relatedness is recognized and the fact is acknowledged that its meaning changed as the contexts of its use changed.

A more sensitive example is the way in which some New Testament writers, particularly John's Gospel, speak of "the Jews." In John's Gospel "the Jews" are presented as virulently hostile to Jesus; Jesus even calls them children of the devil (John 8:44). Such usage, when taken absolutely, becomes an incitement to and justification for anti-Semitism—as the history of Christian anti-Semitism demonstrates all too clearly. Only when such texts are read within their historical context, as of limited reference, that is, probably as directed against the local Jewish leadership hostile to the Johannine churches, only then can their anti-Jewish potential be defused. That is, only an acknowledgment of such texts' context-conditioned character prevents their abusive use beyond that context. The price of a Christian fundamentalist certainty achieved by ignoring that context is to open the door to a continuing Christian anti-Semitism.

In short, the fundamentalist desire for certainty runs directly counter to the particularity and context relatedness of the biblical texts. At the end of the day it can only be satisfied by riding roughshod over the historical character of these texts. What starts as a concern to honor these texts as scripture ends up by abusing them, by forcing them to do service for which they were never intended.

(c) A third feature of scripture that runs counter to the desire for certainty is the fact that scripture consists of different kinds of literature and different literary forms. This, too, is a facet of the character of biblical writings as human words written at particular times and with a view to

different historical contexts. So the point is basically the same. The point is that different literary forms make their truth-claims in different ways. The truth-claim of a poem or a hymn is not to be appreciated or evaluated in the same way as the truth-claim of a legal ruling or a dogmatic assertion. The truth-claim of a parable or a metaphor has to be perceived differently from the truth-claim of a historical statement. In contrast, the tendency in any claim to certainty is to ignore such differences, precisely because they give room to uncertainty. The temptation confronting fundamentalism is to elide these differences, to homogenize the different literary forms, to treat the different truth-claims as all on the same level. In Protestant fundamentalism, for example, the tendency has been to reduce the Bible to a book of doctrinal propositions.

To be fair, this critique can be overstated. No fundamentalist, I presume, would want to take literally the prophet's talk of trees clapping their hands or the psalmist's talk of mountains skipping like rams (Isa. 55:12; Ps. 114:4). The presence of poetry and thus of nonfactual statements is recognized in at least some measure. Fundamentalists, however, usually begin to agonize over the question as to whether the accounts of Genesis 1–3 or the visions of the seer of Revelation should be treated as straightforward history: if the Bible says God created in six days, and that a snake spoke, then so be it; why should Revelation not provide a blueprint for the course or the end of history?[5] Any other course could be a step down the slippery slope.

Perhaps the classic confrontation between critical scholarship and Christian fundamentalism takes place over the nature and status of the truth-claims made by John's Gospel. The contrast between the portrayal of Jesus in the Fourth Gospel and that of the other three Gospels is well known and unavoidable. In Matthew, Mark, and Luke we are confronted with a Jesus who speaks rarely of himself and much about God's kingdom. In John the picture is completely the reverse. In John we have a Jesus who makes amazing claims about himself (e.g., "I am the bread of life"; "Before Abraham was I am"; "I am the resurrection and the life") and who talks constantly of his having been sent from heaven. And these claims are at the heart of fundamentalist apologetic and evangelistic claims regarding Jesus. But such claims are notable by their absence in the other three Gospels. The most obvious solution to such striking discrepancy is that John's truth-claims are of a different order from those of the Synoptics: John's portrayal of Jesus is probably more in the order of meditations on the significance of Jesus than of a historical account of things Jesus actually did or said; his truth-claim thus presumably rests much more on the nature of early Christian experience and worship and much less on the historical facticity of the narratives and discourses he records. In contrast, fundamentalism's lust for certainty causes it to treat all four Gospels on the same level; by insisting that the truth-claim of John's Gospel has to be of the same order as the truth-claim of the other three the distinctiveness of John's Gospel is lost and the richness of its truth-claim diminished.

A similar controversy focuses on the speeches in the Acts of the Apostles—Peter's speech on the day of Pentecost, Paul's sermon in Antioch, and so on. Critical scholarship has noted the historiographical convention of the day regarding such speeches: that speeches could and would rarely be verbatim, that speeches would regularly be intended to fill an artistic or aesthetic role and not primarily an information role, somewhat like arias in an opera. Consequently the readers for whom Acts was written would only expect the speeches of Acts to represent what was said on the occasion or what the author had deemed appropriate to the occasion. In contrast, the Christian fundamentalist's natural instinct is to insist that these speeches record just what was said on the occasion recounted: unless we can be assured that Peter or Paul actually said the words attributed to them how can we trust the narrative at all? But that would leave us with a surprising fact: that the first Christian preachers seem to have preached for no more than about five minutes! For that is how long it takes to speak the sermons recorded. By everything else we know of Christian preaching from the beginning till now, that would be surprising! Nor will it do to say that what has been recorded are outlines or summaries of the actual speeches. For in fact the sermons in Acts are complete in themselves, little cameos, exquisite miniatures. It makes most sense of the evidence therefore to conclude that Luke intended the speeches to be representative and not verbatim. In which case, to continue to insist, despite the evidence, that the Acts sermons must either have been spoken on the occasion or else be false and untrustworthy is not to defend the integrity of scripture but to undermine and destroy it. In this case too the price of certainty is the forced conformity of scripture to artificial rules of consistency, the narrowing of the word of God not simply to human speech but to a limiting kind of rigid human logic.

In short, in its desire for certainty, fundamentalism shows itself unwilling to accept the unavoidable inadequacy of human speech to express God's self-revelation, the degree of historical particularity in most biblical texts that prevents their being absolutized, and the different kinds of literature in scripture and the different conventions behind them, all of which should caution a modern reader from straightforwardly reading off historical fact and Christian doctrine from these texts simply because they are in the Bible. The lust for certainty turns the icon into an idol, pulls the living word from the soil in which it was rooted, turns the metaphor into a mathematical formula, and abuses the scriptural authority it seeks to affirm.

III

The outcome of this triple failure is easily seen in the way fundamentalism actually handles scripture.

(a) For one thing, it ignores or discounts the problem of *interpretation*. For most of the past hundred years or so it was assumed in conservative Christian circles that the main issue was the question of inspiration: How is the mode and character of the inspiration of scripture to be conceived? The assumption seems to have been that if only they could get the liberal critic to acknowledge the inspiration of scripture, the battle for scriptural authority would be over. This assumption, of course, will have reflected the then still dominant idea of scientific objectivity: that an inspired text had an objectivity of meaning which was transparent to inquiry; once grant the status of the text as divinely inspired and its meaning, uncovered by standard historico-grammatical techniques, would carry its authority in its face.

It is only in the last few decades, however, that it has come to be appreciated that the real problem is that of interpretation. Even granted the inspiration of a scriptural text, the question still remains: What does it mean? The current debate on this topic is running through a range of themes—structuralist criticism, narrative criticism, rhetorical criticism, deconstruction, reader response, and so forth. To this debate fundamentalism per se can make no contribution. For the motivation behind the hermeneutical debate is the recognition that the meaning of a text, particularly a historical text, is *not* certain, *cannot* be finally tied down in fine detail. The questions, rather, are whether the interpreter can get beyond a shifting and debated ambiguity of meaning, how far meaning can be pinned down as substantively inhering in the text, how much the interpreter contributes to or even helps bring about a text's meaning. All this is instinctively anathema to the fundamentalist.

(b) A second weakness of fundamentalist hermeneutics is the tendency to homogenize the whole. The desire for certainty is the more readily satisfied when everything fits together within a single integrated system. And the assumption of a single author for all scriptures (God's Spirit) understandably encourages the idea that individual scriptures are constituent elements of a single vision and scheme of things. The natural corollary is that texts can be taken from several different biblical books and put together to form a coherent biblical teaching. The result is that the distinctive teaching of each book is often lost sight of, and a uniformity of teaching is derived which pays too little respect to the diversity of the documents and the purposes and contexts for which they were written.

For example, one might think that Christian fundamentalists would have been happier had there been only one Gospel and not four. But the fact remains that the New Testament contains four Gospels, four *different* Gospels. The Jesus who is presented in them is different, particularly, as we have seen, in the case of John's Gospel, but the differences between the presentations of the other three Gospels cannot be ignored either. It was evidently important for the first Christians that Jesus should be seen to be presented in different ways, to different groups of Christians, themselves with different backgrounds and constituencies. It is precisely the adaptability of the portrayal of Jesus with a view to different contexts that the four Gospels demonstrate. In contrast, the fundamentalist desire for consistency between these different portrayals, the fundamentalist tendency to play down these differences in the hope of making their own single picture of Jesus the more certain works against this manifest function of the canonical Gospels. Seeking to be loyal to scripture they have actually set themselves to counteract one of its purposes.

In North American fundamentalism the classic example of a homogenizing tendency is what many Christian fundamentalists would regard as the biblical doctrine of the second coming of Christ, particularly in regard to the millennium and the "rapture." This doctrine, disputed in its detail, is derived in fact from a combination of a range of passages drawn from the Gospels, 1 Thessalonians, and the Apocalypse of John. It emerges from the assumption that Paul's assurance to the Thessalonian believers, that "we who are alive shall be caught up in the clouds to meet the Lord in the air" (1 Thess. 4:17), must fit with the seer's talk of Christ's thousand-year reign (Revelation 20)—must fit, because the same author (God's Spirit) draws these diverse details from a single final scenario. The desire for the certainty of a single schema dismisses the possibility that different (human) authors were responding to different needs in different circumstances and in different ways, which should not simply be run together. Consequently, the possibility of a scriptural comfort not dependent on some of the frightening portrayals of the "rapture" is lost and the pastoral potential of scripture is cancelled out.

(c) Third, and correlated with the desire to homogenize, is the desire to harmonize divergent details of different accounts of the same episode. As far as Christian fundamentalists are concerned, this applies particularly to the Gospels, but also, for example, to divergences between historical books in the Tanakh or between the Acts of the Apostles and Paul's letter to the Galatians in the New Testament. The lust for certainty refuses to see what is obvious when the Gospels are put side by side—specifically, that the evangelists were usually not concerned with secondary details. It was not of first importance for the gospel they were retelling whether the centurion sent his servants to speak to Jesus or came himself, whether Jesus healed one blind man or two, whether he did so on entering Jericho or on leaving Jericho, whether there was one crowing of the cock at Peter's denial or two, and so on. Similarly with

regard to the tensions between Acts and Galatians: as soon as we allow that both Luke and Paul had their own axes to grind, were writing from their own perspectives, to make their own points, the divergences cease to be much of a problem. The problem, in fact, is not the divergences themselves but the threat they pose to a certainty of knowledge about what actually happened, what Jesus actually said or did. The lust for certainty undermines faith precisely because it makes faith dependent on the accuracy of such details. If indeed Christian faith is equally dependent on whether Jesus rode into Jerusalem on one donkey or two as it is on the claim that Jesus was raised from the dead after three days, then faith is indeed vulnerable. If it is equally important to faith whether Jesus was crucified on or before Passover as it is that Jesus was crucified "for our sins," then faith becomes dependent to a frightening degree on the findings of the historian and archaeologist. If the whole of faith is indeed a seamless robe, so that to pull one thread is to cause the whole to disintegrate, what sort of faith is that? The truth is, as anyone who has taught students from a fundamentalist background will testify, that the all-or-nothing approach is all too often pastorally disastrous. All too often the slippery slope threat becomes a self-fulfilling prophecy, as good students find that the text forces them to question one or two minor points and conclude that since they can no longer hold to the all, the only alternative for them is nothing.

In short, to make faith dependent on matters of little or minor consequence for the biblical writers themselves is to exalt a particular understanding of faith above scripture and to destroy faith itself. This is why terms like inerrancy and infallibility applied to all the statements of the Bible are so unsuitable. They put the emphasis in the wrong places, they make the word of God subservient to a narrow human logic, they encourage a weak and immature faith that has not yet begun to discern what are the things which really matter.

IV

To sum up, if it is indeed the case that fundamentalism is driven by the desire for certainty, then, despite fundamentalism's other admirable concerns, the price of such certainty has to be reckoned with. It is the price of confusing the human words that bring God's word to expression with God's word itself, the making of an icon into an idol. It is the price of absolutizing the particularity of God's word that renders it all the less able to speak to the particularities of other ages and generations. It is the price of merging the rich harmony of the different kinds of literature in the Bible into a single monotone. It is the price of making salvation dependent on a closely defined meaning for texts whose meaning is not susceptible to such certainty. It is the price of losing the distinctive message of different texts. It is the price of making salvation dependent on an all-or-nothing attitude that so often condemns the one who has been so taught to nothing.

In short, the price of fundamentalism is too high.

8. THE BIBLE AND SCHOLARSHIP: BRIDGING THE GAP

Is THEOLOGY A THREAT TO FAITH? There are still students who come to departments of theology and/or religious studies in British universities who have been warned that studying theology at university level will be harmful to their faith.

And indeed there are students who find this to be the case. They have been discouraged from asking searching questions. And when such questions are asked, as they must be at university-level education, they begin to find the foundations shifting under their feet. Not so much by the answers that might be given, but by the fact that the questions have to be asked, hard questions that cannot be ducked or dismissed.

Or they have been told that truth is a seamless robe, so that to doubt any part of it is to doubt the whole. And when they find doubts arising, even on some minor point, they follow the logic that they were taught, and begin to doubt the whole.

But most students who come to academic theology with a living faith find that the study of the Bible at university level is an exhilarating, eye-opening experience. The asking of searching questions helps to inform and even correct their early or inherited faith formulations, to deepen and mature their faith.

They also find that a living faith is what makes academic theology so exciting and sometimes life changing. Of course, theology can be studied as just another academic subject, with interesting intellectual puzzles to be solved, facts to be learned, and questions to be debated with like-minded intellects. But such theology is a pale shadow of the real thing. For the real thing is dealing with the big questions of life and meaning. It can only be tackled existentially, by those not only eager to ask questions of the subject matter, but willing also to be questioned by the subject matter.

A faith that is closed to question and dialogue will never grow. A faith open to instruction and reformulation is a faith eager to go on from the A-B-C of its beginnings, a faith on the way to maturity.

And if this is true for university students, it is true also for the churches at large. Too often preachers lack a proper respect for their congregations. They are afraid to preach on difficult subjects or to ask questions hard to answer. They fear to disturb the faith of their congregations. And all too often there are many in these congregations crying out in the silence of their hearts for answers to questions too difficult for them to deal with on their own. By closing their congregations off from the resources that scholarship provides the preachers leave them to sink or swim alone.

Let me give some examples of how scholarship can function as an ally and instructor of faith.

1. Scholarship can save us from the wilder excesses of "popular" scholarship

Christians will hardly need reminding that there are some very wild theories about Jesus and the beginnings of Christianity running around its fringes. The trouble is that it is usually these theories that catch the headlines in the media or are picked up by researchers for television programs on Christianity. It's understandable, I suppose, since the objective of these articles and programs is to be interesting. Whether they represent an accurate picture of scholarship on the subject in question is evidently a matter of less moment. The sensational is all! That's what secures the readers/viewers (not to mention the advertising revenue). I have had occasion to protest at the irresponsibility of some television presentations in the past—to little avail, I fear.

So we've had the origins of Christianity explained by the magic mushroom! The Dead Sea Scrolls had hardly begun to be published when (inevitably) there were those who found in them the answer to the silent years of Jesus' upbringing and before his baptism by John: Where was he all that time? In the Qumran community, of course! Or the Bible is a giant codebook, whose cipher has only now been broken, and reveals now such information as Jesus' marriage to Mary Magdalene and their parenting of several children!

Fortunately, when such way-out theories are propounded there are usually a number of well-informed scholars on hand to set the record straight—if the newspaper or TV company bothers to consult them, that is. And even then, by the time the letter signed by an impressive array of the most respected authorities in the field is received or published, it is too late for many of the more gullible. The damage has been done.

More challenging is the new view that radically challenges traditional views of Jesus and Christian origins and which captures a number of scholars who have earned respect. Here is where the student or the thinking church needs the help of scholars who are as thoroughly grounded in the subject matter and who can therefore put the new view to an appropriately critical testing.

The best example of this in recent years is the impact of the Jesus Seminar in California. Through shrewd use of the media themselves, the findings of the Seminar have been widely publicized, though too often presented as more representative of the sweep of New Testament scholarship than is actually the case.

One of their principal findings/claims is that Jesus was primarily a teacher of wisdom, whose main mode of teaching was in aphorisms and parables. For several of the leading members of the Seminar this finding is the outcome of a belief that the Galilee of Jesus was quite distinct from the more southerly Judea, centered on Jerusalem and the Temple. Galilee, it is argued, had been settled by a mixed population following the transportations of the residents of the Northern Kingdom (Israel) to Assyria. So Galilee had become much more Gentile in character ("Galilee of the Gentiles"!). It had Hellenistic cities built in it—Sepphoris and Tiberias. It was much more urbanized than had previously been thought. It was such information which had provided the basis for one of the more infamous monographs of the Nazi period in Germany, arguing that Jesus was a Galilean and *not* a Jew!—a theory attractive to Nazi audiences.

Add to this the fact that Sepphoris lay just over the hill from Nazareth (only five kilometers distant), and was being rebuilt during Jesus' youth, and a quite appealing picture begins to emerge. A picture of the young Jesus mixing with the Hellenized citizens of Sepphoris on market days, or of helping to build the new theater (now uncovered by archaeologists)—as a carpenter, of course—but presumably drinking in some of the atmosphere, and perhaps attending performances. "Hypocrite," after all, basically means "play-actor." So where might Jesus have learned such language?

Add to this also the fact that a fair amount of Jesus' aphoristic/proverbial teaching seems to echo the criticisms of society attributed to wandering Cynic philosophers. And the fact that some famous Cynics are remembered as coming from Gadara to the east of the Jordan. Out of this potent brew a fascinating possibility emerges: that Jesus was himself like a wandering Cynic, that what he taught was influenced as much (or more) by Cynic thought than by his Jewish heritage, and even that what he taught was a kind of Cynicism.

What is the student or the person in the pew to make of all this when confronted by it in what appears to be a well-informed article in the press or program on TV? It is precisely here that knowledge of scholarship can provide the necessary response. The way to answer the challenging questions of scholarship is to provide or consult better scholarship. In this case archaeology has come to the aid of the perplexed believer. The most recent finds repay close attention.

First, it is now clear that Galilee was devastated by the Assyrian conquest. It was depopulated, but not repopulated. The evidence of villages being reestablished does not begin to appear till the end of the second and beginning of the first centuries B.C.E. That is when the now independent kingdom of Judea reconquered Galilee—and resettled it. The population at the time of Jesus was predominantly and properly described as "Jewish."

Second, the archaeological evidence of Galilee for the time of Jesus includes many examples of what one archaeologist has described as the four indicators of Jewish identity. These are ritual baths (*miqwaoth*), stone vessels (which do not communicate impurity), absence of pig bones, and burial practices distinctive of Jews. The inhabitants were evidently devout Jews, careful for the most part to observe the Torah.

Third, the same evidence is found in the two cities, Sepphoris and Tiberias. At the same time, they lack extensive evidence of most of the signs of Hellenistic culture. They were only "lightly Hellenized." In fact, they were much smaller and unlike the major Hellenistic cities elsewhere in the region, like Caesarea Maritima (on the coast), or Scythopolis (south of the Sea of Galilee), or Caesarea Philippi. They were administrative centers for the tetrarch, Herod Antipas, provincial capitals. Not the sort of places to evidence the kind of luxury that attracted Cynic hostility. And indeed we know of no Cynics actually functioning as such in Galilee.

Add the serious question marks that hang over the date of the theater in Sepphoris (probably not built till the second half of the first century C.E.). And most of the pillars of the wilder hypotheses regarding Jesus the non-Jew, Jesus the Cynic, have been so heavily undermined as to be able to bear little or no weight.

The answer to threatening scholarship is not to denounce all scholarship, but better scholarship.

2. Scholarship can save us from damaging features of our own (Christian) traditions

Protestants are heirs to the recognition that the developments of historic Christianity were not always for the best, and could go seriously wrong. This recognition that the church needs to be properly critical of its past—*semper reformanda* (always needing to be reformed)—is a crucial part of being "Protestant."

The Enlightenment, whatever wrong directions it took Western culture in, was also important for a similar reason. It taught us all that to accept assertions simply on some august authority is never going to be enough for the mind eager to discover and to delve deeper into truth. We have to appropriate our heritage critically, otherwise we simply compound any errors or imbalances of its earlier expressions. To be critical, of course, is not the same as to criticize. It does not mean finding fault, as though that was an end in itself. It means to scrutinize, to check and test for ourselves, and if faults are discovered, to seek to rectify them. It is the best kind of pedagogy. And to be properly critical—too many "critics" forget this—means also to be *self*-critical.

Now it so happens that Western Christianity, or better, Christian scholarship, has one of the best records in the exercise of self-criticism of all academic disciplines. Because it has had to defend its right to a place in the academy in an era of increasing secularization, it has learned that it must be totally honest about itself, its presuppositions and claims. Its language must be as transparent as possible.

It is that academic dialogue which helps keep Christian scholars honest. But it also helps Christian scholarship to maintain its place within the academy and to demand that its voice be heard in the forums of public debate. And it is that openness to criticism that helps secure the right of Christians to proclaim their gospel, and helps to ensure that what is said is able to be heard, its language understandable by those outside the Christian tradition.

Probably the best example of Christian self-criticism in recent decades is the realization that Christianity had some measure of responsibility for the Holocaust.

One of the most distressing features of historic Christianity has been the virulent strain of anti-semitism that runs through it from early days. "Anti-Semitism" is probably not the best term to use, since it implies a hatred of the Jewish (Semitic) *race*, and that only became a feature in the nineteenth century. Prior to that a Jew could escape persecution by conversion. The antipathy was directed toward Judaism rather than Jewishness, if we might put it so; that is, against the religion, not the race. So the better term is probably "anti-Judaism."

The roots of Christian anti-Judaism lie in the very early claim that Christianity has "superseded" Judaism. From the second century on, the loudest voices among Christian apologists claimed that the old covenant was dead and gone, and with it Judaism's claim to continuing existence. Christianity was now the new Israel. There was no rationale or place for the old Israel.

This attitude continued for decades after the Second World War in the description of first-century Judaism as "late Judaism." The underlying rationale is that first-century Judaism was *late* Judaism, because the only proper function for Judaism was to prepare for the coming of Christ and of Christianity. Once Jesus had come, once Christianity had appeared, there was no further need for Judaism, no further role for Judaism. It may baffle us now how the phrase could have been used for so long, by highly respectable Christian biblical scholars. But it was indeed so used, and still appears in some textbooks.

It wasn't just this dismissive attitude that constituted Christian anti-Judaism. Much more serious, however, was the strain of antagonism, even hatred, that followed in its train. Jews were accused of not simply rejecting their Messiah, but of killing him. They were treated as "Christ-killers," as deicides, the scum of the earth. There are Polish Jews alive today who can recall being abused in their pre-war childhood as Christ-killers. The pogroms that often followed continue to be a black stain on Christian history. One of the most gut-wrenching features of Nazi persecution of Jews in the 1930s and '40s was that they could quote Martin Luther in justification. Synagogues could be pulled down and Jews killed on the authority of one of Christianity's greatest sons.

So one of the redeeming features of Western Christianity in the second half of the twentieth century has been its repudiation of that heritage. The Second Vatican Council, itself led by the wave of theological and biblical scholarship that had grown steadily in the previous decades, showed the way by condemning as false all such accusations and attacks on Jews in the name of Christ. And in his 2000 expression of repentance for Christianity's history of anti-Judaism, Pope John Paul II spoke for all Christians. All this has come about because it has been possible for scholars to take a properly critical look at Christianity's own history.

But now, what do we do with those texts in the New Testament that seem to give some ground to these ancient expressions of anti-Judaism? What about the sermons in Acts where Jews are accused of crucifying Jesus (Acts 2:23)? What about the words of the crowd before Pilate in Matthew 27: "His blood be on us and on our children" (27:25)? What about the passages in John's

Gospel where "the Jews" are shown as resolutely hostile to Jesus and described by Jesus as children of the devil (John 8:44)? I have sat, cringing, under a famous pulpit not far from where I write, when John 8 was the reading for the day, and the exposition could only see an unqualified condemnation of Jews and Judaism.

What do we do? Do we simply read the text at face value and accept, in effect, that the strain of Christian anti-Judaism is rooted deep within the New Testament itself? God forbid. It's precisely at such a point that we need to be able to turn to specialists in these texts to counsel us on how we should hear them. And how does such counsel run?

It points, for example, to the historical context in which these words were written. We naturally read them on the assumption that these were the words of the dominant religion (Christianity) denigrating its lesser rival (Judaism). That is how it has been for most of the last two millennia, when these words have been heard within cultures long shaped by the dominant Christendom. But the situation was very different in the first two centuries. The new Christian movement for most of that time was operating in small house groups, whereas Judaism was the long-established, and usually widely respected, national religion of the Jews, with the synagogue sometimes serving as a major architectural edifice in one of the main squares of a city where Jews were populous. In such a context, the smaller, newer movement may understandably use strong language to shape and defend its emerging identity. It should not be read in the same tones in a different historical context, when the boot is on the other foot.

It notes that any accusation that Jesus was crucified by Jews is factually inaccurate. Under the Roman Empire the Jews never had that power. Crucifixion was a peculiarly Roman means of executing slaves and traitors, and they jealousy retained its use within their own power. So language like Acts 2:23 (read it carefully) has to be read as an imprecise way of attributing some responsibility for Jesus' death to Jews. But not to all Jews. And certainly not to all Jews of all time. Even Matthew 27:25 limits the blood-guilt to one generation, not to the third or fourth generation more typical of Jewish self-condemnation (Exod. 34:7). Any guilt indicated applies only to the people present at the time, and particularly the Temple authorities. As regards John's Gospel, most recognize that the phrase, "the [hostile] Jews," refers to the Jewish authorities in their strongest antagonism to the new small movement related to Jesus. But remember, there are more or less an equal number of references to "the Jews," meaning the crowd, in between, whose final response to Messiah Jesus is still contested and awaited.

Specialist scholarship is also able to note that the language of accusation and vilification which makes such passages so grievous to us today was much more run of the mill at the time of writing. We flinch at a canonical text that can call blessed those who mercilessly kill the infant children of their enemies (Ps. 137:8-9). The curses that the Qumran covenanter was expected to utter against outsiders, fellow Jews, are blood curdling. And we should not forget that Paul could speak of competing Jewish Christian missionaries with scathing dismissal and crude allusion (2 Cor. 11:13-15; Gal. 5:12). In days when heretics could be burnt at the stake (for their own good!) and the Pope vilified in terms that seem outrageous to almost all Christians today, the fierceness of the polemic against the stronger Jewish groups in Mediterranean cities would hardly seem strange. But for us today, with consciences sensitized by the horrors perpetrated in the past in the name of religion, it is no longer possible to read such texts without something of a shudder.

So what do we do? Simply read such texts when they occur in the lectionary, without comment? Here we need to look to expert translators: Can the texts be properly translated in terms that are less offensive and misleading today? Or we look to expert liturgists: Can we ensure that such texts are never read without comment and at least minimal explanation? Or we look to responsible preachers to ensure that some time, some space is given to explaining how historical texts need to be heard with historical sensitivity and not just read as though they expressed timeless truths.

In all this the church looks to its scholars to inform and to advise.

3. Scholarship can save us from the dangerous tendencies of fundamentalism

One of the main thrusts of Christian fundamentalism is good: it wants to insist that there are key issues and beliefs which are fundamental to Christian identity and faith. For example, the reality of God as far more complex than can be expressed in a straightforward monotheism. The centrality of Jesus as the clearest expression (embodiment) of what God is like. The role of the New Testament scriptures as providing the definitive definition (canon) of Christianity.

The trouble with fundamentalism, however, is that it itself is a slippery slope. From such assertions about the fundamentals as most Christians would accept, it finds it necessary to become more and more prescriptive.

(a) Fundamentalism wants to see truth as a whole, and all interconnected. So not just the central claims need to be affirmed, but a much larger range of supporting claims. As the rabbis sought to build a fence around the Torah, to ensure that the Torah itself would not be breached, so fundamentalists seek to build a fence around the fundamentals. And as the fence around the Torah often became as if not more important than the Torah in the disputes that the fence building engendered, so often with Christian fundamentalists. When everything is fundamental we have forgotten one of the gifts of the Spirit most to be cherished—the ability to discern what really matters from issues about which one can (and should) be indifferent (e.g., Rom. 12:2; Phil. 1:10).

Here the churches need professionally skilled and sensitive leadership, such as Paul provided. He did not treat the words of Jesus forbidding divorce simply as a blanket prescription for all time and all circumstances. His counsel in 1 Corinthians 7 was more realistically lenient. Similarly, he did not cite the authority of the Lord, that the laborer was worthy of his hire, as a prescription to be obeyed willy-nilly. In 1 Corinthians 9 he explains that his own priorities and the circumstances of his mission pointed to a different practice. Similarly, when confronted with an issue where fundamentals were at stake—covenant identity on the one hand (as marked by laws of clean and unclean, and the sabbath), and Christian liberty on the other—he did not ruthlessly press the logic of one or other fundamental. Rather, in Romans 14:1—15:6 he followed the logic of love and called both for full respect for the view that he himself had abandoned and for willingness to limit the liberty that he himself so cherished.

The tendency of fundamentalism is to suppress or override such sensitivities and divergences, to insist on conformity and consistency without regard to the circumstances such as Paul displayed. Fundamentalism needs to learn to listen to the voices of scholars who are as well or better versed in the scriptures than its own gurus and who recognize the shade as well as the light, the diversity as well as the unity in the New Testament writings.

(b) Fundamentalism wants to see truth in black-and-white terms. It tends to be eager, even desperate for *certainty*. It wants to know the certainty of that in which it believes. So the tendency is to insist on certain formulae, or rituals, on the understanding that they alone provide the certainty that they lust after. A typical argument, which trades also on the first feature (a), is that if we cannot be certain at one point of faith, then we cannot be certain at any point of faith. Certainty is the glue that is thought to prevent the whole pattern of faith from unraveling. And so the necessity of certainty becomes in effect yet another of the fundamentals to be preserved as all costs.

In this not least we need to hear loud and clear the wiser voices of those long steeped in the Christian tradition who warn us that such certainty is never possible—particularly not in formulations. Words are at best an imperfect form of rendering meaning and effecting communication, because individual words mean slightly (sometimes very) different things to different people. There is an element of interpretation in the hearing and grasping of any communication. Those who are familiar with the problems of translation from one language to another know full well that there is no such thing as a perfect translation.

And when it comes to talk of God and of the work of God, how on earth can human language be adequate to speak of God and of that work? It is the scholars who are able to remind us that most descriptions of God and of God's work have a heuristic element. That is, they use language to indicate something of what is there, but not in any hope of providing an adequate description of it. When, for example, the Fathers distinguish the eternal "generation" of the Son from the "procession" of the Spirit, it is not because they know what these words signify. They know that there is a difference to be taken into account, but the words used are simply labels to indicate the fact of the difference, not to describe the difference itself. The simple fact is that it is not possible to achieve certainty in the verbal definition of any of the fundamental elements of the Christian faith.

But should that concern us? Do "certainty" and "faith" actually go together? It is Paul, after all, who reminds us that "we walk by faith, not by sight" (2 Cor. 5:7). The point is that "certainty" belongs to a different "language game" from "faith." Certainty is a term that lives and moves and has its being in the artificial world of mathematics. When there are only a very limited number of variables, then it may indeed be possible to achieve a "certain" outcome—QED. But "faith" belongs with the language of relationship. Its partners are trust, confidence, assurance. At no point in our typical daily lives is it realistic to speak in terms of "certainty"—whether eating beef, or crossing the road, or getting married. But trust, assurance—faith—is what enables us to live at all. A community that makes "certainty" its watchword is very different from the community where "faith" is the watchword. I'm very confident that the latter is a much more appropriate description of the community around Jesus, the communities established by Paul, than the former.

(c) Things begin to become rather frightening when fundamentalism slides still further down its slippery slope. For a characteristic of the modern fundamentalisms of all the three main monotheistic religions (Judaism, Christianity, Islam) is the conviction that their fundamentals are *alone* right. Any who disagree with them are therefore simply wrong. For the fundamentalist, I cannot be *right* unless you who disagree with me are *wrong*. Fundamentalists by predisposition do not recognize that there may be different ways of expressing what is actually the same, much more complex truth. Since their faith depends on the certainty of that which they believe, any alternative or counter faith is a threat to that certainty. The tendency of fundamentalism, in other words, is to build monolithic blocks of faith, all held together with the same certainties, and all denying the validity of alternative formulations of faith, even within the same religion, even of the same fundamentals.

The real horror begins when the logic is further played out (one of the curses of the fundamentalist tendency is its reliance on a rigid logic). When the alternative, or different viewpoint is seen as a threat to faith (faith thus rigidly conceived). When the alternative or different formulation is seen as culpable heresy. When the securing of the fence around the fundamentals, the safeguard of faith's certainties, are seen to require a uniform obedience from the wider society, and to justify violent opposition to and suppression of any alternatives.

That is the fundamentalism of the Taliban in Afghanistan. But in their heart of hearts, many Jewish fundamentalists long for the restoration of the theocratic state centered on the Jerusalem Temple, just as many Christian fundamentalists long for something equivalent to the Puritan Commonwealth. But it is also the fundamentalism of the Inquisition and the stake!

My point here is that it requires a good knowledge of the key texts of the Bible, and of the history of Christianity, if we are to be aware of such fatal tendencies in Christian fundamentalism. A better knowledge of the texts, in their historical context, would make it clearer that Jesus and Paul were themselves opposed to such fundamentalist tendencies. A better knowledge of Christian history would remind us of how often Christians in the past have gone well down that slippery slope, with consequences most now abhor. And it is precisely the work of scholarship to make the wider church aware of the character of "New Testament Christianity" and of the lessons to be drawn from history.

***

I have focused my primary attention on the traffic going only one way across the bridge (between academy and church)—the contribution of scholarship to the needs and concerns of the church. Perhaps too much attention. So let me conclude by taking up one of my initial points and bringing it more fully into focus—and thus recall that the bridge is two way.

I have already stressed that academic theology needs the vitality of living faith to breathe life into what otherwise would most likely be dead and deadly dull discussions. The point is that theology, including academic theology, is itself about faith. A large part of it has to take account of value systems and ethical principles in discussion of major issues of politics and medicine. It can hardly exclude the role of worship and liturgy in the whole business. Faith and history cannot be put into separate compartments, because the history of Christianity, of its influence in the world, is the history of faith.

So it is important for faith to speak as faith, not just as scholarship. For it has played, and needs to continue to play, an important part in the shaping of individual and community lives, and in informing the values and the principles that enable us to decide wisely, at both public and private level. To bracket out faith, as some scholars do, is to remove the heart from theology (or religious studies) and to leave it gasping for the breath of life in an alien environment.

To put the same point another way: faith needs to enter into a genuine dialogue with a whole range of academic disciplines and policymakers. It should not only be reactive, responding to an agenda set by others, on their terms. It needs boldly to insist that it, too, has items for the agenda of public and community discussion, and to press the case that a community, academic or whatever, which does not have a faith dimension, is a deprived community, functioning on only three cylinders.

The point which ties the whole of what I have been trying to say together is that the faith which has allowed itself to be instructed in the areas outlined above, by its own Christian scholarship not least, is all the more likely to gain a hearing for what is its real and most enduring message. A properly self-critical faith commends itself to its audience by enabling them thus to recognize faith's own proper humility.

9. WHAT MAKES A GOOD EXPOSITION?

WHAT IS A GOOD EXPOSITION? What are the criteria by which a good exposition may be recognized and applauded or critiqued? As a biblical scholar, more than a preacher, my primary concern is with the specific question of hermeneutics: How to *interpret* the biblical text? What are the appropriate criteria for a wise reading of a biblical text? Since a good *interpretation*, one may presume, is integral to, and arguably the basis of a good *exposition*, this is an appropriate way to make inroads into the larger question. In what follows I have in mind primarily the New Testament, but most of what follows could apply also *mutatis mutandis* to the Old Testament.

Of course, to ask how best to interpret the Bible is not a new question; the same question has been posed in varying terms from before the beginning of Christianity. But it is in the last half-millennium that the answers which still shape the current debate have been most clearly articulated. Treatment of biblical, patristic, and medieval canons of interpretation would require several more lectures—more themes for future years. We will limit ourselves here to the period that has most shaped Scotland's own religious and cultural heritage.

We start, then, by observing that since the Renaissance in Western Europe it is possible to distinguish three overlapping phases or emphases in the quest for a good interpretation, the basis of a good exposition.

1. The Givenness of the Historical Text

The Renaissance gave us two lasting criteria for the appropriate handling of historical texts—historical philology and textual criticism.

Historical philology. The Renaissance was characterized, first, by the urge to read the classics not simply in translation or compendia but in their original tongues. This compulsion gave birth to the new science of *historical philology*—the careful discerning of the meaning of words and sentences in the original language of the text, by reference to the way these words and such sentences were used at the time of writing. Francesco Petrarch (1304–1374), the father of the Renaissance, led the way.

It was Petrarch who first understood fully that antiquity was a civilization apart and, understanding it, outlined a program of classically oriented studies that would lay bare its spirit. The focus of Petrarch's insight was language: if classical antiquity was to be understood in its own terms it would be through the speech with which the ancients had communicated their thoughts. This meant that the languages of antiquity had to be studied as the ancients had used them and not as vehicles for carrying modern thoughts.[1]

It would be a mistake to treat this development lightly, or to assume that it is so obvious that it requires no emphasis. On the contrary, its absolutely fundamental character for any and all reading of biblical texts should always provide one of the beginning points for the hermeneutical task. For were it not for the work of our Renaissance forefathers and their successors we would be unable to read these texts as texts; the Hebrew, Aramaic, and Greek characters would be indecipherable, little more than strange squiggles on the page. In order to be read, these squiggles must first be identified as the ancient languages they are. And in order to convey meaning they must be read within the context of the language usage of their time.

For Friedrich Schleiermacher, the founder of modern hermeneutics, this was the "first canon" of interpretation: "A more precise determination of any point in a given text must be decided on the basis of the use of language common to the author and his original public."[2] Similarly Rudolf Bultmann, the greatest of twentieth-century Protestant Neutestamentlers: "every text speaks in the language of its time and of its historical setting. This the exegete must know; therefore, he must know the historical conditions of the language of the period out of which the text he is to interpret has arisen."[3]

We of the twenty-first century, therefore, dare not forget how indebted we are to the great philologists of earlier centuries, how dependent we are on the fruit of their labor stacked so neatly and so accessibly in our modern lexica. Without such fundamental aids we would hardly know where to start the hermeneutical task.

The corollary of most immediate consequence for us is that the language usage at the time of writing is bound to be determinative in at least substantial degree for our understanding of the language used in the ancient text. The point is perhaps clearer if we put it in terms of translation. The point is simply that there are such things as bad, or even (dare one say it?) *wrong* translations. Presumably even radically postmodern teachers of ancient languages and texts do not dissent from this, and postmodern examiners of such translations mark them down like any other teacher.

To say this, of course, is not to ignore the fact that there is no such thing as a single correct translation of a foreign-language text, far less a perfect translation. Anyone who has had to engage in translation knows that there is no translation without interpretation, that interpretation is an inescapable part of translation.[4] Individual words in both languages have ranges of meaning (polysemic, multivalent), and there is no word in one language whose range and cultural overtones exactly match those of a word in the other language. The abundant diversity of modern translations of the Bible is all the illustration needed.

None of this, however, alters the point that the original-language text is what is to be translated/interpreted, and that each translation has to justify itself as a translation of that text. The historical text cannot determine the exact translation, but unless the text functions as some kind of norm for the translation, unless it is seen to provide a limiting factor on the diversity of acceptable translations, then translation itself becomes irresponsible.

Textual criticism. The second great fruit of Renaissance scholarship was the science of *textual criticism*, the skill of reconstructing from the variant manuscripts available so far as possible the original texts, by identifying and correcting the corruptions caused by centuries of Christian transmission and editing. Here again it is easy to forget how much better off we are than the ancient schools and academies, where before discussion of a text could proceed the class had to agree what the correct text was. Here again, it is easy to forget our indebtedness to the Masoretes of old and to Erasmus and his successors for the texts on which we rely for a minimal assurance that we are all actually reading the same text.

Of course we should not deceive ourselves into thinking that textual criticism gives us "the original text." At best our Hebrew Bible texts and our Aland Greek texts are eclectic in their readings. And we should be equally cautious about talking of the "final form" of the text. Alttestamentlers are constantly confronted with the fluidity of the textual form, with Masoretic text, LXX, and now Qumran Bible often pulling in different directions. Neutestamentlers, too, despite the relative firmness of their text, need to appreciate more than many do that textual variations are not simply to be counted as scribal errors but often attest the way the text was being read in different communities.[5] Strictly speaking, the text was not fixed but, rather, bears witness to its character as living tradition, a tradition that grew and developed.

I think here of the debate between James Sanders and Brevard Childs on how a term like "canonical criticism" should be interpreted: whether what we have in view is the final, canonical form of the text (Childs), or the process by which texts heard to speak authoritatively grew into our present biblical texts (Sanders).[6] As one who sympathizes more with Sanders,[7] I want to see scripture as part of living tradition, to stress (and explore) the continuities between precanonical tradition, canonical text and postcanonical tradition, and not least as the last is attested by textual variations themselves.

All that said, however, it still remains true for the Neutestamentler that the Greek text (even in its modern, eclectic form) is a *given*, given as a historical text. Which is to say that the text is *normative* in regard to any and every translation and to any and every interpretation made of it. Which also means that the Greek text must inevitably be allowed to determine and limit the range and diversity of translation, and so also the range and diversity of interpretation read from or into the text. Without ceding such control and restriction to the text itself, translator and interpreter are always liable to manipulate the text and to sacrifice that legitimacy which only the text can give to translation and interpretation.

In other words, it is simply important to recognize *the character of historical texts as historical texts*. For the Greek text read as an historical text (interpretations as well as translations taking account of accidence, syntax and idiom of the day) inevitably functions as a norm for legitimacy of modern readings too. Without that basic recognition, the particular text becomes no more than a lump of potter's clay, vulnerable to being shaped entirely by the whim of the interpreter (potter). In short, the very identity of the text is at stake, and historical study and scholarly method are unavoidable if the New Testament is to be read at all.

2. The Meaning of the Text

If the first phase in the modern search for criteria for a good interpretation focuses on the *givenness* of the text, the second phase focuses on the *meaning* of the text. I focus here on the themes of "plain meaning" and "intended meaning."

Plain meaning. As the Renaissance introduced the first phase, so we could say that the Reformation introduced the second. For the Reformation was marked precisely by its break with the medieval tradition of exegesis in that it gave priority to the *literal sense,* over against the medieval openness to the text's polyvalency of meaning, as expressed particularly through allegorical interpretation. Already in 1496, John Colet, in his lectures on the

Pauline letters in the University of Oxford, provided the paradigm for the Reformation, by maintaining that the text should be expounded simply in terms of the *sensus literalis* (as understood in its historical context).[8] Martin Luther likewise insisted on the plain or literal or historical sense and dismissed medieval allegorizing as so much rubbish.[9] Most influential of all was John Calvin's emphasis on the plain meaning of the text, with his sequence of biblical commentaries providing classic examples of philological-historical interpretation. As Calvin himself put it, with typical Reformation bluntness, in beginning his treatment of Paul's allegory in Galatians 4: "Let us know, then, that the true meaning of Scripture is the natural and simple one, and let us embrace and hold it resolutely. Let us not merely neglect as doubtful, but boldly set aside as deadly corruptions, those pretended expositions which lead us away from the literal sense."[10]

This, in effect, was the second principle of biblical interpretation to emerge in the modern period—*the primacy of the plain meaning of the text*. In so saying, of course, it must always be borne in mind what had been familiar from the early Patristic debates: that the "plain meaning" may include allegory or symbolism when the particular text is "plainly" allegorical or symbolical.[11] But for Calvin, the abuse of scripture by those "who played this game of allegorizing Scripture" made it essential to reaffirm the key point, the primacy of "plain" meaning, in more antithetical terms.

That said, however, we should not allow the Reformation antithesis to degenerate into a naïvely historicist plea for a literal "literalism." For plain meaning as appealed to by Calvin was not always the literal or verbal sense *tout simple*, but a meaning determined in part by Calvin's faith, by the rule of faith—"plain" to those who shared Calvin's faith. "Plain meaning" as it has operated in practice is already in some measure a product of the reader's perspective, a negotiated outcome. Kathryn Greene-McCreight concludes from her study of the subject that a "plain sense" reading "involves negotiating between the constraints of verbal sense and [what she calls] Ruled reading . . . respecting the verbal and textual data of the text as well as privileging the claims about God and Jesus Christ which cohere with the Rule of faith." "The 'plain sense' reading will result from a conjunction of verbal sense and prior understanding of the subject matter of the text provided by the conception of the Christian faith supplied by the apostolic tradition."[12] Similarly with the Reformation concept of Scripture as self-interpreting (*sui ipsius interpres*). For it implies reading the obscure passages in the light of the passages whose meaning is "plain." But we must always ask, "plain" to whom? For what is "plain" to you is obscure to me, and vice versa; what is plain to your tradition is obscure to my tradition, and vice versa. The fact is that our reading of the text is not determined solely by the text itself.

Nevertheless, there is a "bottom line" that needs to be restated and defended here. That is the basic idea of communication, that *communication is only meaningful if it communicates meaning*. Of course, such a basic model of social relationships has to be endlessly qualified by the reality of irony, deception, misunderstanding, and the like. But these are *qualifications* of the basic character of language as *communication of meaning*. Without the conviction that at least the main point and thrust of what we wish to communicate is in fact communicated, no communication could hope to rise above the first stumbling phrases of someone trying to speak in a new foreign language. Without that conviction all lecturers and authors should abandon the pretense that they can inform and persuade. And the same principle applies to ancient texts and our attempts to understand them. As Hans-Georg Gadamer notes, it "has always been a principle of all textual interpretation: namely that a text must be understood in its own terms";[13] and that must mean in the first place, in the terms which the text itself most plainly invites.

Intended meaning. In the Romantic revival the focus shifted from "plain meaning" to *intended meaning*, and to authorial intention. The hermeneutical objective was to enter into the creative experience of inspiration from which the writing was born, and called for a sense of psychological empathy with the author as creator, interpretation being conceived as recreation of the creative act. This was the other side of the art of hermeneutics for Schleiermacher. ". . . understanding a speech always involves two moments: to understand what is said in the context of the language with its possibilities, and to understand it as a fact in the thinking of the speaker." Later he distinguishes between "the historical and divinatory, objective and subjective reconstruction of a given statement." "By leading the interpreter to transform himself, so to speak, into the author, the divinatory method seeks to gain an immediate comprehension of the author as an individual."[14]

In the twentieth century this objective was justifiably criticized, as "the intentional fallacy."[15] The interpreter should not be concerned with such issues, or allow speculations about the author's mood or historical context to determine the text's meaning. The intention of the author was a private state of mind, which lay behind the text; to enter into that state of mind is neither possible nor necessary. Instead, the text should be allowed to speak for itself.

At the same time, it has proved impossible to dispense with the concept of intended meaning. How far the argument can be pushed in regard to a text consisting in separate oracles or aphorisms is a moot point. But the more substantial, evidently contrived and typically narrative text in effect compels the reader to think in such terms. If it has proved possible to dispense with the "real author" as inputting the intended meaning, the text itself requires us to speak of what Wolfgang Iser has designated the "implied author," that is, the author as inferred from the narrative itself, the rationale which has given the text its present structure and content. Similarly, Iser's twin concept of the "implied reader" is another way of speaking of the effect intended by the author, the meaning evidently intended to be conveyed by the text.[16]

In short, it is neither desirable nor necessary to dispense with the concept of authorial intention, but the realistic goal is the authorial intention *as entextualized*. As Francis Watson puts it, authorial intention "is to be understood not as some subjective occurrence lying behind the text but as the principle of the text's intelligibility," "is to be seen as primarily embodied in the words the author wrote."[17] It is the text as embodying that intention, as a communicative act between author and intended readers/auditors, to which attention is to be given.

3. The Hearing of the Text

The third phase in the ongoing quest for the meaning of a text can be identified most simply with postmodernism—postmodernism as marked by a shift from the text itself and the author behind the text to *the reader* of the text, from reading behind the text to reading in front of the text, from text as window to text as mirror. This hermeneutical shift is epitomized in reader-response theory, which no longer looks for meaning simply "in" the text, let alone by reference "behind" the text, but looks for meaning as created by the reader in the act of reading. Texts do not make meaning; readers make meaning. Texts do not dictate to readers; readers dictate to texts. In Stephen Moore's words, "Prior to the interpretive act, there is nothing definitive in the text to be discovered."[18]

Meaning is not in the past (when the text was produced) or in the text as an object, but meaning is produced in the reader's present when the text is read.[19] For reader-response critics meaning is not a content in the text that the historian simply discovers; meaning is an experience that occurs in the reading process.[20]

There is an obvious threat in all this to any ideas of canons for agreed meanings. If all meaning is contingent to each individual act of reading, then it would appear that every man, every woman makes his or her own meaning, and there is no generally acceptable criteria to enable us to judge whether one reading is good or bad, or wise or foolish, or better than another. In postmodernism pluralism is all.

However, in the debate over reader-response theory two constraints have been put forward. One is the perception of reader-response as more of a dialogue between text and reader, where the text has to be "heard," and listened to, lest reader-response deteriorate into the straightforward manipulation of the text to speak to the reader's agenda. In his debate with Stanley Fish, Iser in particular wishes to maintain an objective status for the text, that there is a "given" to be "mediated': "the 'something' which is to be mediated exists prior to interpretation, acts as a constraint on interpretation."[21] George Steiner's exposition of the "real presence" in a text is attempting to pull the debate in the same direction.[22]

The other is Fish's own recognition that reading is not a wholly isolated, individual experience. In his most influential work, he has emphasized that any reading is conditioned to at least some extent by the reading or interpretive community to which the individual reader belongs.[23] In reference to scriptural texts the emphasis is easily integrateable with an emphasis on the church, the community of faith, as the context within which the text is heard and its meaning perceived. Here the correlation with the "plain meaning" as determined by the rule of faith is obvious: the meaning heard within the community of faith will almost unavoidably accord with the *sensus communis*, the *sensus fidelium*.

With similar effect is Hans-Georg Gadamer's more subtle concept of a text's *Wirkungsgeschichte*, the "history of effect" of the text, the point being that the interpreter and the act of interpretation are themselves caught up in the flow of history, that historical text and interpreter are both part of a historical continuum. Consequently, the interpreter cannot stand above the tradition that links him or her to the past under study, but can only begin to understand adequately as being part of and through that tradition.[24] Gadamer's point is not to be reduced simply to the recognition that the interpreter stands within a history influenced by the text. The key term is actually the more elaborate phrase, *wirkungsgeschichtliches Bewusstsein*, "historically effected consciousness"; not historically *affected* but historically *effected* consciousness. Gadamer's point, then, is that the interpreter's consciousness, or preunderstanding, we might say, is not simply influenced by the text; rather, it has in some measure been brought into being by the text, is itself in some degree a product of the text; it is a consciousness of the text to be interpreted. Only because the interpreter's consciousness has been thus "effected" can it be "effectual in finding the right questions to ask."[25]

I have no wish to dispute any of this—far from it. It is important to understand the effective communicative act in terms of reception as well as of delivery. Prophecy is not simply a matter of inspired speech, but of the speech being received as prophecy. The biblical writings are scripture not simply because they were *theopneustos*, but because they were heard from the first as word of God. Meaning heard in a parable or aphorism depends to considerable extent on how the parable, the aphorism is heard.[26] No preaching can be effective without a responsive audience. For my own part, faith is an integral part of the critical theological dialogue that is the interpretation of the New

Testament. At this point my hermeneutical agenda overlaps extensively with that of my Durham colleagues Walter Moberly and Stephen Barton.[27]

My only concern in regard to the emphases brought to the fore by Fish and Gadamer is lest it be concluded that the meaningfulness of the biblical tradition can be appreciated only within the interpretive community (that is, the church), and within the living tradition (that is, the Christian tradition). This concern is twofold. First, lest scripture be wholly subsumed within tradition, whereas it seems necessary to acknowledge that within the church and within the flow of Christian tradition, the New Testament in particular must be accorded some sort of critical role. Precisely by virtue of the New Testament's pivotal testimony to the incarnation, the New Testament was bound to function as the *norma normans*, the canon within the canon of scripture and tradition, otherwise that pivotal testimony would be devalued and its canonical status be effectively lost.[28] It is this readiness for *self*-criticism in reference to tradition that marks out the Western church—its willingness to recognize and acknowledge when it has departed from its norm, whether in the condemnation of a Galileo or in its centuries-long tradition of anti-Semitism[29]—a dialogue of criticism which, it would appear, remains something of a barrier and bewilderment for the Christianity of East and South.

Second, in the emphases of Fish and Gadamer I perceive a certain risk of locking up the Bible once again within the churches, with a meaning heard clearly enough within the worshiping community, but unable to speak to the world outside, unable to dialogue effectively with other forms of knowledge given to us, and unable to be heard or understood because meaning is thought to reside (only?) in a reading within the continuum and community of meaning.[30] To seek thus to escape postmodernism's pluralism and relativity would significantly diminish the possibility of effective Christian apologetics and evangelism. But Christians belong not only to communities of faith; they also belong to diverse and overlapping communities, of workplace or residence or leisure; and unless they want to live a schizophrenic existence of two disconnected language-worlds, they must learn to speak a common language. A hermeneutic that effectively denies the possibility of the biblical message being heard outside the churches and in the forums of the world's discourses is a hermeneutic of irresponsibility and despair.

4. Hermeneutical Circles

The three phases or emphases that I have identified within the art of interpretation can be summed up in terms of the hermeneutical circle, or better, in terms of the different forms taken by the hermeneutical circle.

In its initial form the hermeneutical circle was the circularity of *part* and *whole*, already noted by Schleiermacher: the parts can only be understood in terms of the whole; but understanding of the whole is built up from the parts. As Schleiermacher was well aware, the "whole" was not simply the whole particular writing, but the whole language and historical reality to which the particular text belonged.[31] It is called a circle, because the hermeneutical process is unavoidably a movement back and forth around the circle, where understanding is ever provisional and subject to clarification and correction as the whole is illuminated by the parts and the part by the whole. As Schleiermacher's pupil, P. A. Boeckh, went on to point out, this hermeneutical circle "cannot be resolved in all cases, and can never be resolved completely." Boeckh continues:

> every single utterance is conditioned by an infinite number of circumstances, and it is therefore impossible to bring to clear communication. . . . Thus the task of interpretation is to reach as close an approximation as possible by gradual, step-by-step approximation; it cannot hope to reach the limit.[32]

A second form of the hermeneutical circle sends the interpreter back and forth between the *matter* of the text and the *speech* used to convey it, between Word and words, *Sache und Sprache*,[33] between *langue* and *parole*, signified and signifier.[34] This form of the hermeneutical procedure has been played out throughout the period reviewed above, particularly in the way in which again and again a definitive subject matter perceived through the text has been used to critique the wording of the text itself. One thinks, for example, of the gospel (*was treibet Christus*) serving as the critical scalpel for Luther,[35] or the universal ideals of Jesus indicating for nineteenth-century Liberalism an "essence" from which the merely particular could be stripped, or Rudolf Bultmann's "kerygma" providing the key for his demytholgizing program,[36] or "justification by faith" serving as the "canon within the canon" for Ernst Käsemann.[37] Or in recent Jesus research an instructive example is Tom Wright's repeated appeal to a metanarrative of Israel in exile and hoped-for return from exile as providing a hermeneutical echo chamber in which the various sayings of Jesus and stories about Jesus resonate with a meaning hardly evident on the face of the text.[38]

The third form of the hermeneutical circle is that between *reader* and *text*, as already implicit in Schleiermacher's recognition of a "psychological" dimension to hermeneutics.[39] Bultmann elaborated the point in his insistence that "there cannot be any such thing as presuppositionless exegesis." "A specific understanding of the subject matter of the text, on the basis of a 'life-relation' to it, is always presupposed by exegesis," hence the term, "pre-understanding."[40] Gadamer makes the same point in his striking "defence" of prejudice.[41]

The point is sometimes missed when more conservative biblical scholars deem it sufficient to declare their presuppositions before embarking on what most of their fellow scholars would regard as uncritical exegesis, as though the declaration of presuppositions somehow vindicated the exegesis itself (since "everyone has presuppositions"). But the point is not simply that any reading of a text is shaped by the preunderstanding brought to it. The point is rather that as the exegete moves around the hermeneutical circle between preunderstanding and text, the text reacts back upon the preunderstanding, both sharpening it and requiring of it revision at one or another point, and thus enabling a fresh scrutiny of the text, necessitating in turn a further revision of preunderstanding, and so on and on.

The most vicious form of the hermeneutical circle, however, has proved to be that between reader and text as it has been developed within postmodern literary criticism. Indeed, deconstructionist hermeneutics attempt in effect to undermine the whole procedure envisaged in the hermeneutical circle by suggesting that the reality is an infinite series of interlocking circles, where the search for meaning is neverending and the play between signifier and signified goes on *ad infinitum*. The image conjured up is of a computer game without an end; or of an Internet search into the infinity of cyberspace as Web pages direct to other Web pages in an endless sequence; or indeed of a computer hacker who has succeeded in so overloading a system that it crashes; or perhaps again of an academic colleague who always insists on the impossibility of any effective discussion of an academic subject or political policy without first resolving the problem of what human consciousness is. Intellectually challenging as such exercises are, they do not much assist in the living of life or the advance of knowledge or the building of community. To conceive the hermeneutical process as an infinitely regressive intertextuality is another counsel of despair that quickly reduces all meaningful communication to impossibility and all communication to a game of "trivial pursuit."

Perhaps it has been the image of a "circle" that has misled us, since it invites the picture of an endless "going round in circles." In fact, however, from its earliest use, the hermeneutical circles were always perceived as a progressive exercise, in which the circles, as it were, became smaller. Alternatively expressed, the circle was seen more as a spiral, the circle in effect as a three-dimensional cone, so that successive circlings resulted in a spiraling toward a common center. Wilhelm von Humboldt expressed the point well (though with nineteenth-century overconfidence) when he talked of history as "a critical practice through which [the historian] attempts to correct his preliminary impressions of the object until, through repeated reciprocal action, clarity as well as certainty emerge."[42] The point is made with regard to historical method, but it is equally applicable to hermeneutical method.

As readers of biblical texts that are also historical texts, therefore, we need not despair over the hermeneutical circle but can hope to find that the reality of a historical-critical, self-critical, community-critical scrutiny of these texts can and does provide a growing appreciation and understanding of why they were written, what they must have conveyed to their first auditors and readers, and how they may still be expected to function today. The meaning intended by means of and through the text is still a legitimate and viable goal for the biblical exegete and interpreter—not *the* meaning, but meaning faithful to the text in its historical givenness, resonant with the community's tradition, and capable of becoming word of God to those with ears to hear.

5. The Expositor as Priest and Prophet

As I indicated at the outset, I have had time here to develop only that aspect of a good exposition of a biblical text which depends on the expositor achieving a good *interpretation* of that text. But it should also be clear from what has been said that a good interpretation, a good meaning of a text cannot be achieved in independence from the community within which the text is to be expounded. A good meaning is meaning-*for-the-community*; the goal is for the community to experience what we might call a good *hearing* of the text in question. So permit me simply and briefly to round off my reflections by drawing out two aspects of good exposition that follow from and complement the exposition already made. I sum them up in terms of the expositor as priest and prophet.

The Expositor as Priest. Toward the end of his magisterial letter to the Christians in Rome Paul describes his ministry as "the priestly service of the gospel of God" (Rom. 15:16—literally, "serving the gospel of God as a priest"). In terms of priestly service, his goal was to offer the Gentile believers as an acceptable offering to God (15:16).[43] Why this language and imagery? Why describe the ministry and preaching of the gospel as priestly service? The reason must be that, as everyone in the ancient world knew, the priest functioned as an intermediary between God and the people of God. In particular, Paul evidently had in mind the function of the priest to represent the people of God in the presence of God—in Paul's case, as "apostle of the Gentiles" (11:13), to bring the Gentiles to God. This role of the priest, to represent the priestly people before God, was fundamental to the reappropriation of the imagery of priesthood in the early church, as my great hero, J. B. Lightfoot, pointed out in a classic essay[44]—though the insight was more often lost to sight subsequently.

The point I want to elaborate here is that in order to fulfill this role in representing the people, the priest must be one of the people, must know the people from inside, as it were. As the Epistle to the Hebrews observes, the priest is able to act on behalf of his people in relation to God, because he himself is beset with weakness, and so can deal gently with the ignorant and the wayward (Heb. 5:1-2).

If we apply this observation to the priestly service of the gospel, to the expositor as priest, it means that expositors must be able to explain and expound scripture as those who know not simply the text, as outlined earlier, but as those who also know their people, know them from the inside. Good exposition should be able to meet the needs and concerns of the people because the expositor as priest can represent these needs and concerns in seeking to expound the text.

Since the image of circles has already proved fruitful, the point can be put in the same terms. The good expositor is involved not only in the several hermeneutical circles indicated above, but also in the circles of a people's multiple questions and aspirations, needs and concerns. And as good interpretation involves a constant circling back and forth round the several hermeneutical circles, so the good exposition involves a constant circling back and forth around what we may simply characterize as the several pastoral circles. The expositor functions as a priest precisely by functioning at the point where these circles, the hermeneutical and the pastoral, intersect or overlap, as intermediary between the circles, bringing together the word of the text and the questing of the people by expounding a meaning relevant and true to both.

The Expositor as Prophet. The final aspect of good exposition to which I wish to draw attention is also prompted by another passage where Paul characterizes his own preaching. Early on in what we know as his first letter to the church in Corinth he recalls the effectiveness of his proclamation of the gospel when he first reached the city. "My speech and my proclamation were not in persuasive words of wisdom, but in demonstration of the Spirit and power" (1 Cor. 2:4). Commentators on 1 Corinthians have been long accustomed to pointing out that Paul here is contrasting the wisdom of rhetoric, the "persuasive words of wisdom," with the effectiveness of Spirit-inspired preaching. That familiar exposition of the verse was transformed for me by the observation of Johannes Weiss that the word translated "demonstration," *apodeixis,* was a technical term in rhetoric to denote a compelling conclusion drawn out from accepted premises.[45] Paul, in other words, took the technical term for a persuasively rational proof and used it for a preaching that was technically deficient, delivered in weakness and trembling (2:3), for a message that seemed foolish to most Greeks (1:23), but a message that nevertheless broke into the hearts and minds of the Corinthian converts with compelling power (2:4-5).

It is this "prophetic plus" that I want finally to emphasize. For the exegesis and exposition of a biblical text could be technically correct in every respect. It could conform to the various criteria discussed above. It could be words of wisdom, alert to historical context, to entextualized meaning, to the traditions of the church—and yet lack the persuasive power of which Paul speaks. It could be "correct" in every respect, and still not convey life to a devitalized people. This is why it is important that prophecy remains a reality in the ministry of the whole people of God. Teaching alone is not enough. Even teaching that provides a good interpretation of the text in terms of the earlier discussion is not enough. The church needs also prophecy. As I have observed in an earlier writing: "teaching preserves continuity, but prophecy gives life; with teaching a community will not die, but without prophecy it will not live."[46]

Now I am well aware that the preacher as prophet is an old Scottish emphasis. But the emphasis is often misplaced: as though all preaching by definition was prophecy; as though any bold, outspoken contribution to some political or social debate was by definition prophecy. No! If we are to remain true to the biblical understanding of prophecy, we must conceive of it as a charismatic gifting, as an enabling beyond human power, beyond the wisdom of words, beyond the persuasiveness of human rhetoric, granted by the Spirit, to speak words that God is able to use to open minds, to move hearts and to engage wills, despite every human defect of expositor and exposition. If you like, the hermeneutical and pastoral circles need to be intersected with the circle of prophetic inspiration from above if the exposition itself is to catch fire, if it is to kindle the flame of sacred love on the mean altar of our hearts.

No one needs reminding that such a prophetic exposition is not a skill which can be learned in college, or from books, or from scholarship old or new. It is more like an art, a gifting, an inspiration. And it is granted more through prayer and humble attentiveness than by any other means. Of course, the skills and the art are not to be set in opposition or contrast. For all his decrying of rhetorical skills Paul shows himself to have been no mean operator as a persuasive speaker and letter writer on his own behalf. It is the union of the two, the skills and the art, that is to be prized above all else by the would-be expositor.

No one can guarantee a good exposition. After all, the study and analysis of the text to be expounded, the exposition can still be dead. But an exposition sensitive to the needs and concerns of the people and open to the Spirit's prompting can still transform mere words of learned wisdom into a word that is truly heard by the people as a word from God.

***

In sum, what makes a good exposition of a biblical text? To answer our question in a single sentence: a deep respect for the text in its historical givenness; a primary concern to hear afresh the meaning or meanings thus entextualized; an informed regard for the way the text has been heard in the past, particularly within the community of faith, but also beyond; a burning desire to speak meaningfully and relevantly to the people addressed; and a prayerful openness to the Spirit of God to speak the word of God through the always inadequate words of the expositor. That is hardly a complete or finished answer to the question. But at least it may provide a first draft for some further reflection.

10. THE BIBLE AS LIVING TRADITION

FOR MORE THAN FOUR HUNDRED YEARS Protestants and Catholics have been divided on the subject of "Scripture and Tradition." To put it (over) simply: at the heart of the Reformation was an appeal to scripture over against the traditions of the medieval church. The criticism was in essence that ecclesiastical tradition had moved too far from the doctrines and practices of the apostles, as definitively set down in the New Testament. It is this role of the New Testament in serving as the canon by which subsequent developments in Christian faith and praxis are to be evaluated and criticized that Protestants continue to count as fundamental in the "Scripture versus Tradition" debate. On the Catholic side of the debate the crucial starting point is the perception that the meaning of scripture is by no means always clear and has to be interpreted. In these circumstances the teaching office of the church has to be determinative of the meaning; otherwise the authority of scripture would in effect be hijacked for every idiosyncratic reading of the New Testament texts, as the fissiparousness of Protestantism and the contemporary explosion of new churches attest.

Central to the Protestant side of the debate has been the sense of the "fixity" of scripture, the sense that scripture provides a fixed point of reference. Over against a changing, developing tradition stood the New Testament texts fixed in writing, a stable "given," the canon closed. Here was a firm and already final authority that all could read for themselves; to exalt the magisterium to the status of equal authority was to compromise and detract from the unique authority of the New Testament canon.

It is, however, this very contrast, between a fixed scripture and a changing tradition, that has come into increasing question over the period of debate, and particularly in the last few decades. Or to be more precise, the sense of a clearly delimited canonical text and a final authoritative meaning to be read from the text have become more problematic, and so the stable basis of the Protestant position has become problematic.

Of course the Protestant/Catholic debate can be seen at this point as a particular expression of the transformations in perception occasioned first by the Enlightenment and now by postmodernism. The former could be seen as intervening on the Protestant side of the debate—a natural extension of Renaissance and Reformation. The reaction against tradition and the search for historical origins and original meanings seemed at first to support the Protestant claim that apostolic meaning and apostolic age could be clearly perceived, and clearly perceived to be univocal in content and significance, while the latter, in calling into radical question both a historicist perception of the past and the univocity of all speech, seems at first sight completely to undermine that Protestant perspective. If meaning depends on the reading community within which the New Testament text is read, then the community of the church can properly claim to determine the meaning to be heard by the members of that community. The trouble is that in a postmodern world all claims to stable meaning and single authority are called in question. So to mount a defense of one over against the other is simply to reinstate the debate in its older terms and to return to the cul-de-sac into which it had long ago entered.

Having reflected on the debate off and on for most of my academic career, a conviction has steadily grown and developed within my thinking that a positive way forward out of any such impasse is to perceive scripture and the New Testament in particular as "living tradition." What I mean by this should become clear as I try to outline my thinking below. But perhaps I should say at once that to reconfigure the older debate into the single phrase, "living tradition," is intended to be equally affirmative of the points of lasting value on both sides of the debate and equally critical of others. In any event, the attempt is made with a sense of indebtedness to, respect for, and friendship with one who understands well both sides of the debate and who will appreciate what I am trying to say, however inadequate my words may be to the task.

My basic thesis is that the scriptural texts embody and crystallize a perception (I am happy to say a God-given perception) of God and of God's dealings with humankind which was expressed through the words of these texts, but never to be simply identified with them. Perhaps the most basic of all Israel's insights was that God could not be imaged. The reality of God escaped and transcended all human representation: "You shall not make for yourself an idol" (Exod. 20:4). But the same applies to the words with which humans speak of God (or hear God speaking). The word of God transcends and escapes all human words. To identify the two *tout simple* is to make an idol of what should be an icon. To insist that any wording or phrase is the only way in which a word from God or an insight into God and God's dealings with humankind can be expressed is to make an idol. To insist that any such wording or phrase can or is to be heard in only one way and must evoke a strictly uniform meaning is to make an idol. A fundamentalist, whether a scripture fundamentalist or a tradition fundamentalist, has locked the word of God into human words or praxis, and is in effect worshiping an idol.

The reality is that the authoritative word for the people of God was never single nor uniform, never fixed nor unchanging. From the first it was a living word, which came to expression in diverse words and in changing terms and practices. This is what I will try to demonstrate and illustrate in what follows: (1) I will draw attention, first, to the canonical tradition behind the Old Testament; then (2) ask, How final was the final form of the text? (3) My appreciation of living tradition has been given much richer content by recent work on the oral tradition behind the Gospels. (4) Even though many of the letters of the New Testament would seem to be restricted by the historical particularity in and for which they were written, the same quality of living tradition attaches to them also. (5) Textual critics have recently joined in by observing that they are dealing not with a fixed text into which mistakes have crept, but a more fluid text constituted by variations, as far back as can be discerned. (6) The diversity of modern translations makes the same point even more clearly. (7) Finally, not least the developing science and art of hermeneutics has reminded us forcefully that meaning is in some degree at least the product of interaction between reader and text and not simply of the text alone and therefore inherently diverse.

I

None of the Old Testament writings should be seen as a once-for-all product of a single inspired (or inspiring) writer. None of them should be seen as coming into existence *de novo*, as a creation *ex nihilo*. Each and every one is, in differing degrees, an aggregation and consolidation of earlier material. Thus, no serious scholar today regards the Pentateuch as anything other than the end product of a long process stretching over several centuries. That Moses was a key figure in that process can be maintained with some confidence. But behind Moses there was already tradition from the patriarchal period. Units surviving from different stages of the process can be readily distinguished— for example, the Song of Moses (Exodus 15), "the Book of the Covenant" (Exodus 21–23), the creed of Deuteronomy 26:5-9. And most would agree that it was only in the postexilic period, under the influence of Ezra, that the Pentateuch assumed more or less its present canonical shape. Likewise the prophets are typically collections of oracles (and other material) spoken out over a longer period. Few today would hold that the prophecy of Isaiah was singly authored; the three Isaiahs are likely to have spanned two or three centuries. The Psalms may have begun as a definitive collection of religious poetry and worship with King David; but no one doubts that the present book of Psalms is a much more extensive collection, again spanning several centuries. And the bulk of the Wisdom literature similarly is best understood as a sequence of aphoristic and commonplace rules for good living, not all exclusively Israel's, collected over time.

The point is that it was not the writing down of this material or its final editing which first gave it an authority which it had not previously possessed. There is an important parallel here with the subsequent process of canonization. Despite casual assertion to the contrary, by recognizing these texts as "canon," the church did not give these texts canonical authority for the first time, except in a formal sense. Rather, canonization was a recognition and acknowledgment of the canonical authority that these texts were *already* exercising; they were already being cherished as providing a definitively authoritative rule for faith and life. Had they not been accorded that authority previously they would not have been candidates for canonization in the first place. So it was with the pre–Old Testament traditions that were not only incorporated into the Old Testament, but which, in developed form, became the Old Testament. It was not the "inscripturation" of these pre–Old Testament traditions that gave them authority as scripture. Rather, it was because they were already functioning as authoritative for life and worship that they formed the warp of the further reflections and editing which became what we know today as the Old Testament texts.

This is what I mean by "living tradition." What was first heard as "word of God," to patriarch, prophet, psalmist, and so forth, was not at once written down, put in a box, and preserved inviolate for future generations. On the contrary, without ceasing to be word of God, these earliest encounters with the divine stimulated further insight, became the vehicle for further revelation, enabled devotees to hear fresh words from God. Each Old Testament writing was not a once-only and only-then inspired writing, but the climax of a process of hearing and responding to what God was being heard to say. The tensions within and among the texts are testimony to the varied ways in which God's word was apprehended and to how changing circumstances called forth different perceptions of what God was saying afresh. But the earlier words were not abandoned as passé or regarded as outmoded, even the prophecies that had failed or been realized only in part. Instead they were the generative seed that flowered into renewed expressions and mutated into different forms. Their preservation within the Old Testament texts bears witness to the lasting influence of the fountainheads of canonical authority—Moses, Isaiah, David, Solomon, and so forth. But the Old Testament equally attests that their authority was not limited to their own time, but stimulated the further reflection and speaking, the further writing and editing which in due course became the Old Testament.

II

The final form of the Old Testament writings did not end the process. The living tradition that had built up into the Old Testament did not cease to be living from that point/these points onwards. The very problem of defining what the Old Testament is, and when it became finalized as the Old Testament, reminds us how just how *un*fixed is the very concept of the "Old Testament."

The most obvious manifestation of the problem is the variation between the Hebrew Bible and the Septuagint (LXX), the Greek Bible. I have used the term "Old Testament" thus far much too loosely, principally because I am writing from a Christian perspective, and partly because it was inappropriate to raise the issue too soon. But now we have to face up to the fact that the "Old Testament" strictly speaking does not have a single form. The Hebrew Bible had become authoritative scripture by the century before Jesus—"the law and the prophets and the other books of our ancestors" (Sir. Prologue; 4QMMT C10); the twenty-two books of sacred scripture (Josephus, *Apion* 1.37-43)—at least for Palestinian Jews. But for the great body of Jews in the Western diaspora, whose *lingua franca* was no doubt Greek, it was the LXX that functioned as Bible, as scripture; this included the overwhelming majority of the early Christians. Moreover, the LXX includes more writings than the Hebrew Bible, writings like Tobit and Judith, the Wisdom of Jesus ben Sira (Ecclesiasticus) and 1–2 Maccabees. The flow of inspiration had not ceased; an authority of near equivalence to canonical authority was accorded to them, too; ben Sira was nearly included in the canon of Jewish scripture. Moreover, the LXX clearly attests the phenomenon of earlier tradition/scripture elaborated or reformulated that we can deduce from the Old Testament itself—the priestly revision of the Pentateuch, the different slant on Israel's history provided by Chronicles. For the LXX includes additional material for the books of Daniel and Esther, and a further psalm (151). The Law and the Prophets were by then more or less stable, but the third division (the Writings) still had fluid boundaries. The tradition continued to live. All this is directly relevant to the Protestant/Catholic debate, since the extra material in the LXX is Apocrypha, considered by Protestants to be distinct from the Old Testament and noncanonical, but incorporated into Catholic editions of the Old Testament.

Less widely appreciated is the testimony of the Old Testament pseudepigrapha and the Dead Sea Scrolls. For both attest the vigor of a fresh stream of revelatory insight that only just touched the Old Testament proper (Daniel), which was evidently flowing with full effect in the centuries spanning the B.C.E./C.E. divide, and which clearly affected Jesus and the first Christians to a significant degree. I refer to what is commonly described as "Jewish apocalyptic." For example, the collection of writings put together as 1 Enoch influenced Daniel, the Qumran sect, at least one level of the Gospel tradition, is a precursor for the Christian canonical apocalypse (Revelation), and is cited as with prophetic authority by Jude 14-15 (1 Enoch 1:9). The book of Jubilees and the Qumran Temple Scroll are now generally regarded as attempts to rewrite scripture, the former Genesis 1 to Exodus 14, the latter legislative material in Exodus to Deuteronomy. And the Dead Sea Scrolls include the sect's own psalms (1QH) and the incomplete psalm scroll from Cave 11 with seven noncanonical poems interspersed among the canonical psalms (11QPs^a).

In all this any simple division between scripture and tradition quickly erodes and begins to disappear. Previously it was fairly easy to regard scripture as fixed, in final canonical form, so that what came afterward is clearly demarcated as reaction to, and interaction with, the scriptural given, as *interpretation* formally different and distinct from the *inspiration* that produced the texts now to be interpreted. For now in the pseudepigrapha and Dead Sea Scrolls we see the text itself, acknowledged as scripturally authoritative, nevertheless being modified and supplemented, as the *interpretation* is in effect given the authority attributed to the text (most clearly in the Qumran pesher on Habakkuk). The living word of God was evidently being heard not so much in the text itself, but in the interpreted text; the text, through its interpretation, still spoke with word-of-God authority. None of this should surprise us, for this was what the Pharisees were doing as the oral Torah began to supplement the written Torah, and the traditions of the fathers came to have *de facto* scriptural authority in matters of daily praxis (cf. Gal. 1:14).

More to the point, Jesus' own use of scripture, as attested for example in Mark 10:2-9 and 12:24-31, indicates one who was ready to hear God's word in scripture but in fresh ways, and in dialogue with his contemporaries equally seeking to discern God's word. The first Christians in effect operated in like manner—Paul, for example, joining with his Pharisaic contemporaries in the interpretation of texts like Genesis 15:6, Leviticus 18:5 and Habakkuk 2:4;

and like them, regarding his interpreted text as the authoritative scripture. The word of God was being heard through these scriptural texts, true enough, but the word of God was the interpreted text, the text as living tradition. So, the puzzle as to where texts like Matthew 2:23, 1 Corinthians 2:9, and James 4:5 were drawn from becomes of less importance if we are willing to recognize a living tradition through which God's word was heard but which was not simply coterminous with the already acknowledged scriptures.

III

Nowhere is it clearer that the canonical form of the text was not perceived as the beginning and end of the inspiration which gave that text scriptural authority than in the case of the New Testament Gospels. For clearly the Gospels are the end product of a process stretching between the ministry of Jesus himself and the actual writing of the Gospels—a period spanning some forty to seventy years. No one really doubts that the initial stage of the process was oral tradition. However early we may feel able to date the first writing down of some of the Jesus tradition, the great bulk of that tradition probably circulated in oral forms for some twenty years. For much the most part of the Synoptic tradition at least, Jesus was *remembered*, not recorded or interviewed with a written transcript to follow.

Recent studies of oral culture have brought home more clearly what that would have meant. For the prevailing characteristic of oral tradition is its flexibility. The same stories are retold with seemingly endless variation; the substance or core of the story is stable, but the detail can vary with each telling. The same teaching is repeated in seemingly endless permutations and combinations, with varying emphases presumably deemed appropriate to the differing circumstances in which performance of the tradition takes place. Traditional material is expanded and elaborated, or contracted and treated in summary fashion. So we may speculate with the Jesus tradition. Teaching was not regarded as something fixed in the final form in which Jesus gave it out; almost certainly he repeated much of his most important teaching in varied forms and wording. This was how teachers taught, then as today. Likewise, stories about Jesus were not fixed in a final form by some single authoritative witness; different witnesses with differing perspectives would have reported the same episode in differing terms. This is how reporting happened, then as today. Nor was the material cherished as a kind of relic, its joints and sinews fixed in *rigor mortis*, processed in the equivalent of a reliquary, to be venerated from a respectful distance. The material was the life blood of the earliest congregations, providing information about the one they called Lord, and guidance on matters of belief and worship, relationships and conduct. It was living tradition in that it was the tradition by which they lived. That was why it took such varied and changing forms—because it was their tradition, because they lived by it, because it spoke to their changing circumstances, and the changing circumstances are reflected in the changing forms in which the tradition has come down to us. Hence, for example, the differing emphases with which Jesus' teaching on divorce or on the laws of purity, by Mark and by Matthew respectively (Mark 7:15, 19/Matt. 15:17; Mark 10:9/Matt. 19:9). But the basic point is immediately evident when one looks at a synopsis of the first three Gospels with any care.

It should not be assumed that the writing down of Jesus tradition somehow ended the flexibility of the oral period or froze the stream of tradition once for all. For the oral tradition continued after Mark and the others had extracted the material they wanted for their Gospels. The forms of Jesus tradition echoed in later books of the New Testament and in the apostolic fathers indicate a knowledge of Jesus tradition not derived from any written source available to us. Moreover, in a nonliterate culture (most of the early Christians would have been illiterate) knowledge of any written Gospel itself would have come through hearing rather than reading. Their own use of, and reference to, a written Gospel would have been an example of "secondary orality." Nor should it be assumed that the writing of one of the Gospels was radically different from an oral performance of the Jesus tradition. On the contrary, to take one instance, the Gospel of Mark can be readily seen as a written example of an oral performance—written to be heard rather than to be read. The particular variations of the Jesus tradition that the written Gospels enshrine should be taken more as examples of *how* the tradition was performed rather than as defining the way in which it should be performed or as the only legitimate form of the Gospel.

The preceding paragraphs, naturally, are somewhat speculative, since all our evidence regarding the use and transmission of the Jesus tradition comes down to us, of course, only or already in writing. But the same point can be made anyway by reference to the Gospels themselves. For whatever the reason, the Gospels attest the same sort of flexibility that I attribute to, and largely explain by reference to, the orality of the Jesus tradition in the earliest phase of transmission. It is an observation of enduring significance that has not been given the weight it deserves: that the gospel of Jesus Christ has come down to us not in a single form, as though the one gospel could be told or preached in only one way, as though its authority depended on a fixity and strict uniformity of content and form. The Gospels are the gospel (singular) indeed, but the Gospel according to Matthew, the Gospel according to Mark, and so on. And none of the four is precisely the same. In basic structure (beginning with the

Baptist and ending with the passion) and overall substance, yes. But not in the detailed content of each. This is simply to recognize that the gospel, written as well as preached (or expressed in practice) was a living form; it adapted to differing and changing circumstances. This is both attested and validated by the testimony of the scriptural texts themselves. By the wisdom of God's Spirit the church did not canonize only one Gospel form, or a single composite form, but *four diverse* forms. It was not a case of "one fits all," or "all must fit to the one." Rather, the gospel was seen as a living tradition that could and evidently did speak with differing emphases to differing contexts and situations. The good news of Jesus Christ was from the first a living tradition.

IV

The letters of the New Testament can be seen in a similar way. It is true that the letters of Paul in particular are the nearest we have in the New Testament, perhaps in the Bible as a whole, to occasional literature—that is, documents written for a specific context and for specific purposes. So they are not fluid and flexible in the same way as the Jesus tradition. But the same living quality attaches to them nonetheless.

For one thing there are sufficient hints that Paul intended some at least of his letters for more than one audience; he instructed that the letter to the Colossians should be read also in the church at Laodicea, and the letter to Laodicea should be read also in Colossae (Col. 4:16). So he recognized that even the particularity of letters to individual churches could be heard with relevance more widely. Moreover, the fact that most of his letters were retained by the churches to which he wrote suggests also that they were not read once only and then forgotten, but functioned as a resource to which the churches referred and on which they drew as the churches grew and developed. Moreover, it cannot have been long before copies of the letters were being more widely circulated and gathered into a collection, for the same reason: even the most targeted of contents could be heard with relevance more widely.

In addition, as with the Old Testament, we can readily discern Paul's use of and dependency on earlier tradition. We need only think of such passages as 1 Corinthians 11:23-26 and 15:3-7. It is true that he insists that his gospel came to him direct from God (Gal. 1:12); but it is equally evident that he thereby refers to his understanding of the gospel as for Gentiles as well as Jews, and to be received by faith alone ("the truth of the gospel"—Gal. 2:4, 14). He makes a point of stressing that his gospel, the gospel for the uncircumcision, was fully acknowledged by the pillar apostles in Jerusalem as gospel, as a valid expression of the gospel (Gal. 2:7-9). In other words, it was central to Paul's understanding of the gospel that it was not something static and unchanging, but living and malleable, able to be experienced as "the power of God for salvation" (Rom. 1:16) by different peoples in their different circumstances.

Paul treated the tradition of Jesus' life and teaching in the same way. He quoted it when necessary, as in the case of Jesus' teaching on divorce, thereby indicating its abiding authority for him, but went on immediately to indicate that the circumstances he was confronting in the church at Corinth necessitated some modification of Jesus' teaching (1 Cor. 7:10-16). At other times, echoes of, and allusions to, Jesus' teaching (e.g., Rom. 12:14; 14:14; 1 Cor. 13:2; 1 Thess. 5:2, 4) indicate no concern to distinguish that teaching as something inviolate, given special weight as stemming from Jesus, and therefore requiring attribution to him as the authority. On the contrary, the teaching has been absorbed into the lifeblood of Christian paraenesis and is used not by evoking some instruction given by Jesus twenty-odd years earlier, but as the contemporary wisdom of his apostolate and of his churches.

Paul's use of the Old Testament has the same character. To be sure, he makes explicit quotation of Old Testament passages much more than he does Jesus' tradition; "as it is written" regularly introduces such an appeal to the authority of Jewish scripture (Rom. 1:17; 2:24; 3:4, 10; 4:17; etc.). In so doing he testifies that he found the Old Testament to instruct him in present concerns, as in passages like Romans 15:9-12 and 1 Corinthians 10:1-11. But the number of echoes of, and allusions to, the Old Testament far outweigh the number of explicit quotations. The Old Testament was a source of living authority for him. Of course, for Paul it was to be read in the light of Christ (2 Cor. 3:12-18), and in that light he construed the demand for circumcision as the mark of commitment to God's covenant (Gen. 17:9-14) differently (1 Cor. 7:19). But such fundamentals as the Old Testament's warnings against idolatry and sexual license remained as much part of his continuing rule for life after his conversion as before. The law, as filtered through the prism of Christ, and as summed up in the demand for neighbor love, as "the law of Christ" (Gal. 6:2), was an ever-valid measure of his everyday conduct.

Nor should we forget that the Pauline corpus attests a tradition that ran on beyond Paul's own death. If we follow the large consensus of scholarly opinion, at least the Pastoral Epistles and Ephesians are post-Pauline. As such they suggest not a concern merely to ape the great apostle, and certainly not an attempt (a successful attempt!) to gain authority for the texts by deception. They suggest, rather, a living tradition of his thought, where fellow workers, assistants, and pupils kept alive what Paul had stood for and labored for and articulated it afresh for the generation following Paul. In this we can see a parallel with the Pentateuch, or the three Isaiahs, or the psalms of David. In each case a living tradition did not cease with the death of the initial voice and originating authority figure but continued to develop in the generation(s) that followed. The living waters flowing from the fountainhead continued through new channels.

V

The oral period belongs to the beginning of the whole process. Even though Papias's high regard for the "living voice" of the first generation of disciples could endure into the second century, it could not be satisfied much beyond that. Paul's fellow workers and pupils in turn died; the school of Paul could not maintain the distinctive Pauline theology in fresh compositions beyond a second generation; the later attempts to provide a 3 Corinthians or to replace the lost letter to the Laodiceans are feeble in comparison. Above all, did not the inscripturated tradition steadily, even if not immediately, supersede the oral tradition? And in so doing, did not the written text give the whole a firmness and fixity that had not been possessed before? The simple answer is that it did to a large extent, but by no means entirely. Which brings us to the science and skill of textual criticism.

As a scholarly discipline, the original goal of New Testament textual criticism was to recover so far as possible the original text penned by evangelist and apostle. Quite quickly that objective was modified into the aim to reconstruct a text which takes account of the measured testimony of manuscript and other witnesses and which can command assent as the best approximation to the texts emanating from the apostolic age and used by the early church. Typical of this early phase was the modern regard for the "first edition" of a great literary work. Typical, too, the assumption that differences between witnesses were the result of careless copying and scribal error. But recently it has come to be more fully appreciated that the concept of a "first edition" is much less appropriate to a document no doubt dictated by a particular author, but whose circulation beyond any single recipient depended wholly on authorized and unauthorized copying. In a day well before the idea of copyright gained hold, there was nothing to stop others incorporating parts of other literary works, adapting material to their own ends, or improving what might be deemed poor style, or modifying views thought not to be quite as they should have been.

So just as the discovery of the Dead Sea Scrolls has raised further questions about differing forms of the Hebrew Bible, behind the Masoretic text on the one hand and the LXX on the other, similar questions are being raised with regard to the New Testament text. What does it signify, regarding "the New Testament," if the Western text, particularly of Acts, was the New Testament for a wide range of Western churches? What if Marcion's freedom in regard to the Gospel of Luke and the letters of Paul was not an aberration, but only an extreme example of what was the general practice? What if "orthodox" as well as "heretic" felt free to modify the text of particular scriptures in order that the scripture might be heard to speak more in accord with their own position? What would be deemed unacceptable in a literary culture, with a high regard for author's copyright, might well be regarded as good practice in a culture where no two manuscripts of a single work entirely agreed as to its wording, and where varied corruptions of a text being considered by a group of students could be taken for granted rather then being an exception. If justification were to be sought for any attempt to bring a group of manuscripts into conformity on a contentious point, it would be enough to argue that this is what the writer surely intended and not the other.

The rather sobering fact, then, is that the writing down of material did not fix it as much as has traditionally been assumed. The so-called canonical or final form of a text was not all that final. The contrast between written text and oral communication, which becomes so sharp and clear in a society long accustomed to the printed page and the "first edition" of, say, five hundred copies, loses all that sharpness and clarity once we move back in history behind Gutenberg and Caxton. Which means that the contrast between fixed text and changing tradition also loses its sharpness and clarity. In a preliterary and preprint age the written text had much more a chameleon-like quality, a living quality, than has normally been recognized.

VI

A still further factor is the whole issue of translation. Islam has been able to maintain its belief in the pristine purity of the Qur'an because it regards only the (original) Arabic as inspired and authoritative. Translations into Turkish or Bengali are not properly speaking the Qur'an. In contrast, it has always been recognized that the scriptures of Israel and Christianity needed to be translated—in the case of the Old Testament, from Hebrew into Aramaic (the Targums) and Greek (LXX and others); in the case of the New Testament into the other ancient languages of the ancient Near East, and particularly into Latin in the West. These translated scriptures were the scriptures for generations of national groups. The Vulgate, the Luther Bible, and the King James (Authorized) Version of the Bible, for example, were the authoritatively canonical texts for centuries in Europe. That perception of a particular translation as having a *de facto* canonical authority has only disappeared in the latter half of the twentieth century, marked as it has been both by an increasing accessibility to agreed Hebrew and Greek texts and by a bewildering plethora of new translations.

The point, of course, is that no translation can produce an exact reproduction of the text being translated. Any word in any language has a range of possible significance, depending on how that word has been used in that language. The nearest equivalent in another language will not have precisely the same range of significance; the range will overlap, making translation possible, but not exactly. Add in the complexity of words in sentences, idiomatic usage, wordplays possible in the one language but not in the other, and so on, and the problem begins to become clear. Any sense of a meaning fixed by particular words in an original text, even if valid for the "original," is at once qualified, if not heavily obscured, when primary reference is to the translated text. The issue ought to have been more serious for earlier generations of Christians who regarded the text of the New Testament as a fundamental authority. For the original teaching of Jesus himself comes down to us almost entirely in translation, and in diverse forms at that. The issue was not seen to be serious, since it was the Greek version of his teaching that was thought of as the inspired original. The problem remained rather academic so long as there was only one translation into the vernacular to be reckoned with. But now that a whole range of translations compete for attention the point cannot be ignored. For all these translations are different. To listen to a Bible reading from one translation while following the passage in another translation can at times be a very disorienting experience, so different can the translations be. Any lingering thought of the fixity of the text soon evaporates.

In other words, translations of biblical texts are one of the clearest contemporary demonstrations of the living quality of the biblical text. The meaning of the "original" Hebrew and Greek simply cannot be pinned down finally and definitively in any single word sequence in English, or German, or Swahili, or whatever. There is an amorphous quality to the very textual form, so that any claim to some translation being the most accurate or as rendering the others redundant is rightly regarded as unrealistic or as mere salesmanship. Twenty-first-century congregations have become accustomed to central liturgies in alternative versions, to a Lord's Prayer in three or four different forms, to eucharistic prayers that vary according to the season, and so forth. This is simply because liturgy is one of the clearest manifestations of living tradition, as the amazing burgeoning of new hymnody in the latter decades of the twentieth century shows with particular clarity. The liturgy is adapting to the changing circumstances and needs of the worshiping people of God; that's what we mean by "living tradition." My point is that the translated biblical text read within the liturgy shares precisely in that living and developing process.

Translations which in their time enabled the biblical text to speak afresh, like the Revised Standard Version, the New English Bible, or the Jerusalem Bible, can quite quickly come to be seen and heard as dated and in need of further revision. The Good News Bible or the Living Bible can bring the Bible to life for a new generation, while leaving an older generation cold. The translated Bible is not a fixed text but a diversity of contemporary performances of the ancient Hebrew and Greek. The Bible in translation has become fully and clearly part of the living tradition of the church.

VII

Underlying all the above is the increasing recognition of the role of *interpretation* in the reading of the New Testament, as of any text. Meaning is not simply to be observed in the text and described by the reader, as one might report and describe the physical features of a mountain or church tower. Reading is engagement with the text, personally involving the reader. That is why teachers encourage children to pay attention when reading or being taught a lesson. Without that personal engagement and concentration, the passage or the lesson will "go in one ear and out the other." But even a modest degree of concentration brings the life experience of the reader into interaction with the text read and to the degree that the text speaks to that life experience and informs or enhances or extends it we may speak of a successful reading or lesson. In such a case the meaning heard or lesson learned is in some degree at least the product of the interaction of text/speaker and reader/hearer. And in such a case there will be at least a degree of distinctive individuality in the meaning gleaned.

Still further complicating the picture are observations about the more deliberate acts of interpretation long familiar to students of history and of significant texts: that "historical facts" are each historian's interpretation of the diverse and often inconsistent data still available from the past; and regarding the various forms of the hermeneutical circle, the part helping to illuminate the whole as the whole helps to illuminate the part, and so on. When we take these hermeneutical issues into consideration we find ourselves still further enmeshed in the problem of the historian's or reader's (subjective) input into the quest for facts and for meaning. The old defenses of the univocity and definitive meaning of scripture simply failed to appreciate that the issue was not the *inspiration* of scripture but the *interpretation* of scripture. The Catholic side of the scripture/tradition debate had right on its side: no meaning from scripture without interpretation; no authoritative meaning from scripture without an authoritative interpreter; no scripture without tradition! But who determines who or what constitutes the authority? Can there be a finally definitive interpretation any more than a finally definitive scripture? The problem with a postmodern hermeneutic is that it undercuts *all* readings that claim a definitive authority over other readings.

Here, I suggest, is where the understanding of scripture as living tradition can point a way through the impasse.

As living tradition, scripture is not static, with a dead meaning to be somehow dissected from the cadaver of the text. Scripture has potential to evoke a range of meaning and reaction, as the differing translations and disagreements among commentators have long made clear. So long as scripture evokes a faith response (but there are other responses) and so long as faith reads/hears scripture with relevance and profit, it will retain its character as living tradition. Expressed differently, scripture is the basis not only for the unity of Christianity but for its diversity, and only for a unity that, like the human body, consists in the mutual recognition, interdependence, and active cooperation of its several and very diverse parts. Without a living tradition the body of Christ will not live.

Since the text is the starting point and point of reference common to all engaged in such faithful reading, the content and structure of the text will itself provide the limit within which the range of meaning can be read/heard. The text is not wholly plastic, vulnerable to being molded into any shape the reader chooses. There is such a thing as a bad reading. Translations can be recognized to be just plain wrong. The historical context of Hebrew and Greek usage will indicate limits beyond which the reading becomes irresponsible. The one gospel had different versions recognized to be legitimate, but other "Gospels" were deemed to be illegitimate, and properly so. The discernment of a responsible reading is not the responsibility of any one person or office, but a matter of the *sensus fidelis*, though individual teacher and prophet may well be called by God to speak the word that illuminates a controversial issue.

It is important that the living tradition be not "frozen" at any point. This was the mistake of the Protestant side of the scripture/tradition debate—in assuming that with the final canonical form of the text the variety and fluidity of scripture's meaning had thereby ceased. But the Catholic side of the debate can fall into the same trap by assuming that the tradition has frozen at various points, into dogma and canonical order. In both cases, the living quality of the tradition means that the tradition must continue to develop and change in response to the changing circumstances of the gospel and the churches. As Jesus saw in regard to "the tradition of the elders" (Mark 7:9-13), as all three Reformations saw with regard to the developed tradition of the medieval church, as Vatican II saw with regard to the long-established tradition of Christian anti-Judaism, tradition can become an excuse to ignore the more obvious meanings to be drawn from scripture. Tradition can give practical expression to the living tradition of scripture, but it can also throttle it and prevent the breath of the Spirit from breathing into fresh life into the scriptures.

In short, when scripture is seen as "living tradition" its function as word of God for the here and now is clarified and enhanced, its interaction with church tradition, both in expressing its own vitality through the tradition and in providing a check to any excesses of the tradition, becomes clearer and more positive, and its role in renewing tradition, in provoking departure from tradition and in stimulating new tradition can be given full play.

NOTES

1. The Task of New Testament Interpretation

1. W. Wrede, "The Task and Methods of 'New Testament Theology'," in R. Morgan, *The Nature of New Testament Theology* (London: SCM, 1973), 68–116; K. Stendahl, "Biblical Theology," in *The Interpreter's Dictionary of the Bible* (New York: Abingdon, 1962), 1:418–32.

2. A. Schlatter, "The Theology of the New Testament and Dogmatics," in Morgan, *Nature,* 117–66.

3. R. Bultmann, "Is Exegesis without Presuppositions Possible?," in *Existence and Faith* (London: Collins, Fontana, 1964), 342–51.

4. A. C. Thiselton, *The Two Horizons* (London: Paternoster, 1980).

5. J. D. G. Dunn, *Unity and Diversity in the New Testament* (London: SCM, 1977).

6. For example, D. A. Carson, "Unity and Diversity in the New Testament: The Possibility of Systematic Theology," in *Scripture and Truth,* ed. D. A. Carson and J. D. Woodbridge (Grand Rapids: Zondervan, 1983), 79; R. Nicole, "The Inspiration and Authority of Scripture: J. D. G. Dunn versus B. B. Warfield," *Churchman* 98 (1984): 200 ("a jarring multiplicity of irreconcilable accounts and teachings"); and even the more sensitive treatment of C. H. Pinnock, *The Scripture Principle* (London: Hodder and Stoughton, 1985), 71. Regretably also B. S. Childs, *The New Testament as Canon: An Introduction* (London: SCM, 1984), 20, 29.

2. The Gospels as Oral Tradition

1. J. D. G. Dunn, *The Evidence for Jesus* (London: SCM/Philadelphia: Westminster, 1985).

3. Was Jesus a Liberal? Was Paul a Heretic?

1. Hyam Maccoby, *The Mythmaker: Paul and the Invention of Christianity* (London: Weidenfeld & Nicolson, 1986).

4. The Problem of Pseudonymity

1. David G. Meade, *Pseudonymity and Canon* (Tübingen: J. B. C. Mohr, 1986).

5. The Authority of Scripture according to Scripture

1. F. W. Farrar, *History of Interpretation* (New York: Macmillan, 1886), 373.

2. Helvetic Consensus 1675.

3. Farrar, *History of Interpretation,* 374f.; A. B. Bruce, *Inspiration and Inerrancy* (Cambridge: James Clarke, 1891), 19–20; J. Rogers, "The Church Doctrine of Biblical Authority," in J. Rogers, ed., *Biblical Authority* (Waco, Tex.: Word, 1977), 31 (see also 36).

4. Though G. Maier, *The End of the Historical-Critical Method,* 1974 (ET, St. Louis: Concordia, 1977), 68f., speaks almost with regret of the abandoning of this view as "the first break in the dam," the highest point of "the slippery slope" (see below, 83).

5. "Inspiration," *The Presbyterian Review* (April 1881), 238. In another statement Warfield affirmed "the complete trustworthiness of Scripture in all elements, even circumstantial statements . . ." ("Recent Theological Literature," *The Presbyterian and Reformed Review* 4 [1893]: 499).

6. Orr edited the *International Standard Bible Encyclopedia* (5 vols., 1930) and was a contributor to *The Fundamentals.*

7. J. Orr, *Revelation and Inspiration* (London: Duckworth, 1910), 197–98.

8. E.g., Fuller Theological Seminary modified its earlier statement of faith (which affirmed the Bible's freedom "from all error in the whole and in the part") in the early 1960s to one which affirmed the Bible as "the only infallible rule of faith and practice."

9. E. J. Young, *Thy Word is Truth* (Grand Rapids: Eerdmans, 1957), 48.

10. Quoted by Bruce, *Inspiration,* 4. In a similar vein to Orr's protest (above, 70) is G. C. Berkouwer's comment that when error in the sense of incorrectness is used on the same level as error in the biblical sense of sin and deception, "we are quite far removed from the serious manner in which error is dealt with in Scripture". "In the end it (the postulate of biblical inerrancy) will damage reverence for Scripture more than it will further it" (*Holy Scripture* [Grand Rapids: Eerdmans, 1975], 181, 183, cited by Rogers, *Biblical Authority,* 44).

11. Fuller has responded with a special issue of its *Theology, News and Notes* on *The Authority of Scripture at Fuller* (1976), which includes several important corrections and clarifications on points of fact cited by Lindsell. Lindsell has responded in *The Bible in the Balance* (Grand Rapids: Zondervan, 1979), chap. 5.

12. J. M. Boice, ed., *The Foundation of Biblical Authority* (Grand Rapids: Zondervan, 1978/London: Pickering & Inglis, 1979), 10. The Chicago Statement, signed by 250 evangelical scholars and leaders in October 1978, is more carefully phrased: "Being wholly and verbally God-given, Scripture is without error or fault in all its teaching, no less in what it states about God's acts in creation, about the events of world history, and about its own literary origins under God, than in its witness to God's saving grace in individual lives." But the insistence is still strong that "Holy Scripture . . . is of infallible divine authority in all matters upon which it touches" (the full statement is printed in Lindsell, *Balance,* 366–71, and in N. L. Geisler, ed., *Inerrancy* [Grand Rapids: Zondervan, 1980], 493–502). See also P. D. Feinberg, "The Meaning of Inerrancy," in ibid., 267–304.

13. J. M. Boice, ed., *Does Inerrancy Matter?,* ICBI Foundation Series 1 (1979): 13.

14. Ibid., preface, 3. Contrast those evangelicals who continue to affirm infallibility without inerrancy—see, e.g., S. T. Davis, *The Debate about the Bible: Inerrancy versus Infallibility* (Philadelphia: Westminister, 1977), and those attacked by Lindsell, particularly in his second volume (above, n.11).

15. "The authority of Scripture is inescapably impaired if this total divine inerrancy is in any way limited or disregarded . . ." (Chicago Short Statement). "It is clear that for the conservative understanding, inerrancy is the total basis for the authority of Scripture. To deny inerrancy . . . is to deny any authority of any kind to the Bible" (P. J. Achtemeier, *The Inspiration of Scripture* [Philadelphia: Westminster, 1980], 54f.).

16. See, e.g., G. L. Archer, "The Witness of the Bible to Its Own Inerrancy," in Boice, ed., *Foundation,* 94f.; Lindsell, *Balance,* 12f. Cf. D. Hubbard, "The Current Tensions: Is There a Way Out?" in Rogers, ed., *Biblical Authority,* 172–75.

17. B. B. Warfield, "God-inspired Scripture," *The Presbyterian and Reformed Review* 11 (1900): 89–130; reprinted in *The Inspiration and Authority of the Bible* (London: Marshall, Morgan & Scott, 1951), 245–96. He is followed by the NIV.

18. Arndt and Gingrich, *Lexicon,* ōphelimos.

19. Cf. D. Guthrie, *The Pastoral Epistles* (London: Tyndale, 1957), 164. In response to Lindsell's repeated insistence that "error cannot be profitable," therefore "profitable" here means inerrant (*Balance,* e.g., 12, 217), it must simply be repeated that that is *not* exegesis. For it to qualify as exegesis, it would have to be demonstrated that any New Testament writer regarded what Lindsell calls error (e.g., whether or not the mustard seed is the smallest of all seeds) to be unprofitable, disadvantageous to salvation. Such a demonstration has *not* been forthcoming.

20. A distinction denounced in Article XII of the Chicago Statement on Biblical Inerrancy. Is it so difficult to distinguish between matters pertaining to faith and

conduct, and matters of science and history, as Lindsell repeatedly asserts (e.g., *Balance*, 53, 214)?

21. The argument in John 10:34-36 is most obviously understood as assuming that at the time of Jesus (or John) the words had been addressed to men (those to whom the word of God came)—whatever the original reference might have been (Yahweh's heavenly host?).

22. L. Morris, *John*, New London Commentary (London: Marshall, Morgan & Scott, 1972), 527. Lindsell repeatedly asserts that inerrancy was clearly taught by Christ (*Balance*, 44, 83, 91, 209–11)—even that Jesus taught "the view of error-free autographs" (122)!

23. R. E. Brown notes that "in reference to Scripture *lyein* is contrasted to *plēroun*, the passive of which means 'to be fulfilled,' and that therefore *lyein* means 'to keep from being fulfilled.' In rabbinic usage, *battēl*, which seems to be the Aramaic equivalent of *lyein*, means 'to nullify, render futile' . . ." (*John*, Anchor Bible [Garden City, N.Y.: Doubleday, 1966], 404).

24. Warfield, *Inspiration and Authority*, 140.

25. See Strack-Billerbeck, *Kommentar*, 2:543; M. de Jonge and A. S. van der Woude, "11Q Melchizedek and the New Testament," *NTS* 12 (1965–66): 301–26.

26. Boice, "The Preacher and God's Word," in Boice, ed., *Foundation*, 135; cf. the earlier statement of Archer, "Witness," in Boice, ed., *Foundation*, 94.

27. See, e.g., the discussion in R. Banks, *Jesus and the Law in the Synoptic Tradition* (Cambridge: Cambridge University Press, 1975), 213–20. In Matt. 5:17 Jesus says, "I came not to destroy but to fulfill." That is, he spoke of a fulfilling which is not a destroying, but is evidently not a leaving unchanged, either. Rather, it is a transforming which involves an abandoning of particular injunctions given to regulate worship and life in specific ways, a fulfilling which is a bringing to completion of the law so that part at least of its earlier role is left behind.

28. See further ibid., with summary statement on 234.

29. I am aware of the literary critical discussion of intentionality and the "intentional fallacy" (cf. E. D. Hirsch, *Validity in Interpretation* [New Haven: Yale University Press, 1967]; also *The Aims of Interpretation* [Chicago: Chicago University Press, 1976]) but would wish to argue that uncovering the author's *intended meaning* is the primary goal of New Testament exegesis, whatever *significance* later interpreters might recognize in his words within some wider hermeneutical context.

30. See B. B. Warfield, "Inspiration and Criticism," in *Revelation and Inspiration* (Oxford: Oxford University Press, 1927), 420. Packer puts the point well: "The question which the interpreter must constantly ask is: What is being *asserted* in this passage? The infallibility and inerrancy of Scripture are relative to the intended scope of the word of God. . . . The concepts of inerrancy and infallibility . . . are not hermeneutical concepts, and carry no implication as to the character or range of biblical teachings" (*"Fundamentalism" and the Word of God* [London: IVF, 1958], 97–98). Contrast,

e.g., the Exposition of the Chicago Statement: "We affirm that canonical Scripture should always be interpreted on the basis that it is infallible and inerrant" (Geisler, *Inerrancy*, 500). The charge is thus entirely justified that "the hermeneutical principle of conservative exegesis is Scriptural inerrancy, and no method or conclusion may be tolerated which would conflict with the principle"; "any interpretation that might threaten inerrancy must be ruled out in advance" (Achtemeier, *Inspiration*, 58f.; see also J. Barr, *Fundamentalism* [London: SCM, 1977], 40–55).

31. The Chicago Statement, Article XIII. Having recognized that God's honor is not compromised by use of irregular grammar, etc., why is it so difficult to accept that God's honor can be equally unaffected if God chooses to use equivalent irregularities in historical and scientific detail?

32. The resulting confusion in the definition of "error" ("incorrectness" or "sin and deception"?) makes the concept "inerrancy" at best unclear and unhelpful, and in most cases dangerously misleading. See further C. Pinnock, "Three Views of the Bible in Contemporary Theology," in Rogers, ed., *Biblical Authority*, 64f.; Achtemeier, *Inspiration*, 61ff.

33. See above n.19. Cf. Pinnock, in Rogers, ed., *Biblical Authority*, 63f., who describes himself as "a defender of biblical inerrancy" but who makes a similar point.

34. Boice, *Does Inerrancy Matter?* 20. See also Barr, *Fundamentalism*, 84f.; Achtemeier, *Inspiration*, 50, 54.

35. "God uses fallible spokesmen all the time to deliver his word, and it does not follow that the Bible *must* be otherwise" (Pinnock, in Rogers, ed., *Biblical Authority*, 64).

36. See my discussion of this issue in "Prophetic 'I'-Sayings and the Jesus Tradition: The Importance of Testing Prophetic Utterances within Early Christianity," *New Testament Studies* 24 (1977–78): 175–98.

37. Cf. J. Goldingay, "Inspiration, Infallibility and Criticism," *Churchman* 90 (1976): 13.

38. See, e.g., P. Borgen, *Bread from Heaven,* Supplements to *Novum Testamentum* X (Leiden: Brill, 1965). See also above 31 and 62.

39. Contrast the Chicago Statement, Article XVIII: "We deny the legitimacy of any treatment of the text or quest for sources lying behind it that leads to relativizing, dehistoricizing, or discounting its teaching, or rejecting its claims to authorship."

40. Tertullian, *Adversus Marcionem* 4.5 (with reference to Mark's Gospel being regarded as Peter's, and Luke's narrative being ascribed to Paul).

41. B. M. Metzger, "Literary Forgeries and Canonical Pseudepigrapha," *Journal of Biblical Literature* 91 (1972): 22 (Tertullian quotation on 14). See further above chap. 4.

42. E.g., God is creator, whether in six days or not. Jesus is the good shepherd, whether he said these words or not during his life on earth.

43. See further Pinnock, in Rogers, ed., *Biblical Authority*, 65–67: "Minute inerrancy may be a central issue for the telephone book but not for psalms, proverbs, apocalyptic and parables. Inerrancy just does not focus attention correctly where the Bible is concerned" (67); Achtemeier, *Inspiration:* "Diversion of attention from the Bible's witness about God's saving acts to questions about the precise accuracy of minor details is, in the end, perhaps the most serious defect in the conservative equation of Scripture with its supposed inerrancy" (74).

44. The point is expressed here in terms most appropriate to New Testament exegesis. For a more careful statement see my "Levels of Canonical Authority," chap. 6 below.

45. B. D. Chilton, *God in Strength: Jesus' Announcement of the Kingdom* (Freistadt/ JSOT: F. Plöchal, 1979).

46. K. Stendahl, *Paul among Jews and Gentiles* (London: SCM, 1977); E. P. Sanders, *Paul and Palestinian Judaism* (London: SCM, 1977).

47. See my *Christology in the Making* (London: SCM, 1980), chap. 7.

48. Cf. the Westminster Confession I.VII: "All things in Scripture are not alike plain in themselves nor alike clear unto all; yet those things which are necessary to be known, believed, and observed, for salvation, are so clearly propounded and opened in some place of Scripture or other, that not only the learned, but the unlearned, in a due use of the ordinary means, may attain unto a sufficient understanding of them."

49. "Particularly interesting is Paul's use of the word *apodeixis,* the sole occurrence in the New Testament. It is a more or less technical term in rhetoric and denotes a compelling conclusion drawn out from accepted premises. But Paul's point is precisely that the *apodeixis* of his message was nothing to do with his skill as a rhetorician, nothing to do with arguments and proofs; it was *apodeixis* of Spirit and power. That is to say, their experience was not so much of intellectual persuasion, but rather of being grasped by divine power, of being compelled with a wholehearted conviction to accept and affirm Paul's message, despite Paul's obvious deficiencies as rhetorician!" (J. D. G. Dunn, *Jesus and the Spirit* [London: SCM, 1975], 226f.).

50. Hence the slightly naughty question in my review of Boice, ed., *Foundation*, in *Expository Times* 91 (1979–80): 312: "Does Jim Packer worship in accordance with 1 Cor. 14:26?"

51. See further J. D. G. Dunn, *Unity and Diversity in the New Testament* (London: SCM, 1977), 374f. Maier, *Historical-Critical Method*, protests vigorously against the idea of a canon within the canon: "Scripture itself does not offer a canon in the canon, but the latter is exacted forcibly and against its will" (49). But later on he readily acknowledges that "every interpreter establishes for himself a more or less conscious total impression of Scripture, which in this or that manner usually comes through when he interprets individual portions" (88). Since this "total impression of Scripture" will differ from individual to individual, or at least from tradition to tradition, it is in effect just another name for a "canon within the canon."

52. "The confession of inerrancy . . . does make a full and faithful articulation of biblical Christianity possible *in principle* . . . it commits us in advance to harmonize and integrate all that we find Scripture teaching, without remainder . . ." (Packer, "Encountering Present-Day Views of Scripture," in Boice, ed., *Foundation,* 78f., my emphasis)—the claim I would have to say of the systematic theologian, not of the exegete. In similar vein Maier, *Historical-Critical Method,* 71.

53. Cf. Barr: "The 'evangelical doctrine of scripture' is largely a fiction imposed upon the Bible by human tradition" (*Fundamentalism* [London: SCM, 1982], xviii).

54. Note again the criticisms of Barr and Achtemeier mentioned in n.30 above.

55. To this extent, at any rate, James Barr's earlier criticism of "Fundamentalism" still seems to be on target: "There is no more severe self-indictment of fundamentalism than that it has produced no really interesting discussion of biblical interpretation" (*Old and New in Interpretation: A Study of the Two Testaments* [London: SCM, 1966], 203).

56. E.g., J. H. Gerstner criticizes Berkouwer's willingness to allow that the Bible may contain errors in the sense of "incorrectness" (see above n.10). "This can only mean that if the Bible is the Word of God, then God can be incorrect, can err, can make mistakes, though he cannot deceive. This does more than 'damage reverence for Scripture'. This damages reverence for God" ("The Church's Doctrine of Biblical Inspiration," in Boice, ed., *Foundation,* 49f.).

57. Maier completely ignores or misunderstands this unavoidable character of the hermeneutical task when he repeats too simplistically that "the correlative or counterpart to revelation is not critique but obedience" (*Historical-Critical Method,* 19, 23, 53f.; followed by J. B. Payne, "Higher Criticism and Biblical Inerrancy," in Geisler, ed., *Inerrancy,* 95). The necessary middle term between revelation and obedience is interpretation. See also the criticism of Maier by P. Stuhlmacher, *Historical Criticism and Theological Interpretation of Scripture,* 1975 (ET, Philadelphia: Fortress Press, 1977/London: SPCK, 1979), 66–71.

58. A classic example is Lindsell's assertion that Peter actually denied Christ not just three times but *six* times in all (*The Battle for the Bible,* 174–76). Achtemeier's comment at this point should not be ignored: "If what he [Lindsell] has constructed is the actual course of events, then *none* of the Gospels has given a true picture of objective reality. He has thus convincingly demonstrated that none of the four is inerrant, since none of them know what *really* happened, i.e. six denials. All claim three" (*Inspiration,* 67).

59. Cf. Pinnock, in Rogers, ed., *Biblical Authority,* 60–62, who notes that "a false piety has grown up which would seek to protect the Bible from its own humanity," and who warns against "an excessive veneration and overbelief about the Bible . . . an almost superstitious regard for every detail of it" (62). Cf. also B. Ramm, "Is 'Scripture Alone' the Essence of Christianity?" in Rogers, ed., *Biblical Authority,* 112. G. R. Lewis, "The Human Authorship of Inspired Scripture," in Geisler, ed., *Inerrancy,* admits Pinnock's charge that conservative scholars have not paid enough attention to the human side of Scripture (229f.).

60. The danger was brought home to me in my student days when I read Adolph Saphir, *Christ and the Scriptures* (London: Morgan & Scott, n.d.), 151–66 (a section entitled "Bibliolatry"). For example, he comments on the phrase "The Bible is the religion of Protestants": "Paul never would have said that the Scripture was the religion of the Christian. Christ was his Light and Life" (157f.). And again, "The Holy Ghost is above Scripture. Not that there is anything in the Scripture which is not in accordance with the Spirit's teaching, for all Scripture is inspired of God, but the Church is in danger of ignoring the existence of the Holy Ghost and her constant dependence on Him, and of substituting for the Spirit the Book. And now commences the reign of interpreters and commentaries, of compendiums and catechisms; for if we have the Spirit's teaching in the Book instead of the Spirit's teaching by the Book, men wish to have it extracted, simplified, reduced to a system, methodised. And then practically speaking, the creed is above the Bible" (158f.).

61. This argument recurs for example in the essays of Packer, Archer, and Sproul in Boice, ed., *Foundation,* 66, 92, 116; cf. 18.

62. See Arndt and Gingrich, *Lexicon, diapherō, dokimazō.*

63. One response to an early outline of this paper posed as alternatives the New Testament doctrine of Scripture and New Testament phenomena (how the New Testament handled the Old Testament), and objected that I was preferring possible inferences drawn from the latter to the (presumably clear) teaching of the former. My point is precisely: (1) that the New Testament doctrine is not as clear as such an objection presupposes, and that, in particular, the idea of inerrancy is itself at best a possible inference drawn from these passages; and (2) that in order to clarify what the doctrinal passages mean, we must observe how Jesus and the New Testament authors used the Old Testament. To characterize this approach as "perverse and essentially unbelieving" is surely unjustified, on scriptural grounds to mention no other.

64. As Maier argues (*The End of the Historical-Critical Method,* 11).

65. *The Presbyterian and Reformed Review* 10 (1899): 472–510, reprinted in *Inspiration and Authority,* 299–348.

66. *Inspiration and Authority,* 316.

67. Note how the two strands separate in Gen. 12:3, 7, are woven together in Gen. 18:18; 23:17f.; and 28:13f.

68. Note how Paul elsewhere understands "seed" (singular) in similar contexts in its usual collective sense, viz. Rom. 4:13, 16, 18; 9:7; 2 Cor. 11:22; Gal. 3:29.

69. See particularly D. Daube, *The New Testament and Rabbinic Judaism* (London: Athlone, 1956), 438–44.

70. Since the Warfield school tends to make much of the fact that Paul counted the individual word of scripture (seed) as of authoritative significance here (cf. above, 75), we should perhaps just point out the corollary: to build an argument for inerrancy on that fact here gives indefectible validity to a particular style of rabbinic exegesis which we no longer regard as acceptable exegesis.

71. *Does Inerrancy Matter?* quotes Warfield with unqualified approval at this point. There is a similar weakness in the Warfield school's presentation of the views of Luther, Calvin and other Christian leaders of earlier centuries. A fully rounded appreciation of Luther's views, for example, must take into account his comment in his preface to the Revelation of St John: "I can in nothing detect that it was provided by the Holy Spirit. . . . I stick to the books which give me Christ clearly and purely. . . . If anyone can harmonize these sayings [of Paul and James] I'll put my doctor's cap on him and let him call me fool" (quoted in W. G. Kümmel, *The New Testament: The History of the Investigation of its Problems*, 1970 [ET, London: SCM, 1973], 26). What on earth can it mean that Luther believed the whole Bible to be inerrant, when he could say such things about books historically held to be part of the New Testament?

72. This remains true, even if talk of the Old Testament at this stage is rather imprecise (see my *Unity and Diversity*, 81).

73. See also J. W. Wenham, *Christ and the Bible* (London: Tyndale, 1972), 16–29.

74. Dunn, *Jesus and Spirit*, 53–62.

75. See discussion in Dunn, *Unity and Diversity*, 35–40; also *Christology*, 82–87. Jesus' use of, and dependence on, further Old Testament figures and material is discussed by R. T. France, *Jesus and the Old Testament: His Application of Old Testament Passages to Himself and His Mission* (London: Tyndale, 1971).

76. See further my "The Birth of a Metaphor—Baptized in Spirit," *Expository Times* 89 (1977–78): 135–38.

77. J. Jeremias, *Jesus' Promise to the Nations*, 1956 (ET, London: SCM, 1958), 46.

78. So, e.g., H. McArthur, *Understanding the Sermon on the Mount* (London: Epworth, 1961), 45–48; J. Jeremias, *New Testament Theology: Vol. One: The Proclamation of Jesus*, 1971 (ET, London: SCM, 1971), 206f.

79. Wenham, *Christ and the Bible*, 35.

80. Cf. N. B. Stonehouse, *The Witness of Matthew and Mark to Christ* (London: Tyndale, 1944), 208.

81. See particularly J. Neusner, *From Politics to Piety: The Emergence of Rabbinic Judaism* (New York: Prentice-Hall, 1973), 78–80, 82–90; A. Oppenheimer, *The Am Ha-aretz* (Leiden: Brill, 1977), 51–66, 83–96, 121–24; Emil Schürer, *The History of the Jewish People in the Age of Jesus Christ*, vol. 2 (London: T. & T. Clark, 1979), 475–78.

82. As Wenham points out, there is "no denial of the divine origin of the law that is now repealed" (*Christ and the Bible*, 31); similarly Wenham, "Christ's View of Scripture," in Geisler, ed., *Inerrancy*, 25. But the point remains that the law *is* "repealed."

83. In Mark's version we can defend the continuing authority of Deut. 24:1f. only by criticizing and qualifying the authority of Mark's rendering of Jesus' words.

84. He denies the continuing force of Deut. 24:1 itself, not just of "the traditional interpretation of Deut. 24:1," as Wenham puts it (in Geisler, ed., *Inerrancy*, 28).

85. Cf. Wenham, *Christ and the Bible*, 34. "The commandment was contingent, not absolute; it was temporary and positive rather than permanent as an expression of God's moral will" (Stonehouse, *Witness*, 205).

86. Cf. Barr, *Fundamentalism:* "It is in the defensive apologetic situation, where opposition to critical scholarship becomes the one supreme goal, that conservative writers find themselves forced to deny the critical character of Jesus' use of the Old Testament, in order to make the Old Testament, and through it the New Testament also, absolutely and unqualifiably authoritative in all respects for the church" (82f.).

87. D. Hay reckons that the New Testament contains over 1,600 citations of the Old Testament (*Interpreter's Dictionary of the Bible,* Supp. Vol. [Nashville: Abingdon, 1976], 443).

88. See the full treatment of W. Rordorf, *Sunday: The History of the Day of Rest and Worship in the Earliest Centuries of the Christian Church,* 1962 (ET, London: SCM, 1968).

89. See, e.g., F. F. Bruce, *The Book of the Acts,* New London Commentary (London: Marshall, Morgan & Scott, 1954), 218f.

90. See, e.g., F. F. Bruce, *Romans* (London: Tyndale, 1963), 79–81; C. E. B. Cranfield, *Romans,* International Critical Commentary (London: T. & T. Clark, 1975), 1:100–102. See also the briefer argument in Galatians 3 (Hab. 2:4 cited at 3:11).

91. See further my *Christology,* 184–86.

92. Not only is the interpretation different from that intended by Deuteronomy 30, but it is also somewhat at odds with the original; for part of his apologetic against Jewish understanding of the law is that the Jews had *not* found it easy to keep the law (e.g. Rom. 2:21-24).

93. R. Longenecker, *Biblical Exegesis in the Apostolic Period* (Grand Rapids: Eerdmans, 1975), 123, 125.

94. Since Paul shows himself to be such a sharp exegete elsewhere, it would be unwise to assume that in the above cases it was only the Targumic rendering of the texts he knew, and not also the Massoretic and LXX forms. Longenecker's thesis is that Paul may have selected one variant form out of more than one known to him (n.93 above).

95. See, e.g., S. Jellicoe's reference to the studies of D. W. Gooding on the LXX text of Samuel-Kings: "LXX reflecting 'disquieting features' and a very questionable methodology, and at times making 'factual nonsense' as in 3 Kings 6:17-21" (*The Septuagint and Modern Study* [London: Clarendon, 1968], 285).

96. See further my *Unity and Diversity,* 92–93.

97. See further ibid., 94–96, with bibliography in n.24.

98. Cf. Longenecker's conclusion: ". . . they looked to Jesus' own use of the Old Testament as the source and paradigm for their own employment of Scripture. . . . All treated the biblical text with some degree of freedom. . . . What was distinctive in the exegesis of the apostolic witness to Christ was a pesher approach to Scripture which felt both compelled to reproduce Jesus' own understanding of the Old Testament and at liberty to develop it further along the lines he laid out" (*Biblical Exegesis,*

207–12). Cf. also G. Hughes, *Hebrews and Hermeneutics* (Cambridge: Cambridge University Press, 1979), 47–53: "the Old Testament text must be made present as *logos* usually through the creative, interpretative, reflective activity of one member of the congregation for the others ... the way in which the *logion* becomes *logos* when it is brought into relationship with Christ ..." (51).

99. I assume Markan priority, with the majority of New Testament scholarship. For slightly fuller treatment of the following passages, see my *Unity and Diversity*, 247f.

100. See, e.g., D. Hill, *Matthew*, New Century Bible (London: Oliphants, 1972), 279; D. R. Catchpole, "The Synoptic Divorce Material as a Traditio-historical Problem," *Bulletin of the John Rylands Library* 57 (1974–75): 92–127 (particularly 93–102); J. A. Fitzmyer, "The Matthean Divorce Texts and some New Palestinian Evidence," *Theological Studies* 37 (1976): 197–226.

101. Cf. C. K. Barrett, *1 Corinthians* (London: A. & C. Black, 1968), 162f., 166; D. L. Dungan, *The Sayings of Jesus in the Churches of Paul* (Oxford: Blackwell, 1971), 92f.

102. E.g., E. E. Ellis finds nearly twenty Old Testament citations in Paul which seem to be "a deliberate adaptation to the New Testament context" (*Paul's Use of the Old Testament* [Grand Rapids: Eerdmans, 1957], 144); see also n.98 above.

103. For further examples of the way the Gospels handle the traditions of Jesus' words and deeds, see my *Unity and Diversity*, 70–76.

104. We might well compare the fact that Luke records a word inspired by the Spirit to Paul through others (Acts 21:4), which Paul nevertheless did not regard as of binding authority on himself (cf. Acts 20:22). Even here the link between an utterance's inspiration and its authority in a particular situation can never be simply assumed: a word may be inspired by God's Spirit and yet be judged irrelevant to the decision made in a particular situation!

105. See also Achtemeier, *Inspiration*, 112–14: "Scripture itself apparently thinks it can be inspired as witness to God's saving deeds without having to be regarded as inerrant in matters not central to that witness" (113f.).

106. The necessity for fuller exposition of this point became clear at the consultation to which this paper was delivered—the 1981 Anglican Evangelical Association in London. The following paragraphs and the final paragraph in section (d) below (101f.), are the only substantial modifications to the text of the original paper.

107. Only so can the Christian abandonment of the sabbath and its replacement by Sunday as the Christian holy day be justified in the face of a clear Old Testament (including prophetic) commandment and a New Testament which leaves the position unclear.

108. Maier recognizes the point about covenant relativity (*Historical-Critical Method*, 56, 84–86) but, like most of those who overplay the significance of Matt. 5:18 (see above, 75–6), fails to inquire into, or to spell out, what this must mean for

the "indefectible authority" of the Old Testament, and for the slogan that "revelation requires nothing but obedience" (above, n.57).

109. The only exception to this rule would be New Testament passages which remained within the limitations of the old covenant as judged in the light of the overall New Testament witness to Christ—a case in point very arguably being Paul's (pre-Christian?) argument about the relative status of man and woman in 1 Corinthians 11 (cf. P. K. Jewett, *Man as Male and Female* [Grand Rapids: Eerdmans, 1975], 111–19).

110. Cf. N. T. Wright, *Evangelical Anglican Identity: The Connection Between Bible, Gospel and Church*, Latimer Studies 8 (Oxford: Latimer House, 1980), 26: "*All* the Bible is 'culturally conditioned' . . . Looking for 'timeless truths' is in fact part of an attempt to distil ideas and principles out of their original contexts and reapply[ing] them in the present day—analogous, in fact, to the allegorical method and to Bultmann's demythologization."

111. N. P. Grubb, *C. T. Studd: Cricketer and Pioneer* (London: Lutterworth, 1933), 40.

112. Cf. F. Hauck, *Theological Dictionary of the New Testament*, 3:423–25: "It is of the essence of New Testament religion that the older, ritual concept of purity is not merely transcended, but rejected as non-obligatory. The idea of material impurity drops way. . . . The purity of the New Testament community is personal and moral by nature."

113. Remarriage of divorced Christians can be given properly scriptural legitimacy once this point is recognized.

114. Those arguing for the ordination of women can develop a properly scriptural case along such lines, particularly in view of Jesus' attitude to women and of the prominent roles filled by many women in Paul's churches. It is difficult, however, to see how a similar case for the acceptance of homosexual practice can be made, since the biblical position is so uniform, and was maintained despite homosexuality's cultural acceptability in the Hellenistic world.

115. See further the valuable study of A. C. Thiselton, *The Two Horizons* (London: Paternoster, 1980), particularly 10–23, 103–14, 304–09.

116. As in E. M. B. Green, *The Authority of Scripture* (London: Falcon Booklet, 1963); more carefully, Packer, *"Fundamentalism" and the Word of God* (London: IVF, 1958), 46–51.

117. Since inerrancy is not an exegetical conclusion, but a logical deduction drawn from a particular understanding of God (above, 77), the inerrancy school itself cannot escape the charge of putting reason above Scripture at this fundamental point (cf. Achtemeier, *Inspiration*, 69, 73f.). Maier does at least recognize the inevitable "subjectivity which necessarily attaches to every theology, 'For we know in part . . . (1 Cor. 13:9),'" while justifiably warning against a "highhanded subjectivity" (*Historical-Critical Method*, 56).

118. Cf. Wright, *Evangelical Anglican Identity:* "We all in fact do read the Bible in the context of our traditions, and evangelicals who fail to realize this are therefore peculiarly in danger of failing to re-check their traditions in the light of Scripture, and of hearing the voice of tradition imagining it to be the voice of the Word itself" (27).

6. Levels of Canonical Authority

1. *Das Neue Testament als Kanon,* hrsg. E. Käsemann (Göttingen: Vandenhoeck & Ruprecht, 1970).

2. See also particularly H. von Campenhasen, *The Formation of the Christian Bible,* 1968 (ET, London: A. & C. Black, 1972).

3. See also particularly W. Marxsen, *The New Testament as the Church's Book,* 1966 (ET, Philadelphia: Fortress Press, 1972); E. Best, "Scripture, Tradition and the Canon of the New Testament," *Bulletin of the John Rylands Library of Manchester* 61 (1979): 258–89.

4. See also J. D. G. Dunn, *Unity and Diversity in the New Testament* (London: SCM/Philadelphia: Westminster, 1977).

5. Among Old Testament scholars G. E. Wright in particular has posed the issue in the same terms—*The Old Testament and Theology* (New York: Harper & Row, 1969), 179–83.

6. Käsemann, "The New Testament Canon and the Unity of the Church" in ET, *Essays on New Testament Themes,* 1951 (London: SCM, 1964), 103; also *Kanon,* 402.

7. Käsemann, *Kanon,* 405; see also particularly S. Schulz, *Die Mitte der Schrift* (Stuttgart: Kreuz-Verlag, 1976), 429ff.

8. S. M. Ogden, "The Authority of Scripture for Theology," *Interpretation* 30 (1976): 258, quoting Marxsen (see n.3 above).

9. Particular mention should also be made of J. Blenkinsopp, *Prophecy and Canon* (Notre Dame, Ind.: University of Notre Dame, 1977).

10. See particularly B. S. Childs, *Biblical Theology in Crisis* (Philadelphia: Westminster, 1970); also *Introduction to the Old Testament as Scripture* (Philadelphia: Fortress Press; and London: SCM, 1979). Childs replies to a series of reviews of his *Introduction* both in *Horizons in Biblical Theology* 2 (1980) and in *Journal for the Study of the Old Testament* 16 (1980).

11. J. A. Sanders, *Torah and Canon* (Philadelphia: Fortress Press, 1972); also "Adaptable for Life: The Nature and Function of Canon," in *Magnalia Dei: The Mighty Acts of God; Essays on the Bible and Archaeology in Memory of G. E. Wright* (New York: Doubleday, 1976), 531–60; also "Text and Canon: Concepts and Method," *Journal of Biblical Literature* 98 (1979): 5–29; also "Canonical Context and Canonical Criticism," *Horizons in Biblical Theology* 2 (1980): 173–97.

12. In *Biblical Theology* and *Exodus* (London: SCM, 1974), Childs does illustrate the use of Old Testament by New Testament authors, but in the latter the treatment is surprisingly selective (e.g., there is no discussion of John 19:36's use of Exod. 12:46), and in the former his assertion of a "dialectical relationship" between the two Testaments (111–14) describes rather than addresses the problem (e.g., can the canon of the Old Testament and the canon of the New Testament or of the Christian Bible *both* be "normative" for the interpretation of Psalm 8?). In his brief response to Sanders's review of his *Introduction* he makes some very sweeping assertions about the early church and the role of the Holy Spirit, which only serve to sharpen the issue (*Horizons in Biblical Theology* 2 [1980]: 202.

13. Cf. J. Barr, "Childs' Introduction to the Old Testament as Scripture," *Journal for the Study of the Old Testament* 16 (1980): 22.

14. Sanders's conception of "canonical criticism" with its regard both for the historical depth of a text *and* its canonical authority at the various historical levels is more able to handle the *additional* level of the New Testament than Childs's much more limited conception of a single canonical context. So too H. Gese's method of biblical theology by examining the process of tradition building (see n.18 below).

15. See, e.g., the bibliography in D. L. Baker, *Two Testaments, One Bible* (London: Inter-Varsity, 1976), 34–40.

16. See particularly L. Goppelt, *Typos: die typologische Deutung des Alten Testaments im Neuen,* 1939 (reprinted Darmstadt: Wissenschaftliche Buchgesellschaft, 1969); R. Bultmann, "Prophecy and Fulfilment" (1949), in ET, *Essays on Old Testament Interpretation,* ed. C. Westermann (London: SCM, 1963), 50–75; O. Cullmann, *Salvation in History,* 1965 (ET, London: SCM, 1967).

17. See, e.g., the discussion in G. Hasel, *Old Testament Theology: Issues in the Current Debate* (Grand Rapids: Eerdmans, 1975).

18. I think here particularly of the new Tübingen Biblical Theology movement (or interaction) of H. Gese and P. Stuhlmacher—H. Gese, *Vom Sinai zum Zion: Alttestamentliche Beiträge zur biblischen Theologie* (München: Kaiser, 1974); also *Zur biblischen Theologie: Alttestamentliche Vorträge* (München: Kaiser, 1977); also "Tradition and Biblical Theology," in *Tradition and Theology in the Old Testament,* ed. D. A. Knight (London: SPCK, 1977), 301–26; P. Stuhlmacher, *Schriftauslegung auf dem Wege zur biblischen Theologie* (Göttingen: Vandenhoeck & Ruprecht, 1975); also "Das Gesetz als Thema biblischer Theologie," ZTK 75 (1978): 251–80; also "The Gospel of Reconciliation in Christ—Basic Features and Issues of a Biblical Theology of the New Testament," *HBT* 1 (1979): 161–90; also *Vom Verstehen des Neuen Testaments: Eine Hermeneutik* (Göttingen: Vandenhoeck & Ruprecht, 1979), "Diese Sache einer biblischen Theologie des Neuen Testaments ist mit dem Evangelium von der Versöhnung identisch" (246). See also K. Haacker, et al., *Biblische Theologie heute* (Neukirchen-Vluyn: Neukirchener, 1977); K. Haacker, *Neutestamentliche Wissenschaft: Eine Einführung in Fragestellungen und Methoden* (Wuppertal: Brockhaus, 1981),

87–97. Other literature in H. Hübner, "Biblische Theologie und Theologie des Neuen Testaments," *Kerygma und Dogma* 27 (1981): 1–19, particularly 1–5.

19. B. Kittel, "Brevard Childs' Development of the Canonical Approach," *Journal for the Study of the Old Testament* 16 (1980): 2–11, draws attention to the difficulty this problem poses for Childs's concept of a normative canonical form.

20. Cf. R. E. Brown, "'And the Lord Said'? Biblical Reflections on Scripture as the Word of God," *Theological Studies* 42 (1981): 3–19, who distinguishes literal meaning (what a passage meant to the author who wrote it), from canonical meaning (what it meant to those who first accepted it into a normative collection), from what it means today in the context of the Christian church (17–18).

21. The debate among *Alttestamentlers* has been recently reviewed by B. W. Anderson, "Tradition and Scripture in the Community of Faith," *Journal of Biblical Literature* 100 (1981): 5–21, with a strong plea for recognition of the continued importance and priority of tradition-history analysis. See also the plea, more sympathetic to Childs, of R. Smend, "Questions about the Importance of the Canon in an Old Testament Introduction," *Journal for the Study of the Old Testament* 16 (1980): 45–51.

22. Sanders, *Torah and Canon,* 16–17.

23. Ibid., 20.

24. I am not, of course, implying that the use of material by biblical writers *ipso facto* demonstrates its previous canonical authority—no more than quotations attributed to Satan in Job or quotations from secular writings by Paul have canonical authority per se. My point is simply that with the present documents we can recognize earlier material which in its earlier form had been treasured by the community of faith, that is, had already exercised canonical authority in its earlier form.

25. There would be dispute as to whether P provides a coherent sequential narrative which can stand on its own without reference to J and E, or is essentially a redaction of J and E (see Childs, *Introduction,* 147–48).

26. Childs, *Introduction,* particularly chapter 3. Unfortunately Childs does not clarify the confusion between his earlier "canonical context" (*Biblical Theology,* 99–100 = our "canonical level," below I(c), and his later "canonical shape" (*Introduction*); and the confusion is only made worse by his talk both of "canonical process" (which merges into our "tradition-history level") and of "canonical intentionality" (which poses the problem of "final author/redactor" discussed below). See also Barr, who accuses Childs of "lumping together all sorts of process under the vague heading of canon" ("Childs' Introduction," 13–14, 17). The confusion is not much clarified by Childs's response—*Journal for the Study of the Old Testament* 16 (1980): 52–55.

27. Childs, *Introduction,* 97, 100–101. The point is made by Kittel (above n.19), 5.

28. See also Barr, "Childs' Introduction," 18.

29. I am thinking particularly of the current research of H. D. Betz in this area which he shared with the New Testament Seminar at Nottingham in November 1981.

30. Bultmann's postulated "ecclesiastical redactor" would have provided a coherent final redaction which could be stripped away more confidently, but the hypothesis has found no favor outside the Bultmann school. R. E. Brown, *John*, Anchor Bible 29 (Garden City, N.Y.: Doubleday/London: Chapman, 1966) also allows a substantial role for a redactor, but the problematic character of the hypothesis is shown by the fact that he allows that much of the redaction material actually stemmed from the Evangelist himself (xxxvi–xxxvii).

31. Childs, *Introduction*, 361.

32. G. M. Landes, "The Canonical Approach to Introducing the Old Testament: Prodigy and Problems," *Journal for the Study of the Old Testament* 16 (1980): 32–39, cites Jonah and Lamentations as the only Old Testament documents where it can be maintained that "the original author and the final canonical editor were virtually the same" (38).

33. In *Biblical Theology* Childs proposed "a form of Biblical Theology that takes as its primary task the disciplined theological reflection of the Bible in the context of the canon" (122).

34. Childs's brief discussion of the relation between Hebrew scriptures and Old Testament simply fails to grapple with this point (*Introduction*, 664–66)—as when he asserts that "the theological issue at stake is the maintenance of a common scripture, between church and synagogue as witness to Jesus Christ, which is threatened if the Hebrew text is abandoned as the normative Old Testament text by the church" (665).

35. See also Barr's criticism ("Childs' Introduction," 21).

36. I do not find it necessary or helpful to distinguish a futher level—the *intentio textus ipsius*, what the text itself communicates—see, e.g., D. Patte, *What Is Structural Exegesis?* (Philadelphia: Fortress Press, 1976); G. O'Collins, *Fundamental Theology* (London: Darton, Longman & Todd, 1981), 251–59. Where such "synchronic exegesis" illuminates the final composition level, well and good; otherwise the meanings discovered at the "deep structures" of the text are better classed among the ecclesiastical levels, since they can claim as much, or as little justification as other post-Enlightenment hermeneutical techniques. Despite Gadamer, I still wish to regard *intended* meaning as the proper goal of exegesis—cf. particularly E. D. Hirsch, *Validity in Interpretation* (New Haven: Yale University Press, 1967).

37. See R. E. Brown, *Jerome Biblical Commentary* (London: Chapman, 1968), 71:56–70.

38. See also the valuable discussion of R. E. Brown, "The Meaning of the Bible," *Theology Digest* 28 (1980): 305–20, particularly 311–18.

39. Cf. Childs, *Introduction*, 41: "It is constitutive of Israel's history that the literature formed the identity of the religious community which in turn shaped the literature." Cf. also the discussion by D. A. Knight, "Revelation through Tradition," in *Tradition and Theology in the Old Testament*, ed. D. A. Knight (London: SPCK, 1977), 143–80.

40. Sandmel, "On Canon," *Catholic Biblical Quarterly* 28 (1966): 207. See also R. B. Laurin, "Tradition and Canon," in *Tradition and Theology in the Old Testament,* ed. D. A. Knight, 261–74, with his distinction between a legitimate "canonizing of tradition" and "canonization" as "an unfortunate freezing of traditional growth" (271); Best, "Scripture, Tradition and the Canon," 277—"a decision within the fourth century represents a freezing in the fourth century at that point, but it cannot claim an absolute position as over against other freezings of the tradition at other points."

41. On the significance of the "qualitative jump" from spoken to written word see, e.g., the discussion of R. Lapointe, "Tradition and Language: The Impact of Oral Expression," in *Tradition and Theology in the Old Testament,* ed. D. A. Knight, 125–42.

42. Cf. G. M. Tucker, "Prophetic Superscriptions and the Growth of a Canon," in *Canon and Authority,* ed. G. W. Coats and B. O. Long (Philadelphia: Fortress Press, 1977), 56–70: "While the superscriptions to the prophetic books do not represent the stage of canonization, they do reveal the decisive turning point when—at least for certain circles in Israel—the spoken prophetic words had become scripture" (70).

43. G. T. Sheppard, *Wisdom as a Hermeneutical Construct,* Beihefte zur *Zeitschrift für die alttestamentliche Wissenschaft* 151 (Berlin: De Gruyter, 1980) claims that Sirach and Baruch interpret Torah consciously as "canonical" (109–16).

44. Sanders, *Torah and Canon;* see also, e.g., W. Zimmerli, "Prophetic Proclamation and Reinterpretation," in *Tradition and Theology in the Old Testament,* ed. D. A. Knight, 69–100; Laurin (as in n.40 above).

45. Dunn, *Unity and Diversity,* 247–48, 251.

46. Ibid., 109–16, 352–56.

47. Cf. particularly A. C. Sundberg, "The Bible Canon and the Christian Doctrine of Inspiration," *Interpretation* 29 (1975): 364–71.

48. For recent discussion on what "the inspiration of scripture" means see P. J. Achtemeier, *The Inspiration of Scripture* (Philadelphia: Westminster, 1981); Brown (n.20 above); W. J. Abraham, *The Divine Inspiration of Holy Scripture* (New York: Oxford University Press, 1981).

49. Both Childs and Sanders have rightly emphasized the role of the community in "the canonical process" (see particularly Sanders, "Canonical Context," 181–86). Cf. Gese, "Tradition and Biblical Theology," 317: "Only preaching which was heard, understood, and received constitutes the truth which sustained the life of Israel."

50. Cf. Blenkinsopp's thesis that the tension between normative order (Torah) and prophecy is "a constituent element in the origins of Judaism" (*Prophecy and Canon,* 2).

51. Sanders makes much the same point when he emphasizes "adaptability" as "the primary characteristic of canon" (see his "Adaptable for Life," particularly 539–52).

52. Cf. also J. A. Sanders, "Hermeneutics in True and False Prophecy," in *Canon and Authority,* ed. G. W. Coats and B. O. Long (Philadelphia: Fortress Press, 1977), 21–41.

53. This rule of course will be least applicable where a text was deliberately intended to have a more timeless character, as is the case particularly with so much of the wisdom material.

54. Cf. Anderson, "Tradition and Scripture," 21: "To separate the prophecy from its historical moorings not only leaves us with language that would make no sense, or would make whatever sense the reader cares to bring to the text, but blunts the cutting edge of the word that the prophet spoke in the name of God." K. Stendahl has repeatedly insisted that in biblical hermeneutics we can never ask, "What does it mean?" without adding, ". . . to whom?"

55. See further "The Authority of Scripture according to Scripture," chap. 5 above.

56. It is surprising the *Alttestamentlers'* discussions of the problem of false prophecy have not paid more attention to the New Testament, particularly Paul, whose treatment of the problem is the most perceptive and valuable within the Bible as a whole—a theme if ever there was one for a "biblical theology" study; cf. J. D. G. Dunn, "Prophetic 'I'-Sayings and the Jesus Tradition: The Importance of Testing Prophetic Utterances Within Early Christianity," *New Testament Studies* 24 (1977–78): 175–98.

57. Cf. again Childs's *Introduction,* chap. 3—"the normative status of the final form of the text" (75).

58. Cf. also O. Cullmann, "The Tradition," in *The Early Church* (ET, London: SCM, 1956), 75–87.

59. Childs, *Biblical Theology,* 99–101, argues that this level is normative for biblical theology—a case which is certainly more arguable for *biblical* theology. But to the extent that biblical theology ignores diversity within the canon and abstracts from the historical contexts of the final compositions, to that extent the biblical theology itself must become less normative for either exegesis or faith. Cf. Barr's criticism: "The basic fault . . . is that Childs reads into the minds of the redactors and canonizers his own passionate hermeneutical interest" ("Childs' Introduction," 17).

60. We may speak of the New Testament as "the goal and end, the *telos* of the path of *biblical* tradition" (as does Gese, "Tradition and Biblical Theology," 322), but can the same phrase be used *simpliciter* if we substitute "Old Testament" for "biblical"?

61. See also Barr, "Childs' Introduction," 17–19.

62. Cf. Brown, "Meaning of Bible": "Even when the quest of a larger sense has uncovered spiritual and theological possibilities that go beyond the literal sense and those possibilities have been accepted in Christian thought, the literal sense (= my final composition level) remains a conscience and a control" (311).

63. Contrast G. T. Sheppard's exposition of Childs's earlier views: "To the degree that historical-grammatical or historical-critical exegesis is successful in reviving a 'lost' historical context, it effectively decanonizes the literature by putting it in some other context than the canonical"—"Canon Criticism: the Proposal of Brevard

Childs and an Assessment for Evangelical Hermeneutics," *Studia Biblica et Theologica* IV.2 (October 1974): 13.

64. J. D. Smart, *The Past, Present and Future of Biblical Theology* (Philadelphia: Westminster, 1979), 151.

65. Cf. and contrast the views of Anderson who asserts forcefully, "The 'canonical Isaiah' is no subsititute for the 'historical' Second Isaiah or the 'historical' Isaiah of Jerusalem" ("Tradition and Scripture," 19); and Gese, "Biblical theology must also see that the biblical Isaiah is not the historical Isaiah but the dynamic force, the Isaiah tradition which stems from Isaiah and achieves its effect traditio-historically, stretching from the first redaction all the way to the New Testament view of 'fulfilment'" ("Tradition and Biblical Theology," 325).

66. E.g., W. Wrede, "The Task and Methods of 'New Testament Theology'" (1897), ET in R. Morgan, *The Nature of New Testament Theology* (London: SCM, 1973), 68–116; W. Wink, *The Bible in Human Transformation* (Philadelphia: Fortress Press, 1973).

67. I wish to express my gratitude to members of our New Testament postgraduate seminar at Nottingham (particularly the *Alttestamentlers*) for helpful criticism of an earlier draft of this paper. The defects that remain are entirely my own work!

7. God's Word in Human Speech

1. M. E. Marty and R. S. Appleby, *Fundamentalisms Observed* (Chicago: University of Chicago Press, 1991), suggest that the unifying feature of the different Fundamentalisms observed in "The Fundamentalism Project" is this militancy.

2. As reported by one of the participants in the conversations, Dr. Elizabeth Templeton in *Trust* 11 (July 1993), the Newsletter of SCM Press Trust.

3. In the same edition of *Trust*.

4. See elsewhere in this volume.

5. A recent example is the interpretation of the seven seals in Revelation by David Koresh, leader of the ill-fated Branch Davidian sect in Waco, Texas.

9. What Makes a Good Exposition?

1. D. Weinstein, "Renaissance," *EncBr* 15.664.

2. F. D. E. Schleiermacher, *Hermeneutics: The Handwritten Manuscripts by F. D. E. Schleiermacher*, ed. H. Kimmerle (ET, Missoula, Mt.: Scholars, 1977), excerpted by K. Mueller-Vollmer, *The Hermeneutics Reader* (New York: Continuum, 1994), 86.

3. "Is Exegesis Without Presuppositions Possible?" (1961), in *Existence and Faith* (London: Collins, Fontana, 1964), 342–51 (here 344).

4. The word *hermeneutics* comes from the Greek *hermêneia*, which can mean both "translation" and "interpretation."

5. See particularly B. D. Ehrman, *The Orthodox Corruption of Scripture: The Effect of Early Christological Controversies on the Text of the New Testament* (Oxford: Oxford University Press, 1993); D. C. Parker, *The Living Text of the Gospels* (Cambridge: Cambridge University Press, 1997).

6. The first round of the debate was B. S. Childs, *Biblical Theology in Crisis* (Philadelphia: Westminster, 1970), and J. A. Sanders, *Torah and Canon* (Philadelphia: Fortress Press, 1972).

7. See "Levels of Canonical Authority," chap. 6 above.

8. J. H. Bentley, *Humanists and Holy Writ: New Testament Scholarship in the Renaissance* (Princeton: Princeton University Press, 1983), sums up Colet's significance thus: "Though routinely hailed as a harbinger of Reformation exegesis, Colet's real achievement was simply to provide a running literal commentary in the patristic fashion, abandoning the late medieval style of exegesis, which often subordinated the scriptures to the needs of scholastic theology" (9–10).

9. See, e.g., the extracts in W. G. Kümmel, *The New Testament: The History of the Investigation of its Problems* (London: SCM, 1972): "all error arises out of paying no regard to the plain words"; "This is the method I now employ, the final and best one: I convey the literal sense of Scripture . . . Other interpretations, however appealing, are the work of fools" (23). See further A. C. Thiselton, *New Horizons in Hermeneutics* (London: Marshall Pickering, 1992), 179–84, who also points out that Luther preferred the term *plain* (or "natural") meaning, though he did use the term *literal* (184). In private correspondence (9/10/2000) Thiselton observes: "Although it is true that he [Luther] dismissed mediaeval allegorising, . . . in his earlier work he was not above such 'mediaeval allegorising' himself, and it was part of his developmental process of insight that as his work progressed he came to realise increasingly that such allegorising carried epistemological consequences which were unhelpful for a view of revelation."

10. *The Epistles of Paul to the Galatians, Ephesians, Philippians and Colossians* (Edinburgh: Oliver & Boyd, 1965), 84–85. Similarly in the dedication to his commentary on Romans: "Since it is almost his only task to unfold the mind of the writer whom he has undertaken to expound, he misses his mark, or at least strays outside his limits, by the extent to which he leads his readers away from the meaning of his author" (*Epistles of Paul the Apostle to the Romans and to the Thessalonians* [Edinburgh: Oliver & Boyd, 1961], 1). Thiselton comments: "Calvin is even less tolerant of allegorical interpretation than Luther" (Thiselton, *New Horizons*, 185).

11. Thiselton cites John Chrysostom in noting that "the 'literal' may include the use of metaphor or other figures of speech, if this is the meaning which the purpose of the author and the linguistic context suggest" (*New Horizons*, 173; also 183). R.

Williams, "The Discipline of Scripture," in *On Christian Theology* (Oxford: Blackwell, 2000), 44–59, observes that Thomas Aquinas also insisted on the primacy of the literal sense, but also that for Thomas the literal included metaphor and allowed for a plurality of genres within it (47–48).

12. K. E. Greene-McCreight, *Ad Litteram: How Augustine, Calvin, and Barth Read the "Plain Sense" of Genesis 1–3* (New York: Peter Lang, 1999), ix, 244.

13. H.-G. Gadamer, *Truth and Method* (New York: Crossroad, 1989), 291.

14. Quotations from Mueller-Vollmer, *Hermeneutics Reader,* 74, 83–84, 96.

15. Thiselton, *New Horizons,* 58–59, citing R. Wellek and A. Warren, *Theory of Literature* (1949), and W. K. Wimsatt and M. Beardsley, "The Intentional Fallacy" (1954).

16. See further Thiselton, *New Horizons,* 516–22, referring to W. Iser, *The Implied Reader: Patterns of Communication in Prose Fiction from Bunyan to Beckett* (Baltimore: John Hopkins University Press, 1974); also *The Act of Reading: A Theory of Aesthetic Response* (Baltimore: John Hopkins University Press, 1978).

17. F. Watson, *Text and Truth: Redefining Biblical Theology* (Edinburgh: T. & T. Clark, 1997), 112, 118.

18. S. D. Moore, *Literary Criticism and the Gospels* (New Haven: Yale University Press, 1989), 121. See further 71–107.

19. R. C. Murfin, "What is Reader-Response Criticism?" in *Heart of Darkness,* ed. R. C. Murfin (New York: St. Martin's, 1989), 142.

20. G. Aichele, et al., *The Postmodern Bible* (New Haven: Yale University Press, 1995), 42, citing Murfin, "What Is Reader-Response Criticism?" See further Aichele 24–38.

21. Aichele, *Postmodern Bible,* 41, citing W. Iser, "Talk Like Whales: A Reply to Stanley Fish," *Diacritics* 11 (1981): 82–87 (here 84).

22. G. Steiner, *Real Presences: Is There Anything in What We Say?* (London: Faber & Faber, 1989).

23. S. Fish, *Is There a Text in This Class? The Authority of Interpretive Communities* (Cambridge: Harvard University Press, 1980).

24. Gadamer, *Truth,* 300–307.

25. Ibid., 340–41, 301.

26. See particularly S. I. Wright, *The Voice of Jesus: Studies in the Interpretation of Six Gospel Parables* (Carlisle: Paternoster, 2000).

27. R. W. L. Moberly, *The Bible, Theology, and Faith: A Study of Abraham and Jesus* (Cambridge: Cambridge University Press, 2000), chap. 1; S. C. Barton, "New Testament Interpretation as Performance," in *Life Together: Family, Sexuality and Community in the New Testament and Today* (Edinburgh: T. & T. Clark, 2001), 223–50. Both acknowledge indebtedness to N. Lash, *Theology on the Way to Emmaus* (London: SCM, 1986), particularly chap. 3.

28. Cf. the criticism of Vatican II's "Dogmatic Constitution on Divine Revelation" acknowledged by J. Ratzinger, in response to Protestant critique by J. K. S. Reid, among others, in H. Vorgrimler, ed., *Commentary on the Documents of Vatican II*, Vol. 3 (London: Burns & Oates/New York: Herder & Herder, 1968), 192–93.

29. It should however also be confessed that the historical method as applied in the 19th century did *not* prevent anti-Judaism in Christian presentation of Jesus; the recognition of subjectivity in interpretation did not extend sufficiently to take account of anti-Jewish bias (S. Heschel, *Abraham Geiger and the Jewish Jesus* [Chicago: University of Chicago Press, 1998], 73, 122).

30. Here may be heard overtones of an ongoing dialogue within the Department of Theology in Durham!

31. In Mueller-Vollmer, *Hermeneutics Reader*, 84–85. Gadamer notes that "this circular relationship between the whole and the parts . . . was already known to classical rhetoric, which compares perfect speech with the organic body, with the relationship between head and limbs" (*Truth*, 175).

32. In Mueller-Vollmer, *Hermeneutics Reader*, 138.

33. *Sachkritik* (the English "content criticism" is not really adequate) builds on the older theological distinction between the Word of God which is heard through the words of scripture (but is not to be simply identified with them), by distinguishing between the real intention (*die Sache*, the matter or subject) of a text and the language in which it is expressed (*die Sprache*). *Sachkritik* is linked particularly with the name of Bultmann.

34. Referring to Ferdinand de Saussure's influential distinction between the language system (*langue*) and concrete acts of speech (*parole*) and idea of the text as an encoded sign-system (see Thiselton, *New Horizons*, 80–86).

35. Luther's famous criticism of the epistle of James: "What does not teach Christ is not apostolic, even though St. Peter or Paul taught it" (Kümmel, *New Testament*, 25).

36. R. Bultmann, "New Testament and Mythology" (1941), in H. W. Bartsch, ed., *Kerygma and Myth* (London: SPCK, 1957), 1–44.

37. E.g., E. Käsemann, ed., *Das Neue Testament als Kanon* (Göttingen: Vandenhoeck, 1970), 405.

38. N. T. Wright, *Jesus and the Victory of God* (London: SPCK, 1996).

39. Mueller-Vollmer, *Hermeneutics Reader*, 8–11.

40. Bultmann, "Exegesis without Presuppositions," 343–44, 347.

41. *Truth*, 270–71, 276–78.

42. From Mueller-Vollmer, *Hermeneutics Reader*, 112–13.

43. Paul evidently had in mind the surprisingly still contentious point that in the new covenant, priestly service is no longer restricted within the sacred space of temple and cult; on the contrary, *all* service of the gospel of whatever kind, can (and should) be seen as priestly service; see further my *The Theology of Paul the Apostle*

(Grand Rapids: Eerdmans/Edinburgh: T. & T. Clark 1998), 543–48.

44. J. B. Lightfoot, "The Christian Ministry," *St Paul's Epistle to the Philippians* (London: Macmillan, 1868), 179–267.

45. J. D. G. Dunn, *Jesus and the Spirit* (London: SCM, 1975), 226, referring to J. Weiss, *Der erste Korintherbrief*, Kritisch-Exegetischer Kommentar über das Neue Testament (Göttingen: Vandenhoeck & Ruprecht, 1910), 50.

46. Dunn, *Jesus and the Spirit*, 284.

INDEX OF BIBLICAL REFERENCES